Criminal Justive/Forensic Science
Office No. 419-434-4308
E-Mail: lucasp@findlay.edu

ETHICS in
FORENSIC SCIENCE
Professional Standards for the
Practice of Criminalistics

Protocols in Forensic Science Series
Keith Inman and Norah Rudin, Series Editors

Principles and Practices of Criminalistics: The Profession of Forensic Science
by Keith Inman and Norah Rudin

Ethics in Forensic Science: Professional Standards for the Practice of Criminalistics
by Peter D. Barnett

ETHICS in FORENSIC SCIENCE
Professional Standards for the Practice of Criminalistics

Peter D. Barnett

CRC Press

Boca Raton London New York Washington, D.C.

Library of Congress Cataloging-in-Publication Data

Barnett, Peter D.
    Ethics in Forensic Science: Professional Standards for Practice of Criminalistics/Peter D. Barnett.
        p. cm.—(Protocols in forensic science)
    Includes index.
    ISBN 0-8493-0860-7
    1. Forensic sciences—Moral and ethical aspects—United States. 2. Forensic
scientists—Professional ethics—United States. I. Title. II. Series.

    HV8073 .B3557 2001
    174′.93632—dc21   2001025704

Visit the CRC Press Web site at www.crcpress.com

© 2001 by CRC Press LLC

No claim to original U.S. Government works
International Standard Book Number 0-8493-0860-7
Library of Congress Card Number 2001025704
Printed in the United States of America   5 6 7 8 9 0
Printed on acid-free paper

Foreword

At first it may seem odd to find a book about ethics in forensic science included in a series entitled *Protocols in Forensic Science*. However, we find it entirely appropriate because the generation of data and the use to which that data is put fall under the general rubric of good professional practice. In the introductory volume of this series, *Principles and Practice of Criminalistics: The Profession of Forensic Science*, we provided a general introduction to the topic of ethics and accountability. In *Ethics in Forensic Science: Professional Standards for the Practice of Criminalistics*, Peter D. Barnett, a pioneer in this facet of the forensic profession, expands on these ideas and puts them in context.

The profession of forensic science, sometimes perceived by the public and practitioners alike as a *cowboy science*, or worse yet a *bastard science*, has yet to achieve the ubiquitous credibility of such time-honored professions as medicine and law. This continuing unease with criminalists as a group derives in equal parts from the perceived power of science to influence matters of law with regard to guilt or innocence, from fear of the unknown (science), and from an historical lack of self-government of the profession. Several aspects of self-government define a profession: accreditation of agencies, certification of individuals, a minimum program of education and training, and a set of rules by which the profession operates (Kirk, 1963). This set of rules usually takes the form of a code of ethics, a standard by which members of the profession agree to abide. Although several codes of ethics exist in forensic science at both the national and regional levels, they differ greatly in their specificity, breadth, and length. This makes the profession appear rather fractured. To which of these standards should a practitioner be held? Who decides if an ethical violation has been committed? Who determines the consequence?

In this seminal volume about the ethics of forensic science, Mr. Barnett reviews the history of ethical codes in forensic science and compares them to those in other professions. He discusses the unique requirements and limits of a code of ethics for a profession that straddles the boundary between two almost antithetical professions — science and law. He boldly aims straight for the heart of the matter and asks, why do we need one? He outlines the basic requirements of utilitarian codes of ethics, including not only general and specific models for the code itself but also methods of enforcement, without which a code is toothless, if not useless. Finally, Mr. Barnett applies various codes of ethics to the day-to-day work of the criminalist. The meat of this volume comprises several ethical dilemmas taken from actual casework. For each, the facts are set forth, the specific ethical dilemma is articulated, and possible solutions are suggested. Then several existing codes of ethics are examined for their abilities to provide guidance. The conscientious reader will certainly find himself or herself squirming in an attempt to reach a just, equitable, professional, and, yes, ethical decision about the action to be taken in each of these real-life situations.

Like *Principles and Practice*, we hope that the present volume will inspire thought-provoking discussion among practicing criminalists and between forensic scientists and legal professionals.

Reference

Kirk, P. L., The ontogeny of criminalistics, *J. Criminal Law Criminol. Police Sci.*, 54, 235–238, 1963.

Preface

In reviewing this manuscript, it seems that I have asked a lot of questions — and have left most of them unanswered. Why? First, the answers to many questions can only be given within the context of the details of a particular situation. Codes of ethics, rules of professional conduct, and committees that investigate and judge cases of alleged misconduct exist just for that reason — because the answers are not simple and must be considered within the context of the specific case. Second, I don't know many of the answers.

When the first code of ethics for criminalists was written by members of the California Association of Criminalists nearly 50 years ago, the face of the profession was considerably different than it is today. Contributors to the CAC code of ethics had academic training in criminalistics, were employed in law enforcement agencies, worked in laboratories with a one- or two-person technical staff, performed the entire range of examinations and analyses, and were responsible for developing many of the procedures they used. The past half century has witnessed an evolution, if not a revolution in the practice of forensic science. The majority of criminalists today have no formal criminalistics education, work in large laboratories with highly specialized responsibilities, are restricted to examining only specific types of evidence or conducting specific types of analyses, and are required to follow detailed protocols in virtually every phase of their jobs. While most criminalists are employed by law enforcement agencies, an increasing number work for private laboratories ranging in size from a one-person lab to a large, multi-disciplinary, full-service, and for-profit forensic science laboratory.

If the face of criminalistics has changed over the past five decades, the capabilities of science have changed even more. In the foreseeable future, it will be possible to identify essentially every individual who has been at an incident scene. Whether this analysis will be done by machines in the forensic laboratory operated by people with white lab coats — or by machines carried on a Sam Browne belt and operated by people wearing blue shirts and gold badges — remains to be seen. In any event, it seems that the identification of the perpetrator in many cases — at least in enough cases to keep all of the prosecutors and investigators busy — will be routine. What then will be the role of the forensic scientist, other than to keep the genetic analyzers running smoothly? Questions such as *When were those people at the scene? What did they do when they were there? What was their intent? Were other people there from whom no biological evidence has been recovered?* will probably not be as easy to answer. Nor will the answers be as clear cut as *Whose DNA is this?*

Not to be outdone by advances in science, the practice of law has evolved over the past 50 years. In the 1950s the only case that forensic scientists thought was significant was *U.S.* v. *Frye*. If scientific evidence could meet the *Frye* test (or if an argument could be made that the evidence did not need to meet the standard established in *Frye*), the forensic scientist was home free. Cases in the 1950s and 1960s, such as *Ake* v. *Oklahoma* or *Brady* v. *Maryland*, which have an impact on the practice of criminalistics, were not and are not well known to many practitioners. Since the 1970s a series of cases (*People.* v. *Nation, Arizona* v. *Youngblood, Daubert* v. *Merrell-Dow, Kumho* v. *Carmichael*, etc.) have affected the interactions among science, forensic scientists, and the law in a variety of ways. Practicing criminalists should be familiar with these cases. Even though the *Nation* case is no longer the law in California (due to the ruling in *Youngblood*), the *Nation* court expresses an enlightened view toward the preservation of physical evidence. These cases are included in the appendices. As a profession, criminalists had little impact on these decisions.

If the field of criminalistics is to evolve as a profession, it is necessary to consider the issue of appropriate guidelines, standards of professional practice, or codes of ethics. Whatever the title, it is necessary to define the appropriate criteria for distinguishing the competent from the incompetent, the appropriate from the inappropriate, or the acceptable from the unacceptable practices. Ethics, the written rules that prescribe or proscribe certain aspects of professional activity, are but one of the criteria by which professionals are judged — by their peers, their clients, and the public they serve. This book is an effort to stimulate thought on this subject and to provide some guidance to people who are faced with the problem of deciding whether a proposed course of action (theirs or someone else's) would be considered ethical.

Acknowledgments

I would like to express my appreciation to the editors of the series *Protocols in Forensic Science*, Norah Rudin and Keith Inman, not only for their support and encouragement in writing this book but also for their concept of the series and their dedication to it. There is substantial literature on forensic science directed toward an audience of lawyers, investigators, mystery afficionados, or the general public. There is an increasing number of books devoted to specific technical subjects. These are useful reference works for the specialists in the field who devote themselves to specific technical subjects. There is not, however, a unifying literature that provides a cohesive paradigm for what transpires in the modern forensic laboratory. It is hoped that this series will fill that void.

Over the years I have had a number of discussions with colleagues that have helped shape my own views on what constitutes good and ethical criminalistic practice. My colleague, Edward Blake, never fails to point out what he considers poor or inappropriate practice when he sees it. My own views are in substantial measure a result of his incessant demand for excellence. George Sensabaugh, Charles Morton, Carol Hunter, Peter DeForest, and John Murdock have all, over the years, provided information and insight that have been most valuable. I must also express my debt to the late V. Parker Bell, who started his professional life as a criminalist and changed to the law; but he never forgot the dichotomy between the responsibility of the scientist and the obligation of the lawyer.

Finally, I thank my wife Dana. As a teacher, she is a member of a profession with a significantly longer history than that of criminalistics. She continues to remind me that there should be no quarter given to those who would ask anyone to violate a professional obligation in favor of some temporary convenience or popular movement. For over 30 years she has patiently listened to my harangues, contributed to my views, and supported my decisions.

In the end, though, the views expressed in this volume are my own. I am aware that there are those who will claim that my views are wrong or that the idea of ethics for criminalists is either absurd or trivial. I can only hope that those who both agree and disagree will enter into the discussion.

The Author

Peter D. Barnett is a criminalist in private practice with Forensic Science Associates in Richmond, California. He earned a B.S. degree in criminalistics from the University of California at Berkeley, where he studied under Paul Kirk. He worked briefly for the San Diego Police Department, and he has been in private practice for the past 30 years. He is a member of the California Association of Criminalists and has served as Editorial Secretary and President of that organization. He is also a Fellow in the Criminalistics Section of the American Academy of Forensic Science. He is a long-time member of ASTM Committee E30 on Forensic Science and has served as Chairman of the Criminalistics Subcommittee and the main E30 Committee. He has been the CAC representative to the Examination Committee of the American Board of Criminalistics. He continues to make efforts to preserve the notion that everyone who works in a forensic science laboratory ought to be familiar with all of the work that goes on in the laboratory.

Table of Contents

Section I
BACKGROUND, HISTORY, AND REVIEW OF ETHICS IN FORENSIC SCIENCE

1 Introduction   3

Ethics Are Important   4
Purpose of This Book   6
Existing Codes of Ethics   7
Enforcement of Codes of Ethics   8
Sanctions   9

2 Why Are Professional Ethics Necessary?   11

Importance of Codes of Professional Ethics   11
Legal vs. Scientific Practices   12
Ethics and Morals   14
Credibility as a Reason for a Code of Ethics   16
Obligations of the Expert Witness   19
Other Rules Are Not Enough   21
Competence   22
General Societal Obligation   24

3 Development of a Code of Ethics   27

Various Models of Codes of Ethics   27
Making a Complaint   32

4 Application of Codes of Ethics: How Ethical Requirements Impact the Daily Work of a Forensic Scientist   43

The Ethical Requirements for Work Done on a Case   43
Interactions between the Forensic Scientist and the Client   45
Interactions with Colleagues   48

Section II
ETHICS IN ACTION

5   **Ethical Issues Involving Professional Practice**   **53**

Introduction   53
Recovery of Physical Evidence by a Defense Investigator   53
Criticism of Work Not Done   60
Selective Evidence Examinations   65
Identifying Another Examiner's Markings on Evidence   70
Agency Proposes to Retain an Incompetent
     or Unethical Criminalist   74
Attempting To Avoid the Rigors of Cross-Examination   78
Evidence Is Discovered by a Defense Criminalist   82

6   **Ethical Issues Involving Technical Competence** **89**

Wrong Gun Identified   89
Attacking Incorrect or Incompetent Work   94
Ambiguous Blood Stain Analysis   99
Preservation of Test Results   111

Appendices   **121**

1 *Code of Ethics and Conduct, American Academy
    of Forensic Science*   123
2 *The Code of Ethics of the California Association
    of Criminalists*   125
3 *Procedure for the Code of Ethics Enforcement of the
    California Association of Criminalists*   131
4 *American Academy of Forensic Sciences Good Forensic
    Practice Guidelines*   143
5 *American Society of Crime Laboratory Directors Code
    of Ethics*   145
6 *American Board of Criminalistics Code of Ethics*   153
7 *Council for the Registration of Forensic Practitioners
    (England) Code of Conduct*   155
8 *Daubert v. Merrell Dow Pharmaceuticals*   157
9 *Kumho Tire Company v. Patrick Carmichael*   169
10 *People v. Donald Richard Nation*   183
11 *Arizona v. Larry Youngblood*   193

Index   **213**

Section I

Background, History, and Review of Ethics in Forensic Science

---

Introduction

When the topic of ethics comes up in a conversation among criminalists, it is often stated that a criminalist who tells the truth and is of good moral character will not run into any ethical problems. When situational details are described, however, those who hold this view recognize that ethical issues can arise for which there are no obviously correct answers. Others will assert that they have the right answer and that there is no ethical alternative. This book is an effort to demonstrate that there are ethical issues that arise in the practice of criminalists that cannot be easily dismissed by admonitions to tell the truth or to be of good moral character. That such ethical issues do arise should not be a surprise. What is surprising is the fact that many practicing criminalists fail to recognize the potential for such issues.

Unlike the practitioners in most professions, and particularly unlike practitioners of law and medicine with whom criminalists have the most frequent professional contact, criminalists have little common professional background or training. The vast majority of individuals who work in criminalistics laboratories come from college or university science programs where matters of professional ethics in forensic science are simply not part of the curriculum. A brief discussion of ethics may be part of the orientation to their new jobs. This may consist of nothing more than a copy of the code of ethics of the regional forensic science professional organization, or it may involve a more formal discussion of the topic. But in any case, of the many things a new employee in a forensic laboratory must learn, the subject of professional ethics is often given only cursory attention.

Most criminalists work in forensic science laboratories associated with law enforcement or other governmental agencies that have ethics codes developed specifically for their organizations. The forensic science portion of any law enforcement agency is but a small cog in the large wheel of the agency. Codes of ethics developed for police or prosecutorial agencies address those areas of professional behavior that are important to the bulk of the people

3

within that agency. If the agency is a police agency, the ethics codes are designed for police officers. If the agency is a prosecution agency, the ethics codes are designed for prosecutors and lawyers.

The point is not that ethics codes designed for police officers or lawyers are inapplicable to forensic scientists — some may be. But the forensic scientist needs to have ethics codes that provide guidance in situations that result from the type of work the criminalist does and the types of ethical issues that arise. An ethics code that is applicable generally to a wide variety of occupations is of little use to the practitioner in a specific field who is looking for information on which to base a decision as to the appropriate course of action in a particular circumstance. General statements such as, "The employee will do nothing that will reflect poorly on the organization" provide little in the way of guidance to the criminalist who is asked to assist a prosecutor preparing to discredit an opposing expert.

Another important reason to develop and adopt ethical codes of conduct for criminalists is that such codes are hallmarks of professional status. In the same way that scientists agree upon procedures for conducting scientific inquiries, as professionals we need to agree on procedures by which we govern our professional practices. Discussions among criminalists reveal many topics about which we disagree. For example, is it appropriate for the criminalistics laboratory to prepare fake cocaine or methamphetamine samples that narcotics investigators can use for undercover operations? Is it unethical for the criminalist to synthesize controlled drugs for use in such situations? What about preparing false reports that investigators can use during interrogation of suspects? What information should be included in a report? What is the obligation of the forensic scientist to provide discovery information to opposing counsel? Is that obligation different for criminalists working for law enforcement agencies, prosecutorial agencies, or private practices?

The questions that arise when considering alternative courses of action in matters of professional practice may not all be considered truly ethical in nature. What is an ethical issue to one person may be a non-issue to another person; and to yet another, the appropriate course of action may appear obvious. But in situations where these types of questions arise, one source of information that may help guide a criminalist's action is a code of ethics.

Ethics Are Important

The practice of criminalistics lies at the confluence of science and the law. With the exception of forensic psychiatry, no other area of forensic science has such an intimate relationship with the law. The science of criminalistics can establish that a crime was committed, who committed the crime, whether witnesses are lying or telling the truth, and what happened in an incident to which there were no eyewitnesses and can, to paraphrase a common saying, give words to the mute physical evidence from a crime scene. The work of the criminalist is often critical to determining what will happen to the defendant in the dock or the plaintiff at the bar.

At first glance it may seem that the ethical issues facing a criminalist can be resolved by following simple rules. In court, the criminalist, like all witnesses, takes an oath to "tell the truth, the whole truth, and nothing but the truth." What could be simpler? There is no such convenient rule for other phases of the criminalist's professional life. Outside of court there are a variety of simple rules that might be relied upon: *do unto others as you would have them do onto you, principles of justice, the right way, be a good scientist,* or *Brady v. Maryland* are all apparently simple rules that, if followed, would probably keep criminalists free of ethical quagmires. But a code of ethics is more than a mere reliance on moral principles. A code of ethics, like a code of laws, has written rules governing behavior in certain circumstances. What are the ethical requirements for work done in the laboratory or in the field? What are ethical considerations that govern the criminalist's relationships with his colleagues, supervisors, lawyers, litigants, the press, and the public? Even the simple courtroom maxim to "tell the truth, the whole truth, and nothing but the truth" is not so easy to apply in practice. What is the correct response to the instruction from the court to provide a *yes* or *no* answer to counsel's question? What should the criminalist do when an important question is not asked? Does the obligation to tell the *whole truth* mean that all *possible*, all *probable*, all *reasonably probable*, all *highly probable*, or only the *most probable* alternatives must be given in response to a question?

The criminalist's work may be considered by judges, juries, or lawyers, who make decisions that profoundly affect other people's lives. The fact that the criminalist does not have to decide guilt or innocence, pass judgment of death or life without parole, or determine the amount of liability for civil damages does not mean that the criminalist can ignore the fact that the results of the work done in the laboratory may be used, sometimes correctly and sometimes incorrectly, as the basis for such decisions. In the same way that the criminalist cannot escape responsibility for the consequences of the work that is done in the laboratory, neither can the criminalist escape the responsibility for ensuring that the work is used appropriately. There are many circumstances in which the work of the criminalist is capable of misuse by those who either do not understand the implications of the laboratory results or are willing to misrepresent the work to further their own interests. The credibility of the forensic scientist and the profession in general is wholly dependent on the confidence that the users of these services have in the reliability and accuracy of the work performed.

The criminalist's work is ultimately published in a report in which an opinion is expressed based on the laboratory results combined with the knowledge and experience of the criminalist. In some situations, the criminalist is assigned evidence that must be analyzed by following specialized procedures in which the criminalist is uniquely trained. In other situations, the criminalist responds to an incident scene and must supervise the entire process of evidence collection and scene documentation. On another day a truck may back up to the door of the laboratory and unload a houseful of items along with a request to "examine for all relevant evidence." No matter what the situation, the criminalist cannot ignore the professional obligations that are defined by appropriate codes of professional practice. Whether undertaking a specialized laboratory analysis, processing an incident scene, or determining what should be done with a truck full of evidence, the criminalist has an obligation to do so competently so that the maximum amount of information is obtained that is relevant to the matter under investigation. The obligation is more than to simply be an analyst — the criminalist must understand the scientific issues relevant to the analysis as well as the relevant forensic (legal) issues.

Purpose of This Book

The development of a code of ethics for a profession is a fundamental attribute that defines a vocation as a profession. Along with the appropriate specialized educational requirements and demonstration of competence by a process developed by the profession, the existence of a code of ethics that defines appropriate behavior in matters involving professional practice is one hallmark of a profession. The requirement for appropriate and specific education is obvious — the specialized work done by a professional practitioner in any field requires some type of specialized training. For most of the traditional professions — law, medicine, accountancy, or teaching — the specialized nature of the work requires some specific training as well as general education relevant to the professional activity.

The criminalistics profession has suffered from the absence of such educational requirements. Persons entering the field from a college or university program in chemistry, biochemistry, biology, or other fields typically required for newly hired criminalists generally have had little, if any, exposure to the field of forensic science or criminalistics. Most agencies that hire neophyte criminalists find it necessary to provide training programs for their new employees. These training programs cover not only technical subjects in the specialty to which the new hires will be assigned but also an introduction to criminalistics and professional responsibilities and ethics. These subjects, which for most professions constitute a part of their formal professional education, must be a part of in-service training for most criminalists.

It is easy to read a document titled *Code of Ethics* or *Standards of Professional Practice*, nod wisely, and think, *I agree with all of that and cannot imagine a situation in which there would be a problem with following the practices specified.* The situations described in this book, most based on actual incidents, should demonstrate that the proper course of action is not always obvious, codes of ethics do not necessarily cover all contingencies, and not all professional standards are necessarily appropriate.

Existing Codes of Ethics

No standardized or generally accepted code of ethics for criminalists exists. The first and perhaps only code of ethics developed specifically for criminalists was developed by the California Association of Criminalists. This code has served as a model for codes of ethics adopted by other professional organizations of criminalists or closely allied practitioners — the American Board of Criminalistics, the Association of Firearms and Toolmark Examiners, and several of the regional forensic science organizations. The other source of an ethics code for criminalists is the American Academy of Forensic Sciences. Their ethics code, different in fundamental structure and content from the CAC's, also serves as the basis for other codes of ethics. The differences between these two codes, and the advantages and disadvantages of one over the other, are described in Chapter 3.

Codes of ethics should not be considered immutable documents. Indeed, only a stagnant profession will not see the need to address new developments as they consider ethical obligations of the profession. Some of the developments in the forensic laboratory that should have an impact on ethical codes include computerized databases, DNA profiling, the war on drugs, and increased narrowing of professional practices (also referred to as specialization). Does the forensic scientist or the laboratory have an obligation to purge databases when individuals are erroneously entered into the database? If DNA profiling reveals unexpected family relationships or genetic conditions, does the forensic scientist have an obligation to divulge this information? Should the forensic scientist become a soldier in the war on drugs by manufacturing actual or fake illicit drugs for use in undercover operations, or producing false reports to further such operations? What should the analytical chemist, trained in glass analysis using the Glass Refractive Index Measurement (GRIM) and mass spectrometer, do when ordered to process a crime scene? Do current codes of ethics provide helpful guidance in these situations?

Enforcement of Codes of Ethics

The application of codes of ethics to any professional activity must accomplish one of two alternatives: The specific activity under consideration must be deemed either ethical or unethical. The code must be constructed carefully, with the understanding that behavior not explicitly deemed unethical will, by default, be accepted as ethical. Professional organizations have the responsibility not only to enforce ethical behavior of their members but also to explain why certain actions are not violations of ethical requirements. The credibility of the profession requires that both of these responsibilities are effectively exercised by the professional organization.

There are many situations in which ethical conduct by a professional is perceived as inappropriate by certain members of the public. Lawsuits seen as frivolous, medical procedures seen as experimental, or expert testimony seen as "junk science" may, by the lawyer, doctor, or forensic scientist, be seen as entirely desirable and ethical professional practices. The credibility of a profession rests largely on its ability to educate and convince the public that the actions taken were appropriate.

It is not enough to adopt a code of ethics — mechanisms must be available to allow allegations of unethical behavior to be brought, investigated, and resolved by the professional organization. The process by which this is done must be fair to the person charged with an ethical violation, considerate of the person who made the allegation, convincing to all concerned, and helpful in allowing other members of the profession to conform their conduct to expected requirements in similar situations in the future. The primary objective of a code of ethics and enforcement of its provisions with respect to individual practitioners is not to rid the profession of bad apples. The goal is to provide a mechanism by which all members of the profession can gauge their conduct in certain situations in which alternative courses of action are possible. Ultimately, of course, a practitioner may decide on a course of action that is so contrary to the requirements of the code of ethics that expulsion from the professional organization is seen as the only reasonable alternative. In some professions, expulsion means legal disqualification of the person from practice. The consequences of being expelled from a forensic science association are not generally so drastic since membership in a forensic science organization is generally not required.

Fundamentally, a code of ethics and adherence to its principles are for the benefit of the public. Only in limited circumstances does unethical behavior affect other practitioners directly. The public perception that a profession has a reasonable code of ethics, and a reasonable process for making sure that its members abide by its requirements, is critical to the credibility the profession. Allegations of ethical violations by one practitioner may not have a direct impact on other practitioners. However, the overall credibility of the profession and its image depend on the public perception of how it responds to allegations of unethical conduct. One need only read the daily newspaper or listen to dinner table conversations to understand how a profession's image is influenced by the public perception of a particular individual's actions as ethical or unethical. Further, if the profession is not seen as reacting swiftly and appropriately when unethical conduct has occurred, the public concludes that such behavior is condoned or even endorsed by the profession.

Sanctions

There is a general belief among some criminalists that unethical behavior is akin to a mortal sin and that no punishment short of professional excommunication is appropriate. This belief is held by the same people who assert that there is no real need for a code of ethics for criminalists because, if the criminalist simply follows a few simple moral rules (usually rules that the person making this argument supports), there would be no need for a code of ethics. Any violation of these moral rules would, of course, be such a gross violation of appropriate professional behavior that banishment from the profession should be the least of the sanctions that are exacted.

This simplistic view fails to address the complexities and subtleties inherent in enforcing a code of ethics. While ethical rules may be based in part on moral principles, they are also influenced by other rules — in the case of criminalists, at least legal and scientific rules. As a consequence of various and often conflicting values that must be accommodated, not all violations of codes of ethics deserve the ultimate sanction. Furthermore, if the ultimate sanction were to be the only one available, what would one do in cases of minor violations of acceptable professional behavior?

In the same way that the law has a variety of punishments designed to fit the crime, so must there be a variety of sanctions available when a practitioner has violated an ethical requirement. At the present time the available sanctions are limited because the ability to engage in a professional criminalistic practice is not under the control of professional organizations. What sanctions are available, how they are applied, and the consequences of their application will be discussed in Chapter 3.

The value of a code of ethics is not to prevent or even punish the most egregious violations. Practitioners who commit such ethical violations — lying about qualifications, failing to actually perform the tests they claim to have done, or putting material from evidence into their own pockets — will not be dissuaded by a code of ethics. If adherence to a code of ethics is a condition of employment, such violations might be cause for dismissal; but these types of egregious acts need no ethics code to make them unacceptable — they are in most cases illegal, or at the very least a clear violation of employer policies.

The primary value of a code of ethics is to provide a ruler against which to measure proposed actions in certain situations. Codes of ethics should enable practitioners to justify a particular course of action in a particular circumstance. For example, there is a recurring debate among forensic scientists concerning the appropriateness of crime lab personnel preparing cocaine or methamphetamine "look-alike" samples in kilogram quantities for use by undercover narcotics investigators. There are mixed views on this issue. One way to resolve the issue may be to refer to a code of ethics and determine if such activity would be, or could be, considered unethical under that code. There is obviously no clear right or wrong answer to this question; but for the undecided person, reference to a code of ethics might provide some guidance for a personal decision. In addition, if a practitioner relies on a section of the code of ethics to follow some particular course of action, the organization has an obligation to support that member's decision if, in its opinion, the member made the ethically correct decision.

Section II of this book will present a number of ethical dilemmas and discuss their resolutions. Many of these were presented by the author in a series of brief notes in the newsletter of the California Association of Criminalists published 20 years ago. Much of the discussion of these issues is based on comments received from readers when these dilemmas were first published. Other dilemmas will be presented that come from more recent sources, and some are entirely hypothetical in nature. The purpose of these dilemmas is to provide some concrete examples of how codes of ethics can be applied to actual situations that arise in professional practice.

Lest anyone think that this book is meant to be the final or definitive word on the subject of ethics for criminalists, rest assured that I have no such intention. Since ethics are basically no more than a set of arbitrary rules that define appropriate behavior, the rules can only apply to the situations for which they are defined. Being arbitrary, they can be changed. Ethics rules are not moral imperatives — they may be an attempt to apply moral imperatives to real-world situations, or they may simply be arbitrary rules established to try to make some operation or function work more smoothly. I can only hope that you will consider this discussion in light of the ethical rules you have agreed to follow. When you are faced with ethical dilemmas, I hope this book will help you make a decision that you can defend and live with. If the decision required by the applicable rules seems to be the wrong one, then perhaps the rules need changing. The rules have been changed in the past, and they will be changed in the future. Were this not the case, the criminalistics profession would be stagnant indeed.

Why Are Professional Ethics Necessary?

2

Importance of Codes of Professional Ethics

The consumers of the services of the forensic science practitioner or laboratory are generally police officers, lawyers, investigators, business executives, and the occasional private party. These consumers have problems that they hope to resolve with the assistance of a forensic scientist. Presumably the reason that these consumers require the services of a criminalist is that they are unable to do the work themselves; they may not even be sure that the criminalist can provide any assistance in the matters under investigation. These consumers of the criminalist's professional services, then, are relying on the criminalist to competently provide the services that are expected and required for the matter at hand. While some make fairly routine use of the services of a forensic laboratory, such as police investigators or trial lawyers, it is a mistake to assume that every request, even from an experienced user, will fully clarify the issues that can only be addressed by a thorough and competent examination and evaluation of the evidence.

In some cases, the nature of the required services, combined with the experience of the consumer, are evident — a blood stain on the clothing of a suspect in an assault case, a shoe sole impression under the window where a burglar may have entered a residence, a bullet recovered from the body of the victim — are obvious types of evidence, familiar to any experienced investigator or forensic scientist. Requests for DNA analysis of the blood stain, comparison of the scene impression with the suspect's shoes, or determination of the weapon that may have fired the bullet are obvious to both the consumer and the criminalist. Requests for these analyses can be handled routinely and simply take advantage of the fact that the criminalist has education, training, and experience that the consumer lacks to carry out the requested examinations.

However, it should not be a requirement that the consumer know exactly what services are necessary in order to obtain the most effective assistance from the criminalist. The criminalist has an obligation, in spite of the request being made, to undertake the work necessary for the resolution of the issues that are relevant to the matter under investigation. It is the criminalist's responsibility to determine if there is any significance to the pattern of the blood stain, the trace evidence on the soles of the shoes, or the paint transfer on the bullet. The professional practitioner in any field is expected to know more than the layman about what professional services might be appropriate in any particular case. Is the distribution of the blood or the appearance of individual stains important? Is the stain a contact transfer or a blood spatter? Has it been washed? Is it a mixture? Other than a determination that the shoe sole impression could have been made by the suspect's shoe, or any shoe with a similar sole pattern in a similar state of wear, can anything more be learned about the impression? Are the shoes common or unusual? Is it possible to eliminate shoes with the same sole design but of a different size? Is there anything else about the bullet, or any material on the bullet, that might be of value to the investigator? Is there damage to the bullet indicating a ricochet?

A code of ethics helps to define the relationship between the consumer and the person providing service. The consumer is not expected to know in any great detail all of the professional resources that could be brought to bear in a particular situation. The professional is expected to be aware of the entire gamut of services that could resolve the issues relevant to the case. Codes of ethics may require that the professional practitioner provide a level of service beyond that which was specifically requested by the consumer.

Legal vs. Scientific Practices

Just as the science involved in the examination of physical evidence may be foreign territory to the consumer of forensic services, the legal, investigative, or business environment may involve requirements, policies, or procedures that are alien to the scientist. This is particularly true at the convergence of science and the law, where most criminalists spend a great deal of their professional lives. One does not have to be a criminalist for very long to see that there are many differences in the ways problems are resolved by scientists and the way they are resolved by lawyers. It would be presumptuous to argue that one side has a better technique than the other. The goals are different, and the mechanisms designed by lawyers and scientists work well in their respective arenas. It is when legal issues are decided by scientists, or science issues decided by lawyers, that difficulties arise.

While there are many differences in the approaches taken by lawyers and scientists to resolving issues, there are two areas in which the differences are the most problematic. The first can be referred to as necessity issues: lawyers need to resolve any particular issue in a timely fashion, or the issue may become moot. Arrests must be made before the suspects disappear, speedy trials must be held as prescribed by law, sentences must be carried out in a timely fashion, and verdicts must be rendered or judgments satisfied in order to provide appropriate relief to aggrieved parties. A second difference between science and the law can be referred to as the limited evidence issue: there is only a finite quantity of any physical evidence. The available evidence may be limited by mass or by time, but in any case it does not exist forever in unlimited physical quantity. The necessity of resolving the matter under investigation with a limited quantity of physical evidence often places the lawyer and the scientist in conflicting roles. The scientist would like to approach the problem slowly and methodically and use as much of the sample as necessary, even getting more when the sample is consumed. The forensic world just does not work this way, and the practices of both the scientists and the lawyers should be able to handle these conflicting requirements.

The first step in balancing conflicting requirements is the need for the consumers and providers of professional services to understand the requirements of the other. This requirement exists in any professional relationship, whether it is the doctor and the patient, the lawyer and the client, or the teacher and the student. The key to this understanding is communication. The consumer needs to communicate the legal or investigative requirements to the criminalist, and the criminalist needs to communicate the scientific and technical requirements to the investigator or lawyer. The current legal requirements for scientific evidence are set forth in the U.S. Supreme Court decisions of *Daubert v. Merrell Dow Pharmaceuticals* and *Kumho Tire Company v. Patrick Carmichael* (see Appendices 8 and 9). Unfortunately, there are no technical references that serve to communicate scientific requirements to the lawyer.

With or without good communications, seemingly irresolvable differences sometimes arise. In those situations, one approach to the resolution is by reference to codes of professional ethics or conduct. If a particular course of conduct is required by an ethical code, then the person to whom the code applies has a powerful argument for that course of action. When dealing with other professionals who have codes of ethics they are obligated to follow, the realization that a particular course of action is an ethical requirement is frequently accepted as justification for that course of action. When providers of a professional service simply explain to the consumer that the proposed action is required by ethical rules, this should be sufficient to justify and defend the action taken.

Ethics and Morals

The distinction between morals and ethics is often a difficult one. One primary distinction is that a code of ethics implies that there is a written document containing ethical rules. Moral principles, on the other hand, are generally not written down in a concise list. Moral principles are generally recognized, within the milieu in which they are applicable, as appropriate guidelines for personal conduct. All ethical codes draw to some extent on the generally accepted moral values of the culture in which the ethical codes are developed; but moral principles are, in themselves, insufficient to govern action. What, then, is lacking in a set of moral values that is present in a code of ethics?

In the first place, the code of ethics is in writing. There are specific rules to be followed, and there is a specific document in which these rules are set forth. Moral rules are generally not quite so clearly stated. When moral rules are clearly stated, they may not be accepted by everyone with the same weight of authority. Moreover, moral rules may not be explicitly written; they may be expressed by parables, religious dogma, philosophical exposition, or political rhetoric. Regardless of form, there are always those who disagree over the meaning and applicability of these rules.

Ethical rules derive from mutual agreement. It is not possible to force people to agree to abide by a code of ethics, although some gentle coercion is always possible (*If you want this job, you have to agree to adhere to this code of ethics* or *If you want to be a member of this professional organization, you have to agree to abide by this code of ethics*). For some professions, agreement to abide by the code of ethics, and continuing adherence to those ethics, is a requirement to practice the profession. Such professions enjoy a high degree of admiration because it is correctly assumed that those members of the profession who have been found guilty of unethical behavior are no longer able to practice that profession. For an ethical code to enjoy any general public credibility, it must be perceived by the public as a high standard for the practitioners of the profession to whom it applies.

In discussions of ethics it is often argued that persons who follow basic moral principles will not run into any ethical difficulties. Perhaps if we all agreed to the same interpretation of the same moral rules, such would be the case. The fact that not everyone shares the same moral convictions, however, means that reliance on moral values or rules to govern professional behavior is not likely to be successful. Further, many issues that are addressed by some codes of ethics have no particular moral component. For example, what moral rule would tell us that assisting a lawyer in cross-examining an expert witness (even to the point of discrediting that witness) is ethical, even when it is understood that the opinion offered by the witness is a correct one? While moral rules may have value in our professional lives, they are no more help in deciding ethical courses of action than they are in determining criminal culpability or civil liability. Written codes (statutes) or other written guidelines (regulations, legal precedent) are necessary to apply societal values to the behavior of citizens. Similarly, written codes of conduct are required to codify the behavior expected of professional practitioners.

The general moral principles that form a portion of the underlying principles for a code of ethics for criminalists are not easy to articulate. Volumes have been written by theologians, philosophers, politicians, and academics about what constitutes appropriate moral behavior. It is probably not possible to find a universally accepted set of moral values that can form the basis of an ethics code. Rather, it must be assumed that a group of people who collaborate on developing a code of ethics will do so within the framework of a set of mutually, if not explicitly, agreed upon moral values. When a code of ethics is developed by a collaborative process, it is unlikely that any differences in the content of such a code is based on a moral difference of opinion.

Although moral precepts form a portion of the basis of most codes of professional ethics, they are not the only source of such rules. Only in the most general and theoretical ways are ethics based on morality. Beyond the influence of moral values, there are other far removed considerations that affect a code of ethics. Codes of ethics represent an attempt by a group of individuals to document the shared expectations of others in their group.

For the criminalist, there are several different sources for the rules that guide the formation of a professional code of ethics. First, general moral principles play an important part in the development of a code of ethics. Second, the requirements of science play an important role in the development of a code of ethics in any scientific profession, including criminalistics. The influence of science on the professional ethics of scientists includes technical requirements. For example, a requirement that conclusions must be based on data and techniques that are generally known or published is a typical requirement for a code of ethics for a criminalist. This requirement would probably not apply to a scientist working in a military weapons development program. Another influence of science on professional ethics is the collegial aspect of science. The tradition in the science community is to freely exchange information, to stay abreast of advances in science, and to contribute to the exchange of information. These collegial aspects of science have an important bearing on the development of a code of ethics of a professional scientist. They are not always completely compatible with the interests or ethical practices of others with whom scientists interact on a professional basis.

Credibility as a Reason for a Code of Ethics

By their mere existence, codes of ethics give professions a degree of credibility that they may not otherwise enjoy. The development of a code of ethics is not simple, and the fact that a code has been developed demonstrates that the profession has considered its relationship to society and accepted its responsibility to determine appropriate courses of action in certain circumstances in which more than one alternative appears to exist. For example, when asked by a client to perform a screening test for a substance and then testify in court as to the result, it is helpful to refer to an ethical code when advising the client that more definitive testing needs to be done because it would be unethical to testify solely on the basis of a screening test. (Of course, there are situations when it is technically and ethically correct to do so. In some circumstances, however, ethical requirements to perform adequate testing or to explain results that are less conclusive than they might be with further testing may have a bearing on what the criminalist should do or say.)

The consumer must have confidence that the professional service provider is capable of comprehensive and competent performance. In other words, the consumer of professional services expects to receive a thorough consideration of the relevant issues within the purview of the professional. In addition, the consumer expects that the services are performed with technical competence to produce reliable results.

The customer is often naive about the professional capabilities that might be brought to bear on the problem at hand. The customer may think that a specific analysis or examination is required; but it is incumbent on the professional to understand the nature of the customer's problem and advise how to proceed to maximize the value of the professional service. When consulting with an accountant, for example, a client may request that the accountant "do my taxes." If the accountant fails to ascertain that the client has certain deductions to which he may be entitled, or income that the client does not know should be reported, the client might feel, when the IRS comes knocking, that the accountant did not provide a high level of service. Similarly, assume a forensic scientist is asked to undertake a blood spatter interpretation. After he testifies about his interpretation, another criminalist testifies that the stains examined were not blood but redwood deck stain. The lawyer retaining the first criminalist would probably feel that he had not received the highest level of professional service.

The customer expects technical competence. The missed diagnosis, the unstated objection, or the misinterpreted infrared spectrum undoubtedly leads to a lack of confidence in the medical, legal, or criminalistics professional. One's peers may judge the service as competently performed, but the judgment of the customer is often more damaging to the professional career. After all, it is normally the naive layman who engages the service of a professional practitioner. If the layman believes that the services provided by a particular practitioner — or by practitioners of that profession in general — are of little value, he will not use that practitioner or those services.

A lawyer, investigator, businessman, or private party who uses or is affected by the services of a criminalist is unable to determine whether the service is provided in a competent manner. The consumer must use mechanisms other than a technical evaluation of the service in deciding whether or not to use a particular consultant or technical service. A complete technical evaluation of the service is also not normally possible. The consumer must, then, rely on other criteria for passing judgment on the services that have been provided or recommended. Among the criteria that may be used for evaluation is learning whether a specific practitioner will be allowed to practice. If there are legal or professional mechanisms in place that effectively weed out incompetent or dishonest practitioners, the confidence of the consumer is enhanced. One of the primary mechanisms available to professional organizations to maintain the credibility of the profession is to effectively adopt and enforce a code of ethics.

Since criminalistics is a forensic science and is therefore intertwined with the law, guidelines for the development of a code of ethics should include legal requirements. Legal requirements are often in direct conflict with appropriate values or practices for a scientist. For example, the confidentiality of the lawyer–client relationship (which extends to persons working on behalf of that lawyer–client pair) often requires that data developed by a scientist are made available only to persons who are involved in the same lawyer–client relationship as the scientist. On the other hand, the normal credibility of a scientific conclusion, or the scientist making that conclusion, is based on a public review of the data on which the conclusion is based. The conflict between the desire of lawyers to keep information confidential and the obligation of scientists to make data public gives rise to ethical dilemmas that must be resolved.

Of course, lawyers are not the only people to whom criminalists must demonstrate a high degree of credibility. Since criminalistics is a profession in which the knowledge and skills of a practitioner are applied to the affairs of others, those "others" are entitled to some input into the code of ethics. They may include persons directly influenced by the practitioner's work product, those who utilize the work product in their own professional practices, and, more abstractly, the system (e.g., criminal justice or legal system) in which the professional practices.

The development of an acceptable professional code of ethics requires the participation of all of these diverse groups and careful consideration of the consequences of any prescribed or prohibited courses of action within the context of each of the affected groups. To develop a code of ethics, one must have an understanding of each of the areas from which the code of ethics is drawn. For the criminalist, this means an understanding of general cultural morals and values; an understanding of the values, morals, and principles of science; an understanding of basic principles of the law; an understanding of the rights and concomitant obligations of a professional expert witness; and an understanding of how the work of the criminalist affects the lives of others in the community.

The scientific principles that underlie a code of ethics for criminalists include both the practice of science and the relationship of scientists. The practice of science involves a certain way of looking at the world, a certain way of arriving at conclusions about the real world, and a certain way of interacting with fellow scientists. Scientists are expected to base their opinions on things that can be seen, touched, described, or counted. Scientists arrive at conclusions and opinions by following a process called the "scientific method." The scientific method requires the scientist to make observations using valid methods and use these observations to form the basis of an opinion. Critical to the scientific method is that the scientist's conclusions can be verified by other scientists. This requires that the methods and processes that underlie a scientist's opinion are available to another scientist for review. In developing a code of ethics for practitioners in a scientific discipline, it is necessary to consider how to reflect the features that are deemed essential to the scientific aspects of their work.

Criminalists are not simply scientists — they are forensic scientists. The effect of applying the adjective *forensic* to the scientist's job title is a profound one. It introduces the need for the criminalist to consider the requirements of the law in whatever actions are taken. Interestingly, and not too surprisingly, the proper course of action in most situations is the same whether considered from the standpoint of science or of the law. There are situations in which the requirements of the law and science differ — conflicts may develop in areas of disclosure, compensation, validity, and experimental design. What data developed in the crime lab must be retained or disclosed? Is it appropriate for scientific consultants to work on cases for fees that are contingent on the outcome of the cases? How is the validity of a scientific technique established or, often more importantly, what is required to demonstrate that a scientific technique lacks the validity required by legal precedent, judicial desire, or statutory requirement? Who is to be the judge of appropriate experimental design? Is experimental design subject to judicial review (in other words, is it a matter of law), or is it subject to review by juries (in other words, a matter of fact)? Some specific instances of these conflicts will be described and discussed in subsequent chapters.

Obligations of the Expert Witness

The criminalist enjoys a prerogative that few members of society enjoy — that of expressing an opinion in a court of law. Most witnesses are required to state their observations — what they have seen, heard, felt, smelled, or tasted. Since the jury is assumed to be competent to evaluate these observations, the witnesses are restricted to providing the data upon which the jury (the witness's peers) can reach a conclusion. The expert witness, however, occupies a special place in the courtroom; and the law allows the expert witness to express his conclusions and opinions on certain issues based on data that the witness has obtained. Even further, the expert witness need not even have personally obtained that data. The witness is entitled to rely upon data received from another source — hearsay data — to form an opinion. Generally, the only requirement is that the data are of the type that other experts in the witness's particular field customarily rely on in forming opinions.

Strangely, in return for the privilege of appearing as an expert witness, the law has placed few obligations on the expert witness. It is interesting to speculate on why there are so few restrictions placed on expert witnesses. The obligation of the trial lawyer is to present his client's case in the most effective possible way. This means that the legal profession has little to gain by restricting its ability to call witnesses to the stand to express opinions that are helpful to the case. One would think that lawyers can distinguish an expert with legitimate expertise from one who has none, but this is apparently not the case. It is assumed that the process of *voir dire*, by which experts state their qualifications for the court so that the court can determine their expertise, and the process of cross examination serve to weed out incompetent experts. This is demonstrably not the case. One might suppose that the reason for this is that lawyers are not trained as scientists and simply have a hard time telling the good scientists from the bad ones. While this may be part of the problem, the fundamental problem is that the legal profession does not want to be restricted as to who they can call as a witness when they have a particular point to prove in a case. Since lawyers are reluctant to diminish the pool of experts available for their use, they have never supported efforts to prevent incompetent or unethical expert witnesses from appearing in court.

The lawyer must simply demonstrate to the satisfaction of the court that the witness possesses knowledge, experience, and training in the relevant discipline that are greater than those of the average layman. The judge arbitrates the decision to allow a witness to express an opinion. The trial judge's rulings in such issues are rarely reversed by appellate courts. Scientists who observe the legal process generally agree that the evaluation of a potential witness's expertise is not a notable strength of the legal profession. This is hardly surprising given that most lawyers have little training or experience in the technical matters that come before them. The selection of an expert witness is frequently based on factors other than the witness's expertise. Witnesses may be granted expert witness privileges based on academic or professional degrees, employment, self-defined experience, prior experience as an expert witness, or other factors that may or may not have any bearing on the witness's expertise.

Most professions have developed their own mechanisms for recognition of members who have achieved a level of professional competence. The so-called traditional professions, particularly law, medicine, and teaching, are governed by legally mandated licensing requirements as a prerequisite of entering practice. The legal and medical professions also have specialty certifications; and such certifications may be required, for example, before physicians are granted hospital privileges. Other professions have certification programs that serve as peer recognition of the status of the individual practitioner. These programs vary in quality and credibility, and they may or may not be considered by those who evaluate the expertise of a particular practitioner. Any profession that is perceived to be dedicated to self-regulation, and has mechanisms in place to evaluate the professional competence of a practitioner, generally enjoys an increased level of consumer confidence.

Lawyers are sometimes unable or unwilling to take the steps necessary to prevent incompetent and dishonest experts from appearing as witnesses. But is this the lawyer's responsibility? Whose responsibility is it to see that only competent lawyers have clients, only competent doctors have patients, or only competent accountants complete income tax returns? In some cases the government regulates the professions, and persons without the appropriate governmental recognition (license) cannot engage in a professional practice. But criminalists do not have governmental licensing. (An exception to this in California is licensing analysts who perform blood alcohol analyses in DUI cases.) It is interesting to speculate on the response of courts if governmental licenses were required for expert witnesses. Would a court not permit an otherwise qualified witness from testifying because the witness was not licensed? Would the court accept a governmental license as sufficient proof of a criminalist's expertise?

Consumers generally are unable to evaluate the validity of the work done by the professional. Indeed, one of the best definitions of a professional is "a person with training in some department of knowledge and who applies that training to the affairs of others." One cannot rely on market forces to separate the competent from the incompetent, the honest from the dishonest, or the ethical from the unethical. The evaluation of the work of a professional is most often judged on the outcome of the matter under consideration. A favorable verdict, a nice tax refund, or relief from pain generally results in a satisfactory evaluation by the client or patient. Other professionals may judge the services substandard, but the word of the patient or client undoubtedly has a significant effect on the public's perception of the professional. Conversely, an unanticipated verdict or an analytical result that led to an erroneous arrest may cause the lawyer who has hired a forensic scientist to negatively evaluate the quality of the services provided. Knowledgeable forensic scientists, on the other hand, could well look at the work done in these cases and determine that the services provided were competent. If a profession wants to weed out incompetent practitioners, it must do so on its own initiative. This is preferable to the alternative of allowing an outside organization, which is likely less qualified to rule on professional competence, to impose such decisions.

A member of a profession is obligated to assist in the development of programs, procedures, and policies that will help ensure that only competent people practice in the profession, and that clients have some way to tell the competent from the incompetent, the honest from the dishonest, and the ethical from the unethical. This professional recognition is not something that is accomplished overnight by establishing a code of ethics. Professional certification, laboratory accreditation, standardization of educational criteria, and development of commonly accepted laboratory protocols are all part of a process that will eventually lead to the recognition of criminalists as professional scientists. As an adjunct to all of these programs, a code of professional practice or a code of ethics can serve as a mechanism to ensure that practitioners follow generally professional practices in their technical work, their relationships with their employers or clients, their relationships with other professions, their relationships with the general public, and their relationships with one another.

Other Rules Are Not Enough

It is a common misconception among criminalists that the proper rules of professional conduct are set down for them either by the law, if they are in the courtroom, or by their employer, if they are in the lab. During a criminalist's career, even if every decision could be justified on the basis of a legal rule or a workplace rule, the development of a profession of criminalistics still requires the development of a code of ethics to provide some evidence that issues of appropriate professional conduct have been considered. A code of ethics for scientists, in general, does not exist. Institutions who employ scientists, funding agencies, or other professional associations to which scientists belong (for example, medical associations) may have their own code of ethics. But there is no code of ethics for scientists.

The other aspect of a criminalist's professional activity is the law and, in some case, law enforcement agencies. Lawyers and law offices (whether they be a public office such as a prosecutor or public defender or a private law firm) may have codes of ethics developed by that office or by some related professional organization. Law enforcement agencies have codes of ethics that may have been developed internally or adopted from some other source. It would be naive to think that codes of ethics developed by these agencies or professional associations would be adequate for criminalists. Even if they were, the credibility of criminalistics as a profession relies in no small measure on demonstrated standards of professional practice — a code of ethics — adopted by the profession.

Competence

This brings us to the convergence of ethics and competence. We must first address the question of whether competent professional service implies that the result, advice, or other product is always correct. Clearly that is not always the case. Professional work may be done in a very competent manner but lead to a result that is less than optimum. This may be due to technical limitations in analytical methods, lack of knowledge of relevant information, or unusual circumstances that are not anticipated. The judgment of whether a professional service was competently rendered can only realistically be made by other members of the professional community.

The evaluation of the competence of any professional practitioner generally addresses the performance of that person in the context of a specific professional assignment, or case, or a series of related cases. The review or evaluation of a professional's work may be in the context of a second opinion on a particular case, a normal case review process within the agency or firm employing the professional, a review by a licensing or certification agency pursuant to normal procedure or a specific complaint, or review by a professional organization as a result of a complaint received. In any of these review processes, the reviewers are asked to determine if the professional service was provided in a technically competent manner; and they may be asked to determine if the actions of the professional violated any canons of ethics or codes of professional conduct that are applicable.

During this evaluation, the issue of the relationship between competence and ethics may be faced. Presumably, criminalists can recognize competence and incompetence when they see it. However, some disagreement may exist as to what constitutes competent practice, and a code of ethics may indeed help resolve such issues. Most criminalists would agree that the identification of a stain as human blood based solely on a presumptive color test, basing a bullet identification on the fact that the bullet and firearm both have 6 right rifling with the same land and groove widths, or concluding that a hair came from a particular person to the exclusion of all others based on microscopic similarity would qualify as incompetent work on the part of a criminalist. But do any of those situations establish unethical conduct on the part of the practitioner? In the first instance, if the criminalist explains that the red-brown, crusty appearance of the stain and the proximity of similar stains that were proven to be human blood were other factors on which the opinion was based, does the issue of competence or possible ethics violation change? In the case of the bullet identification, if the examiner had been abruptly transferred to the firearms section, had received no training in firearms identification, and had been assigned this case, would the issues of competence or potential ethics violations be considered differently? In the case of the hair examiner, who was trained by an "old timer" who believed that such opinions were justified, is the analyst either incompetent or unethical? What can reasonably be expected of a professional?

The layman is not able to independently assess the competence of the criminalist. If the work of the professional that the layman has retained is unsatisfactory, the layman may register a complaint. The complaint may be that the practitioner is incompetent, the practitioner is unethical, or just a vague description of dissatisfaction with the work of the criminalist. The response to such a complaint will, in large measure, determine the credibility of the profession. To disregard or minimize the complaint, and especially to ignore it, will result in the consumers of the services becoming convinced that the profession has no desire to solve the problems that the clients perceive.

Since the professional role of the criminalist is to apply his knowledge and training to the affairs of others, it is the criminalist's obligation to provide clients with some means of evaluating the criminalist. Such evaluation may be done before any work is started, such as in making a decision to hire a criminalist to work for a law enforcement agency. The evaluation may be done in the context of a specific case, as when deciding to consult with a criminalist over matters in a lawsuit that are technical in nature. In other cases the evaluation may occur when work is done by a criminalist on a particular case. At the most basic level, the issue of concern to all consumers is competence. But competence cannot be judged by most of the individuals who utilize the services provided by a criminalist. The only thing a potential client has to go on in deciding who to hire or retain is anecdotal evidence, mostly no more than a random name. Just imagine what it would be like if anyone could claim to be a doctor or a lawyer. If you were sick or arrested, on whom would you rely? While it would be foolish to go to a doctor just because the person has an M.D. on the sign outside the office, or to a lawyer who has Attorney at Law on the letterhead, it would be equally foolish to ask someone for legal advice who is not a member of the bar, or to ask for medical advice from someone who is not a licensed physician.

Adherence to a code of ethics does not, of course, ensure competence. Membership in a professional organization with a code of ethics, and a policy and procedure designed to respond to complaints received from consumers, will go a long way to demonstrate that a profession seeks to provide a valuable service and makes efforts to regulate the practices of its members.

General Societal Obligation

The criminalist has an obligation to conform his conduct to appropriate ethical standards. Every person sees ethical standards differently. From the standpoint of the layman, the most important requirement for the criminalist is competence. Other ethical requirements relating, for example, to the relationships of the criminalist with colleagues, attorneys, or supervisors, while perhaps not as important to the layman who is affected by the work done, are also part of the criminalist's obligation.

In order to function effectively in the justice system, the criminalist must enjoy the respect of his scientific colleagues (both those who are forensic scientists and those who are not), as well as other professionals who are involved in the justice system — lawyers, investigators, and judges. Competence is only one of the issues, and may not even be the primary one, by which a criminalist is judged by these colleagues. Scientists may be more interested in process than anything else — the right answer for the wrong reason is not much better than the wrong answer. The lawyer may be more interested in having a witness that can be an asset to the argument presented. The criminalist must decide how to address the sometimes conflicting requirements of this diverse group of people, and a code of ethics is one guideline that can help deal with situations where demands conflict.

The vast majority of practitioners strive to be ethical at all times. In their efforts to follow ethical practices, criminalists are guided by codes of ethics which have been developed by professional organizations of which they are members.

While the practices of the vast majority of criminalists are consistent with established ethical principles, it should not be assumed that there are no situations that call for ethical judgments. Situations develop regularly in criminalistics that require the practitioner to make a judgment on the correct course of action. At times a criminalist will be confronted with a situation in which the alternative courses of action are seen to be troubling. At other times, a course of action, apparently without any conflict, will run afoul of an ethical requirement. It behooves all criminalists to be aware of the code of ethics of organizations to which they belong and use those guidelines for the appropriate course of action. Reliance on ethical guidelines often provides support for a decision that otherwise might be more difficult to defend. For example, a demand on the part of a client or supervisor to complete an examination by an unreasonable deadline might run afoul of an ethical requirement to do all tests necessary for proof.

The codes of ethics developed by most professional organizations have one shortcoming — since they are not often utilized, there is little in the way of history or precedent to guide the application of the ethical codes to the situations in which criminalists find themselves from time to time. Codes of ethics, like codes of laws, are documents written by individuals who are neither prescient nor omniscient. They can neither predict future development nor anticipate every future question. As a consequence, codes of ethics are written with as much or as little foresight as the people involved in the process bring to the table. Like any code governing behavior, codes of ethics must be continually interpreted, revised, and amended to reflect developments and evolution. When such codes are infrequently utilized, and not often even discussed, they cease to provide much guidance to the practitioners.

One of the reasons for the infrequent use of ethics codes is the belief of many practitioners that, by applying some simple moral rules or legal rules, all ethical problems can be resolved. Many criminalists feel that raising an ethical question is tantamount to raising a moral question: to make an accusation of violation of ethical rules is to say someone is utterly immoral. While it is certainly the case that some types of immoral behavior may be considered moral issues, there should be no harm in asking whether some action taken by a colleague is unethical. Professional organizations owe it to their members to develop mechanisms where opinions on questions of ethics can be sought, without the rancor and contentiousness that generally accompany ethical investigations.

Development of a Code of Ethics

3

Various Models of Codes of Ethics

Codes of ethics that have been adopted by various forensic science professional organizations can be broadly categorized into two types — the general type and the specific type. The general type is exemplified by the *Code of Ethics and Conduct, American Academy of Forensic Science* (AAFS) (see Appendix 1). The detailed model is exemplified by the *Code of Ethics of the California Association of Criminalists* (CAC) (see Appendix 2). The *preamble* to the CAC Code is twice the size of the *entire* Code of Ethics of the AAFS. This reflects two fundamental differences between the organizations. The AAFS was formed in an effort to unite a series of professions under a single umbrella. Since most of the professions had previously existing ethical codes, it was not necessary to cover all possible ethical contingencies. It was only necessary to make an ethics code that supplemented the individual ethics codes of the professions who were being united under the AAFS umbrella.

The development of the CAC Code, on the other hand, was an effort by a group of early criminalists in California to help define a profession for the first time. The California criminalists who founded the CAC and adopted its code of ethics were really inventing something that had never before existed: a code of ethics that tried to bridge the gap between one profession with a strong ethical tradition — the law — and another nascent profession that was trying to develop professional recognition and a means of self-governance.

Broad Model

The broad model of the code of ethics as developed by the AAFS is easy to write and covers a wide range of situations, despite its brevity. Whether situations arise in which members of the Academy feel that a colleague has acted unethically, but formally find no ethical violation, is difficult to determine. Generally speaking, situations in which complaints have been made but no ethical violation is found are not reported to the Academy.

The main drawback to the brevity and lack of specificity of the code of ethics of the AAFS is that it has little value as a guide to proper action in a particular circumstance. One of the primary values of a code of ethics, and one of the primary values of a professional organization, is that the code of ethics provides a guide to proper action in certain circumstances; and the member who abides by the code can be assured that the organization will support the decision that the member made. Further, the AAFS code provides little guidance to professionals or laymen who want to know if the actions of a member would be considered by the Academy to be unethical. Indeed, it is apparently not even necessary for the accuser of unethical conduct to cite any particular section of the code of ethics. Charges of unethical conduct against members are brought, and the ethics committee decides if the actions of the accused members fall within the scope of actions proscribed by the code.

In an attempt to provide guidance to practitioners, the AAFS has recently developed the Good Forensic Practices Committee. Apparently in recognition of the deficiencies in the AAFS code of ethics, the first task of the Good Forensic Practices Committee was to develop an ancillary set of professional guidelines that are not intended to be ethical requirements (see Appendix 4). The *Good Forensic Practices Guidelines* are aspirational guidelines, designed to distinguish what is minimally acceptable as defined by the AAFS code of ethics from what is considered good forensic practice. Violations of the standards established by the *Good Forensic Practices Guidelines* does not result in any sanction, unless such violation also violates the code of ethics.

Like the AAFS code of ethics, these professional guidelines are sufficiently vague to provide little specific guidance for the practitioner who is faced with deciding among alternative courses of action. But in any given situation, the alternatives can be evaluated in light of the aspirations expressed in the guidelines. This mechanism provides a unique opportunity for the AAFS to review the actions taken by a member, examine alternatives, and render a judgment as to the best resolution of the issue. If done in a frank and public way, this use of the *Good Forensic Practices Guidelines* would provide a valuable educational opportunity. In fact, one of the guidelines calls for "forensic scientists … [to] strive to instill the highest ethical and scientific standards in their students … ."

This committee's function is to review situations that are presented and reach a consensus as to whether the described actions are consistent with good forensic practice as defined by the guidelines developed by the committee. If these situations were routinely submitted to, evaluated by, and published by the Good Forensic Practices Committee a body of information that would develop over time would help define what *good forensic practices* are. This would be of immense value to the neophytes in the field and to experienced practitioners. One can easily imagine the evolution of these guidelines as changes in technology, law, and policy occur.

Whether this approach will provide adequate guidance to members in cases of allegations of ethical violations or improper professional conduct is yet to be seen. There have been no publicly reported cases of members charged with unethical practices that fall within the acceptable guidelines of the standards for good forensic practice.

The development of the Good Forensic Practices Committee was due to recognition by the Academy that many of its members have different views of what constitutes acceptable professional practice among forensic scientists. The Academy may also have recognized that such views differ from one section of the Academy to the next. At the same time, there are certain standards of practice that can be generally expected of all members of the Academy, and the *Good Forensic Practice Guidelines* are an effort to articulate these expectations.

Detailed Model

The alternative approach to a code of ethics is the type developed by the California Association of Criminalists and adopted in whole or in part by a number of other forensic organizations. This code contains detailed language that deals with ethics in a variety of circumstances the practitioner may face.

The development of a detailed code of ethics for criminalists such as the CAC's is a long and difficult process. It requires a clear understanding of the role of the criminalist in all of its various manifestations — the role of the criminalist as an investigator of incidents, the role of the criminalist as a expert witness, the role of the criminalist as a member of a profession, and the role of the criminalist as a member of society with certain unique privileges and prerogatives. The code of ethics not only proscribes certain types of behavior for those who profess adherence but also prescribes certain types of behavior.

The specific language found in the CAC code of ethics undoubtedly derives in significant measure from the experiences of those criminalists who were involved in drafting the document in the 1950s. The characteristics of those people are rarely found in criminalistics laboratories some 50 years later. They were trained as criminalists. Most had studied at the University of California at Berkeley under Paul L. Kirk. Most of these criminalists had at least started their careers in small laboratories where one person did all of the work that the laboratory produced. Whether the specific language in the CAC code of ethics draws from the collective experience or the collective wisdom of this group of criminalists is difficult to say. In any event, the genesis of any code of ethics is irrelevant. The only issue is the applicability and utility of the code to situations that occur in contemporary practice.

One of the challenges of a detailed and specific code of ethics such as the CAC's is that it is difficult to revise. Of course, some advantages accrue to a document that is not subject to revision whenever there is some slight new development. It is a testimony to the wisdom and foresight of the original authors that, 50 years later, much of what they said can be used to evaluate current practice. Good arguments can be made that sections of the code should be revised due to the development of new techniques, the obsolescence of some techniques, and changes in law, laboratory management, education, and other factors that could not have been foreseen by the original authors.

It is unfortunate that the revision of a code of ethics is so difficult. Especially with a code of ethics such as the CAC's, revision immediately runs into two stumbling blocks. First, there are those who will invariably argue that a behavior proposed for specific inclusion in the code of ethics is already proscribed, at least by inference, in other sections. Second, proposed revisions to one section may conflict with language in another section, requiring revision of that section, and the cycle continues.

One final difficulty with a detailed code of ethics is that it may be difficult to apply to unusual circumstances. A detailed code raises the expectation that whatever is unethical will be described specifically in the code; hence, all one has to do is to describe the offense and peruse the code for the appropriate violations. If the situation under consideration is not specifically described in the code of ethics, some may conclude that the behavior is ethical. Rather than trying to find a section of the code that could be applied, members may be tempted to look for the specific situation under consideration and, not finding it, decide that the behavior is not covered by the code of ethics.

One solution to this problem is to rely on the more general language found in the introductory paragraphs of the code. For example, the CAC code introduction states, "In carrying out these functions, the criminalist will be guided by those practices and procedures which are generally recognized within the profession to be consistent with a high level of professional ethics." This language seems to cover any situation that would be considered unethical by a tribunal — the Committee (established by the bylaws of the CAC to investigate ethics violations), the general membership of the CAC, or some other group within the profession. Contrasting this language with the more specific language used in the enumerated sections of the CAC code raises the issue of whether the language quoted above can be used to support a finding of unethical behavior. It is frequently argued that the introduction is not part of the code of ethics; any violations must be based on language in the enumerated sections of the code, not in the introductory paragraphs.

There have been many changes in forensic practice over the years since the CAC code was developed — large, multi-specialist laboratories; lack of formal education in criminalistics or forensic science for most new practitioners in the field; different requirements for the admissibility of scientific evidence in a court of law; requirements of accreditation of laboratories, certification of personnel, and standardization of methodology; and different expectations and definitions of professionalism on the part of criminalists and users of their services. Such changes will continue in the future — some resulting from evolution in the field, and some, perhaps, from devolution in the field.

Enforcement Issues

In order to implement and support an effective code of ethics, an organization must provide a variety of services to its members as well as nonmembers who might be affected by the ethics code. These services include a method of receiving complaints about members; a procedure for investigating those complaints; a procedure for a hearing in which interested parties may participate; a method for some form of review by the organization; and, finally, there must be a mechanism by which the organization decides whether an ethical violation has occurred. An appeals process, generally to the entire membership, must be available in the event unethical conduct has been found. Likewise, if the conduct of the member has been found to be appropriate, such a finding may be subject to an appeal by the person who brought the original ethics charge. See Appendix 3 for an example of a detailed enforcement procedure.

Once an initial determination has been made that a member of the organization has committed an ethical infraction, it is important that other members of the profession be advised of the results of the investigation so that they have a basis for modification or validation of their own practices in similar situations. The persons originally making the complaint or otherwise bringing the matter before the professional organization must be advised of the outcome of the investigation. The publication of the results of ethical inquiries is critical to the overall success of the adopted ethical practices. Publication of the process of reaching the decision is likewise important. It is only when all parties concerned determine that the investigation has been fairly conducted, the sanctions thoughtfully determined, and the review or appeal process carefully followed, that others in or outside the profession will grant some credibility to the process and the profession. Since it is the credibility of the process that is entirely at issue, the procedures and policies must be well thought out, the agreed processes must have been scrupulously followed, and the sanctions must be seen to be commensurate with the proven offense.

Making a Complaint

The process normally begins with a complaint about the actions taken by a criminalist in a particular situation. Professional colleagues of the criminalist are aware of the ability to bring charges of ethical violations, but other interested parties may not be aware that such a process exists and may not avail themselves of the opportunity. Colleagues are in a position to judge professional actions and generally take appropriate steps. Whether a criminalist in a large law enforcement laboratory or a private consultant, the judgment by peers about professional competence and integrity affects the professional opportunities available. Even if no formal actions are taken, evaluation of professional work by co-workers, colleagues, or clients will inevitably have the same limiting effect. Very often, however, the only people privy to the work of a criminalist are those who have no real basis to judge the work. Such persons, whether a judge who hears testimony, a lawyer who works with a criminalist in preparing a case for trial, or an investigator who requests assistance in an investigation, are unaware that the actions of the criminalist are subject to some form of professional review. When faced with a situation in which the work done by the criminalist fails to meet the expectations of the court, the lawyer, or the investigator, that person simply dismisses the situation as yet one more example of "an expert who, like all experts … ." (The reader can fill in whatever catch-phrase seems appropriate. One hears such things as is *just another hired gun, will say whatever the DA [or defense attorney] wants to hear,* or *is just another lab guy who doesn't understand the first thing about police work.*)

The process of enforcement of ethical behavior in any profession calls for an investigation that is open to all concerned parties and an awareness by all parties that such an opportunity exists. It should not be surprising that codes of ethics for professional associations exist, and the fact that a criminalist is a member of a professional association should be known by anyone who consults with a criminalist. Indeed, a criminalist may sometimes invite review by the ethics committee of the appropriate professional organization of actions personally taken or contemplated. The AAFS Good Forensic Practices Committee provides one example of how such a process might work — a scenario is presented to the committee, which evaluates the proposed action or alternatives and gives its opinion as to whether the alternative, or which alternative, seems most consistent with good professional practice. Such a process is of great value to the practitioner faced with a dilemma — and of great value to other practitioners who can review these situations and begin to develop a feel for what does and does not constitute good practice.

Most complaints are made by a client, a principal, an adverse party, another expert, or a judge who is dissatisfied with the work done by a criminalist in a particular case. Sometimes the complaint includes a variety of issues or extends across several cases. The method for making a complaint should be as simple as possible. Most often, the person making the complaint is unfamiliar with the applicable code of ethics and simply makes a charge of "unethical conduct." The procedures for making the charges should be sufficiently straightforward in order not to intimidate the person making the charge, but they should also be sufficiently demanding to prevent abuse of the process for harassment or intimidation.

One of the most difficult decisions a criminalist may face is to bring a charge of unethical conduct against a colleague. Such an action almost inevitably leads to friction in the workplace, and the situation may degenerate into retaliation by the colleague or formal or informal censure by the employer. Employers and colleagues must remember that one of the requirements of most codes of ethics is that members of the organization who are aware of unethical conduct of a colleague are required by that same code of ethics to bring such matters to the attention of the professional organization to which both belong. Obviously, co-workers prefer that all people who are behaving unethically be corrected; but they are also concerned that bringing an ethics complaint will have unanticipated consequences from their colleagues, co-workers, superiors, agency administrators, or others.

Some laboratories require their employees to attempt to resolve differences of opinion, or instigate action in the event of perceived ethical transgressions, by in-house procedures developed by the laboratory. There are pros and cons to this procedure. The most obvious counter-argument to such a procedure is that it allows laboratories to cover up ethical problems (which often derive from technical shortcomings). The argument in favor of such a policy is, of course, just the opposite: a review of the circumstances by an independent professional body will result in a "fairer" resolution of the issue. Indeed, even the idea that complaining to an outside body is supported by management may have the beneficial effect of encouraging personnel to remain aware of ethical requirements of their professional organizations.

In-house resolution of a problem may be preferable to a solution imposed from the outside, and no organization wants to air its dirty linen in public. However, a policy preventing an employee from making a charge through the professional organization puts the employee squarely on the horns of a dilemma: the employee is ethically required to report ethical violations of a co-worker to the relevant professional organization, yet is also required to first have the record reviewed by the agency for whom both work. Even though the agency may determine that the questioned actions are appropriate, the complainant may still feel that ethical violations occurred (perhaps because the ethical requirements of an agency might differ from the ethical requirements of a professional organization). The obligation under the code of ethics to bring the matter to the attention of the professional organization places the complainant in a difficult position. When the employer has judged the actions of an employee to be proper, to suggest further review of those actions puts the employee in even greater difficulty.

While there is potential for cover-ups by agencies, there is little evidence to establish that such cover-ups in fact occur. Anecdotal evidence suggests that such cover-ups do occur — either intentionally or simply as a result of the fact that complaints are ignored or dismissed. The problem with the system that requires in-house handling of complaints before they are sent to the professional organization is that some procedures (the CAC's, for example) provides for "satisfactory resolution" of the problem, obviating the requirement to send it to the professional group. Effectively this means that the resolution of the problem will remain a private affair. The lessons to be learned will not have been learned, and, for the most part, the fact that the problem had been resolved will not be known except by the few people within the organization who were involved in the investigation.

Bringing the Charge

The actual process of bringing the charge may be as simple as sending a letter to the president of a professional organization saying that a criminalist's behavior in a particular circumstance, or in a variety of circumstances, is thought to be unethical. Such a complaint may or may not include accompanying documentation such as transcripts, reports, and bench notes. Especially in organizations that have detailed codes of ethics, some specificity to the charges is generally required. When charges are brought that are vague in nature and not supported by documentation, the person making the charges may be requested to provide additional information and to state more clearly the nature of the complaint or the specific section of the code of ethics that the complainant believes has been violated. At some point a decision is made whether the charges have merit. If they do not, the accuser is so advised and may or may not have the right to appeal that decision. Once the charges have been decided to have potential merit, a formal investigation is undertaken.

Investigative Procedures

The investigation of a charge of unethical conduct is not a trivial affair. The consequences may be significant, both to the accused individual and to the professional association. The task facing the investigating body is to be as thorough as possible while also resolving the matter as expeditiously as possible. The investigating body generally has no power to compel cooperation in its inquiry; it has no power to compel production of materials that it might want to review; and it has no power to compel cooperation from individuals who may be reluctant to cooperate. In spite of these obstacles, the investigating body must complete a thorough investigation, the results of which must convince at least some skeptics that the committee's recommendations or findings are justified. All the while it must keep in mind that the investigation may have a serious impact on the personal and professional life of a colleague. All in all, this is a tall order for the investigating body.

The formality and scope of an investigation depends, first, on the practices and policies of the organization and, second, on the nature of the charges. Some organizations, such as the CAC, have a detailed procedure to be followed in the investigation and resolution of a charge of unethical conduct of one of its members (see Appendix 2). In the absence of a specific procedure, the investigation follows an *ad hoc* procedure that may result in a less than satisfactory resolution of the issue. There will often be a number of individuals who have a stake in the investigation: the accused individual, the accuser, the presiding officer of the professional association, the person or committee in charge of the ethics investigation, principals in a case from which the charges arise, and employers. These individuals may have their own views of how the investigation should be conducted, who has a right to participate, how the matter should be resolved, and so forth. A pre-established procedure that specifies the steps to be taken in the investigation prevents the entire exercise from bogging down in determining how to proceed, rather than getting to the real issues at hand.

Funding

The first issue facing the investigating committee is funding. Many investigations of criminalists revolve around testimony given in court. Evaluation of such testimony, or consideration of charges based on the testimony, requires the committee to obtain transcripts. This can be an expensive proposition, but it is a necessary step. In some cases transcripts may be supplied by the person making the complaint, but often that is not the case. To require the accuser to provide the transcripts that form the basis of the complaint puts an obstacle in the path of the accuser that is undesirable, especially if the accuser is a private citizen.

Expenses are also expected for committee meetings that may be necessary to discuss the issues, to take statements from interested parties, to allow the accused criminalist an opportunity to respond to the allegations made, or to review physical evidence. The scope of the committee's investigations and the costs involved are primarily dependent on two factors — the nature of the allegations and the response by the accused, and the policies and procedures followed by the committee. The former can hardly be controlled, but the latter can be established by precedent and procedures for the conduct of such investigations.

Composition

The composition and scope of responsibility of the investigating body vary according to the procedures of each organization. In some cases a standing ethics committee is given the accusation to investigate. Its responsibility is to conduct an investigation and recommend a resolution to be approved by the governing body or by the membership at large of the professional organization. In some organizations an *ad hoc* investigating committee may be established, sometimes as an adjunct to a standing ethics committee if one exists.

The investigating committee may simply advise either the governing body or the general membership, or it may have the responsibility of making recommendations to the governing body or membership that can be accepted, rejected, or perhaps modified. Whether the investigating committee's responsibility is simply to gather the facts and present them to the governing body or the membership, or whether it is expected to make a recommendation, the critical issue is that those making the final decision on resolution and/or sanctions should be privy to all of the relevant information and should have the opportunity to review and understand all evidence that bears on their decision. There may be some ethics cases that are straightforward and can be resolved without difficulty; but the procedure to be followed should anticipate that the issues will be complex, with proponents and opponents for many of the issues. To resolve these issues requires thorough investigation and careful consideration of the questions that arise.

In the consideration of a complex matter, involving, for example, multiple items of evidence, or many volumes of transcripts, reports, or other documents, the ability of a large group of people to review the information is limited. For example, if the ultimate decision of whether an action was unethical — or what the appropriate sanction should be — is left to the general membership, some thought must be given to how, in a complex case, the membership can be given access to all of the relevant material. If, on the other hand, the ethics or investigating committee is charged with the responsibility of making a recommendation or presenting the evidence without making a specific recommendation, other issues arise. Is there an opportunity for the accused to present evidence in opposition to the committee's views? Is there an opportunity to examine witnesses heard by the investigating committee in front of the general membership? How can the entire membership review material that may be confidential in nature or voluminous in extent? These questions must be addressed in established procedures for conducting such an investigation.

Representation

At all stages of the process of the investigation and resolution of an ethics complaint, the issue of representation of the accused person is an issue. Here again, rules may differ among different professional organizations. In some cases the accused individual may only be represented by a colleague from the general membership. Other procedures may allow the accused to be represented by an attorney or other person selected by the accused criminalist. As with all stages of the investigation, the parameters of such representation, and the rights and obligations of the representative, must be established before the investigation gets underway.

Cooperation

Cooperation with the investigating committee is essential to its success. Without the power to compel such cooperation, the committee must depend on the voluntary cooperation of people, many of whom have no real stake in the outcome of the investigation. Cooperation is, of course, to be expected from the person making the accusation; but even that cooperation may not be forthcoming. The accuser, whether a colleague, a client, or a party to litigation, may not have the interest or the ability to provide cooperation. If an accusation is made, however, the accusation cannot be ignored simply because of an uncooperative accuser.

For example, a lawyer might complain that a criminalist who testified in a trial misrepresented his qualifications, adversely affecting the lawyer's case. Investigation of this allegation requires review of the entire transcript of the testimony of the criminalist. The lawyer may not feel it is his obligation to pay to have the relevant portions of transcript prepared, yet the investigation cannot proceed without the transcript. To expect the complainant to provide the transcript, and to abandon the investigation when it is not forthcoming, will simply convince the lawyer that the criminalistics profession has no interest in policing its own members. Although one can expect some cooperation from the complainant, it would be unrealistic to expect the complainant to finance the investigation. That is the responsibility of the investigating organization.

Cooperation must also be obtained from individuals or agencies that have information or material that is necessary for the investigation. Exhibits logged with courts, reports filed with agencies, and procedure or policy manuals that might be of interest may not be readily available. It is incumbent upon all involved, whether they are direct participants in the investigation or not, to assist or encourage others to assist in the investigation. Problems in obtaining the necessary cooperation are frequent. Agencies might not want to release procedure or policy manuals, reports, or other necessary documents. Items of evidence may be logged with courts or agencies, and the professional organization may have no official standing for access to that material. There may be issues of privileged communications that impact what information is available and who is able to provide information to an investigation.

While it is desirable to have a totally free and frank exchange of information, unlimited access to all relevant materials, a budget that imposes no restrictions on the investigation, and no conflicting obligations on the part of all concerned, such a situation is unlikely to ever occur. The lack of the ideal, however, should not prevent doing what is possible.

Expansion of Investigation

Investigations of alleged unethical conduct often result in the discovery of additional information — not a part of the original accusation — that suggests the possibility of further violations on the part of the accused criminalist. In some instances the complaint centers on an isolated incident. It is reasonable to assume, however, that practices found in one situation are repeated in similar situations. Whether such practices are unethical is why the investigation has been instigated; but should the investigation be expanded into areas not anticipated in the original accusation? The investigating committee cannot ignore evidence that suggests the possibility of repeated ethical misconduct on the part of the accused individual, but neither can it pursue every hint of misconduct. Policy may set the limits of the investigating committee's inquiry, but in the end common sense is the best rule. Investigating committees must be allowed to follow inquiries to their natural conclusions, but the necessity of ending the inquiry in a reasonable amount of time must not be forgotten.

Hearing/Review Procedures

Any procedure for enforcement of a code of ethics requires a method for a hearing. This hearing may be held under the auspices of the investigating committee (the ethics committee), or it may be held under the auspices of the general membership of the organization. The exact procedure to be followed should be established by standing rules of the organization, or at the very least it should be established at the onset of a particular ethics investigation. Ideally this procedure serves several purposes. First, it provides an opportunity to hear information from the various interested parties. This includes the accuser, the accused, others with particular knowledge of the circumstances that form the basis of the accusation, and any other persons with relevant information. Second, the hearing provides a review of initial decisions made by an investigating committee or individuals. This is particularly important at the stage of a hearing before the general membership of the organization. While some organizations do not routinely bring ethics matters to the floor of general meetings, most organizations provide, at least in theory, a method for the general membership to review and perhaps modify a decision made by the investigative committee or the executive board of the organization. Finally, the hearing provides a valuable learning opportunity for the general membership. Except in the most egregious of circumstances, it is likely that activities of a particular member that resulted in an ethics charge have been repeated by other members. It is only by free and frank debate among professionals that the boundaries of ethical conduct are defined.

Once having decided that there is a legitimate complaint to be investigated the investigating committee is no longer in a position to make an impartial judgment. The accused criminalist should, at this point in the process, have an opportunity to present a defense or rebuttal to the case presented by the ethics committee. Members of the organization should be able to participate in the debate. It must be decided initially whether this is done in the format of a hearing in which various "sides" are present and represented by spokesmen, or whether this is done in the manner of a meeting of the organization. However it is done, this public discussion (public in the sense that all members of the professional organization can participate in or at least observe the debate) serves the vital purposes of educating the profession on the limits of professional conduct and allowing members to participate in the evolution of ethical rules.

Appeal Procedures

Once the final hearing has been held and the determination of violation and sanction has been made, most procedures call for some type of appeal process. This may be an appeal to the general membership in the event the final decision resides with the ethics committee or the governing board of the organization. If the final decision is made by the general membership, an appeal for a rehearing may be permitted by the rules. Once the hearings have been held and the appeals have been decided, some resolution to the matter must be made. The first decision might be that no ethics violation has occurred. That should terminate all further proceedings unless there is some mechanism for appeal by the accuser. Having decided, however, that an ethical violation *has* occurred, the next step is to determine the appropriate sanction.

Sanctions

Like all other stages in the process, the method of determining the sanction to be applied, and the alternative sanctions available, should be established before the investigation begins. The question of sanctions always involves the issue of whether and to what extent the matter will be made public. In some cases, it may be appropriate to keep the entire matter confidential — even to the extent of not informing the general membership of the existence of the charges. Of course, if the ethics procedure calls for some portion of the procedure to take place at a general meeting of the membership, the matter cannot be kept entirely confidential. These are matters of policy that must be carefully considered and decided beforehand, preferably as part of a standing set of rules and procedures for the investigation and resolution of ethics complaints.

The question about whether to make public any part of the process, from the complaint itself to the sanction imposed, is not an easy one to resolve, especially in the abstract before a specific case is resolved. There are many issues to be considered. Will the accuser be advised of the outcome? If the matter is confidential, but the accuser is not a member of the professional organization, how can confidentiality be ensured if the accuser is advised of the outcome? If the accuser is not advised of the outcome, or only advised in a very general way, how does that serve the goal of holding the criminalist responsible and demonstrating that the professional organization is willing to act on complaints of unethical conduct brought against one of its members? If the matter is made public, professional colleagues may be unwilling to make accusations for fear of repercussions from other colleagues or due to reluctance to embarrass the accused over what might be considered a minor, but not insignificant, violation. Further, there is the possibility of legal repercussions to the organization. Matters of internal self-discipline on the part of professional organizations are considered to be legitimate functions of the organizations, and courts are not generally willing to interfere. However, since most criminalistics professional organizations have limited resources, it is intimidating to contemplate the possibility that a member accused of ethical misconduct will file a lawsuit.

The resolution of the public vs. private dilemma is most often reached by a series of sanctions, some of which are public and some of which are private. For example, a reprimand may be a sanction that can be imposed by the ethics committee without review of the membership and without publication of the details of the matter. More serious sanctions, including suspension or termination of membership in the organization, may call for a greater degree of publicity. At some point the nature of the proven violation would seemingly require that the information be made public; otherwise, the behavior of the accused person will not be altered, and there will be little point to the entire exercise.

At the very least, some publication of the circumstances of the allegation should be made public. Failure to do so seriously undermines any confidence that persons outside the profession might have that the profession is able to monitor the actions of its members. However resolved, the publication of ethics investigations to both the professional community and the public serves to establish the limits of professional practice and serves as a valuable educational tool for members of the profession and those who use or are affected by the work of the criminalist.

Whether the accused in the investigation should be publicly identified is a further issue. There seems to be little point in publicly identifying the criminalist who has committed an isolated, and relatively minor, ethical infraction. Having the matter debated by an ethics committee, and having that committee decide that the violation did occur, should be sufficient to accomplish the legitimate goal of modifying professional behavior. On the other hand, there are certainly situations in which most members of the organization want the person publicly identified and associated with the proven acts of misconduct in order to prevent that person from continuing to practice. Again, the various options must be considered beforehand, decided by the membership, and adopted by policy or association bylaws.

Application of Codes of Ethics: How Ethical Requirements Impact the Daily Work of a Forensic Scientist

4

The ethical requirements placed on a criminalist cannot be separated from the technical requirements of the job. Some criminalists may have a job in which they perform a specific analytical procedure on a piece of evidence that has been isolated for them to work on. They produce a DNA profile, a glass analysis, or a drug analysis. Other criminalists may work in a lab where thirty bags and boxes of physical evidence are brought to the front counter along with laboratory analysis request forms that say, "Check for blood, bullet holes, and trace evidence." Still others may simply supervise the work that goes on in the laboratory without any direct contact with or responsibility for the material that comes in or the reports that go out of the laboratory. Some criminalists may work closely with lawyers in preparing cases for court, preparing to examine witnesses on both sides of the case, and preparing for the presentation of the evidence. No matter what the job of the criminalist, no matter what the criminalist's involvement in a particular case, there are ethical requirements that must be met.

The Ethical Requirements for Work Done on a Case

Competence

One of the ethical requirements is that the criminalist must be competent to undertake the tasks that are required in the assignment that has been accepted. Who, or what, determines competence for a particular task? It is not enough to get the right answer to demonstrate competence. Neither is getting the wrong answer necessarily a demonstration of incompetence. Codes of ethics that address the issue of competence generally require that the criminalist not undertake tests or examinations that he or she is not competent to undertake. At first it may seem that this is simply a self-validation of competency; but some thought reveals that the requirement which sounds trivial is, in fact, quite profound. To evaluate one's own competency, one must first understand what competency is in any particular field. One cannot assert competency in an area unless one understands the components that constitute competency in that area. The requirement to understand competency is actually much more stringent than the requirement simply to be competent.

Thoroughness

Thoroughness requires that necessary examinations be conducted and that superfluous examinations be avoided if done simply for the purpose of appearing to bolster one's opinion. Thoroughness goes beyond simply doing what is requested — it includes doing what is necessary. It also includes making sure that what is necessary gets done rather than only doing those things within one's limited scope of responsibility. Requests that are made for laboratory evidence examination are usually adequate. However, it is important for the criminalist to remember that not all persons making requests are familiar with the capabilities of forensic science; the reason they have sought the assistance of a criminalist is precisely because they have a problem (as opposed to a piece of evidence) that they hope the criminalist can help them to resolve.

Relevance

Examinations and tests must be relevant to the issues that are involved in the investigation. Irrelevant examinations and tests needlessly consume evidence or lend a false aura of scientific credibility to the case. The relevance issue may be extended to include a requirement that procedures are done only when they are capable of answering a relevant question. If a procedure is contemplated that is incapable of addressing a relevant issue in the investigation, then it may be considered incompetent and, in some cases, perhaps unethical to conduct such an examination. For example, if an analytical procedure is incapable of distinguishing between evidence with similar class characteristics, applying that procedure has no apparent purpose. If done simply to make it appear that a more thorough testing protocol has been followed, therefore the results are more significant, an ethical violation may have occurred.

Reviewability

Ethics codes for criminalists frequently include a requirement that the work of the criminalist is *reviewable*. This is also generally a legal requirement. This requirement originates from the concept of the scientific method, which essentially requires the scientific investigator to provide experimental verification of hypotheses. The scientist does not simply assert that something is true; he or she provides the process and information by which another observer can independently verify the truth of the proposition. This scientific requirement, reflected in the law and in codes of ethics, means that the data, the methods, and the materials are preserved for review by other interested investigators — the data upon which conclusions were based, the methods by which the data were obtained, and the material that was used for the analysis. Unlike most other fields of science, where the material that is subjected to analysis is generally in plentiful supply, the material available to the forensic scientist is often in very short supply; and the possibility of getting more is usually nonexistent.

The scientific, legal, and ethical requirement for preservation of the evidence does not mean that evidence cannot be consumed, sometimes completely, during an investigation. Evidence should be consumed only if absolutely required for a reliable analysis, and the work should be thoroughly documented to allow for future review.

Interactions between the Forensic Scientist and the Client

As with the issue of competence in the examination of the evidence, at first glance the issue of appropriate communication with the client seems straightforward — just give 'em the facts. The unadorned, unbiased facts. But what are the facts? Are conclusions facts? Is a fact different than an opinion? To whom are these facts or opinions to be given? When and in what format must facts, data, opinions, or conclusions be communicated, and to whom is such communication directed?

Everyone expects a practitioner in any profession to give competent advice. The consultation occurs because the person seeking the consultation, the client, does not have the knowledge or skill to do whatever is being requested. The role of the professional criminalist, unlike that of the laboratory technician, is to solve a problem. Whereas the role of the laboratory technician is to conduct a requested analysis, the role of the professional criminalist is to evaluate the circumstances, understand the relevant issues, and advise the client what can be done to resolve any relevant questions.

Ethical conduct requires that the criminalist give competent advice on what needs to be done to resolve the relevant issues. The criminalist also has the responsibility to avoid procedures that do not serve this purpose. It would appear that performing unnecessary tests, ones that have no chance of resolving any of the issues in the investigation or litigation, is easy to avoid. Unfortunately, experience has shown that this is not always the case.

The ability to give competent advice, like the ability to do competent work, is difficult to evaluate. The simplest solution to this problem is to simply fall back on one's job description. "I can't answer that question," or "I shouldn't have been asked that question because the subject matter is outside of my job description." If the client is advised that the consulting criminalist is not competent to give advice in a particular area, then at least the client can seek out someone from whom such competent advice can be obtained. On the other hand, the criminalist who is silent about work that should be done but has not been requested, or who performs work that has been requested even if the work compromises other evidence or fails to address relevant issues, may be guilty of an ethical violation.

One of the inherent dangers of the current trend toward narrowly trained analysts who conduct specific analyses of particular types of evidence is that they are not always able to recognize when the examinations that they *do* conduct will be useful. More seriously, they are not always able to determine what other examinations might be useful or what damage their analyses might do to other, more useful procedures.

Disclosure

Disclosure is another potential ethical issue which, like competence, seems rather straightforward. By application of the principle of "the truth, the whole truth, and nothing but the truth," all questions of proper disclosure can be settled. But a little thought will provide a broader view of the issue. What about data that have been rejected, for whatever reason, and play no part in the opinion? What about tests that were done that appear irrelevant to the case? What about opinions expressed in response to a question during testimony that are not addressed in a report? What about raw data existing only as a computer record?

During the course of an investigation, whether at a scene or in the laboratory, data are developed or observations are made that are subsequently determined to be irrelevant. These observations may never be recorded, or they may be recorded and ignored. Can an unrecorded observation be utilized when it becomes convenient or necessary to do so? When can a recorded observation be ignored, and when it *is* ignored, must it be divulged? As an example of the former, consider a laboratory with a policy that every bullet identification is confirmed by another examiner in the laboratory. Would it be unethical for the firearms examiner to state in testimony that such a procedure had been followed, even though there is no mention of the fact in the report? Would it be unethical to mention that the procedure had been followed even though no notation of the confirming observation exists in any written document?

For an example of recorded observations that are ignored, consider another case from the firearms section of the laboratory. Weapons seized by officers are routinely submitted to the laboratory for entry into the automated bullet identification system. One of the bullets already in the database is from a particular murder case. Occasionally, one of the submitted weapons is identified by the automated system as a candidate for having fired the bullet from the murder case. The firearms examiner actually compares the test fired bullets from the submitted weapon with the bullets from the murder case and concludes that the weapon can neither be identified or eliminated as having fired the murder bullets. For each weapon recovered, a report is issued from the laboratory with an inconclusive opinion of the examiner. Ultimately, a suspect in the murder is identified by some other method, and a search of his residence results in the seizure of a weapon. Like the others, this weapon is entered into the automated system and (as in some number of other cases) results in the murder bullet's inclusion in a list of possible matches. The firearms examiner compares the evidence bullet with the reference bullet from this latest gun and, again, reports an inconclusive opinion. This report is then forwarded to the prosecutor and defense attorney, neither of whom is aware of the fact that a number of weapons have been submitted that are just as likely to have fired the fatal bullet as the weapon seized from the defendant. Is the disclosure of all of the other *inconclusive* comparisons with the fatal bullet an ethical requirement?

Some believe that the information contained in a report — the primary means of disclosure of the opinions of the criminalist — should include only the data and not the opinions and conclusions of the examiner. If the opinions and conclusions of the examiner are sought, it has been argued, the reader of the report can pick up the phone and speak with the analyst. The reader of the report, however, may not understand that there is more information to be gained than what is in the report. The reader may assume he understand what the report means, or be reluctant to admit a certain lack of understanding — after all, why would anything but the most obvious be left out of a report? The decision of how much information to include in a report is not always an easy one. However, it would seem that the opinions and conclusions of the criminalist with respect to the examined evidence are the most important information to be included in the report — not something that should be omitted. After all, investigators do not submit evidence to a laboratory because they are interested in chemical composition or genetic profile. They want to know what the evidence reveals about the issues that are important to their cases — are the fibers from the victim's sweater and how common are they, or is the blood at the scene from the suspect or the victim?

Interactions with Colleagues

The most perplexing ethical dilemmas arise when scientific and legal values conflict; but these cannot be entirely avoided because, after all, criminalistics is a forensic science. It would be convenient if the criminalist only had to *get the facts*. Unfortunately, the criminalist must *get the facts* in such a way as to satisfy all scientific requirements for validity, reliability, accuracy, and precision (as well as the legal interpretations of these issues). Legal requirements such as due process, the right to confrontation, the right against self-incrimination, and the right of security of one's property and possessions must also be satisfied. Few criminalists are trained as lawyers; many are disdainful of the law and lawyers, and few understand the complexities of the law as it might affect their work. This book is not the place to explore all of the interactions between science and the law as they affect the work of the criminalist, but there are fundamental questions that arise from the interaction of science and the law in the daily work of the criminalist.

Although conflicts between science and the law may occur in a number of ways, the most common are in the area of the right to confrontation and the area of disclosure. Whenever a criminalist embarks on a legal discussion, he is treading on dangerous ground. Discussions in this book that appear to involve legal issues are meant to present the legal issue in its broadest context. For example, the right to confrontation was originally meant to be the right to confront one's accuser. Exactly what the law requires or includes under the right to confrontation is a question for the lawyers — there is undoubtedly no single, universally accepted answer to that question. For the context of this discussion, however, we will assume that the right to confrontation broadly means the right of one party in a lawsuit to have access to the evidence that will be presented by the other side or that is in some way relevant to the issues litigated.

In order to be confronted, evidence must have several properties — it must exist, it must be unaltered, and it must be of proven origin. In some circumstances, one or more of these requirements may not be met. The evidence may have been necessarily consumed in analysis, it may have been altered for the purposes of analysis, or proof of provenance may be in some respect lacking. The ethical responsibility of the criminalist is to make certain that none of this happens unnecessarily; and when it does occur, to keep appropriate records of what transpired.

For example, in testing a small blood stain, a presumptive color test is positive; and the remainder of the sample is consumed in an effort to obtain a confirmatory microcrystal test for blood. Is it unethical to consume the evidence in this way? During examination of a bullet, a fiber is removed and placed on an unmarked microscope slide. No record is made of this operation, and the fiber is never examined. Is it unethical to alter the evidence without notation of that fact, and is it unethical to fail to document the origin of the fiber on the slide?

Disclosure, like confrontation, is used here not in the strictest legal sense, but in the sense that there is a body of information that must be made available to the various parties involved in litigation. Disclosure is not restricted solely to information that is required by discovery. Information required to be disclosed by discovery is a subset of what might be made available through disclosure. For example, discovery might require the prosecutor to provide the defense attorney with a copy of the DNA report in which the analyst concludes that the defendant may be the source of the blood stain. But the fact that analysis of the stain shows a mixture, and that 40% of the population could have contributed blood to that mixture, may not be discovered if the necessary data have not been disclosed in the report. A more subtle form of disclosure comes when the relevant information is buried in data or other records that are disclosed or provided during discovery but is otherwise not addressed in a report.

There are other areas where requirements of law and science intersect and may conflict. One such area is privileged communications. One of the most basic tenets of science is free exchange of information. Scientists believe that the free exchange of information is the only method by which the work of another scientist can be reviewed, validated, or disproved. One of the basic tenets of law, on the other hand, is that certain matters are privileged and are therefore not subject to disclosure to other parties. This conflict is most obvious when evidence is re-examined by criminalists retained by the defense. Most lawyers, and even most criminalists, would agree that the examination results are privileged — at least up to a point. But to what point? Can a criminalist who conducts such an examination for the defense also assist his attorney-client in preparing to cross examine, and attempt to discredit, the criminalist working for the prosecution, even if the defense consultant has found nothing wrong and agrees with the conclusions of the prosecution witness? Does it make any difference if there is an error in the analysis that has been misinterpreted so that the right answer has been obtained, but for the wrong reason?

Another area of potential conflict arises when individuals or organizations refuse to release information based on a claim of proprietary or institutional privilege. A company may refuse to release product formulations, claiming that they are proprietary. Is it unethical for the criminalist to use such materials? A laboratory director may refuse to release proficiency test information, claiming that it is proprietary. An agency may refuse to release information based on the claim that it will compromise ongoing investigations.

Section II

Ethics in Action

Ethical Issues Involving Professional Practice

5

Introduction

This chapter presents a number of scenarios that give rise to ethical issues in professional practice and technical competence. Issues of professional practice cannot clearly be separated from issues of professional competence, but there are issues involving ethical considerations that have nothing to do with the professional competence of the criminalist. These non-technical issues involve legal requirements, employer policies, or relations with colleagues, clients, or the public. Because the issues of practice are more easily understood by laypersons, they have a greater bearing on the perception of the field of criminalists than do issues involving technical matters.

Recovery of Physical Evidence by a Defense Investigator

Facts

A defendant was charged with assault with a caustic substance. He allegedly purchased a bottle of drain cleaner, altered the top of the bottle, and threw it at the victim, intending for the caustic liquid to splash from the bottle onto the victim. In fact, the bottle was thrown at the victim and caustic liquid did splash on the victim, causing serious injuries. The police were called to the crime scene, conducted a minimal investigation, arrested the defendant, and turned the case over to the district attorney's office for prosecution.

The defendant claimed that he had been talking with the victim after a trip to the hardware store to buy the bottle of drain cleaner, which he planned to use for maintenance in his apartment. The victim, according to the defendant, assaulted the defendant; and he reflexively threw what he had in his hand, the caustic bottle, toward the victim. The bottle struck the wall, causing the cap to break and caustic material to splash on the victim. Hence, the defense attorney could argue that there was no intention to throw caustic material at the victim and that, at most, the defendant could be guilty only of an assault.

Several weeks after informing the district attorney's office that she intended to have someone take a look at the crime scene, the defense attorney hired a consulting criminalist to accompany her and the defendant to the crime scene. During the examination at the apartment (which had been unoccupied since the incident), a drain cleaner bottle was found in a closet. The defendant identified the bottle as the one he had thrown at the victim. With the knowledge of the defense attorney, the bottle was seized by the defense consultant for preservation and laboratory examination.

Experiments were conducted by the defense consultant that established that the type of damage to the bottle cap, alleged by the prosecutor to have been intentionally produced by the defendant for his planned assault on the victim, could be produced by simply dropping the bottle. The defense attorney was advised of this fact, but no written report was prepared.

At trial the bottle was produced by the defense consultant, who testified that the bottle appeared to have been broken as a result of having been thrown or dropped and did not appear to have been intentionally altered. The district attorney vigorously objected to the presentation of the bottle, claiming that he should have been advised of its existence and that failure to do so was misconduct on the part of the attorney and perhaps suppression of evidence on the part of the defense consultant.

Possible Actions

Several courses of action were available to the criminalist. The bottle could have been turned over to the investigating agency or the prosecutor. The bottle could have been turned over to the defense attorney, whose legal or ethical obligations with respect to the bottle may have been different from those of the criminalist. The criminalist could have prepared a report and sent it to the defense attorney, who may have had to divulge the report to the prosecutor. Or the criminalist could have informed the judge of the situation.

Discussion

Discovery is a recurring theme, present in many of the critical dilemmas faced by criminalists. Who is entitled to what information or evidence, and when are they entitled to receive it? The laws of discovery place certain requirements on district attorneys, law enforcement officers, defense counsels, and other individuals to provide information in their possession to interested parties. What information needs to be provided to whom, when that information needs to be provided, whether the information needs to be provided, and whether the information has to be volunteered depends on who has the information, the nature of the information, and interpretation of the ever-changing law in this area. The typical response of a criminalist when faced with a question of whether to divulge information is, "Let the lawyers decide." I propose that criminalists need not always defer to lawyers in making decisions of this type. Instead, criminalists need to evaluate the pros and cons of the various approaches to discovery and exercise significant influence on when such discovery is to be permitted or required.

In this case, providing a report and the evidence to the prosecutor may have resulted in the charges being dropped or altered. However, seasoned defense counsels have reason to believe that prosecutors would not take such action, even in the face of incontrovertible evidence that the charges were without merit. Not wanting to give up the tactical advantage of surprise (a tactic that all sides in litigation commonly use to their advantage), the defense attorney elected not to advise the prosecutor of the decision to call the defense consultant as a witness and produce the broken bottle at trial.

In litigation each side is trying to prove its case while simultaneously making it as difficult as possible for the other side to prove its case. There is often tactical advantage to not revealing certain information, or timing its disclosure to gain the best tactical advantage. Recognizing that unfair advantages can be gained by a litigant by failing to disclose information until the most tactically advantageous moment, legislatures and courts have determined that some participants in the litigation process have obligations to turn over evidence or information at various stages of the litigation. The exact details of these obligations vary from jurisdiction to jurisdiction, court to court, and time to time.

It is generally the obligation of the attorneys to turn over discovery materials to the other party. This obligation is placed on those individuals because, as officers of the court, they have an obligation to abide by the rules established by the court in the conduct of litigation. The obligation to disclose information or physical evidence is not absolute. There are categories of material that are excluded from the discovery obligation. Rules of discovery recognize that considerations exist that may dictate that certain types of information are not subject to discovery. One of the types of material excluded from the discovery obligation is that which is the result of the attorney work product, or that which falls under the protection of the attorney–client privilege.

In a criminal case, discovery obligations are not the same for both the prosecution and the defense. The actual discovery laws and rules that might be applicable to a particular situation in a specific jurisdiction can only be determined in the context of that jurisdiction and the particular circumstances.

For the criminalist, the easy way out is simply to wash one's hand of the problem by abdicating all discovery decisions to the attorney, prosecutor or defense. But criminalists, since they are the collectors of physical evidence and the producers of testimonial evidence, cannot completely ignore their roles in the discovery process. If evidence is not collected, if opinions are not written in reports, if records of examinations conducted are not maintained, then discovery of that evidence, in whatever form it exists, is not possible. By failing to collect physical evidence, failing to document observations or examinations that are conducted, and failing to provide all data produced in the laboratory, the discovery process is thwarted.

There are two basic issues to be resolved in this type of case: (1) the necessity of making judgments based on all pertinent evidence, and (2) the necessity of allowing the defendant to vigorously investigate the circumstances surrounding the offense with which he is charged without fear that such investigation can be used against him. Obviously, everybody would like to make decisions based on all pertinent information. On the other hand, if a defendant knew that the results of any investigation he made on his own behalf could be used against him, he would be hesitant to undertake such an investigation. Evaluating this situation from a legal perspective, it is necessary to remember that the state has the obligation to prove the case against the defendant. The defendant is not required to assist the state in fulfilling that prosecutorial obligation. From a scientific point of view, the ability to fully explore the technical issues that arise during the investigation is fundamental to the basic process of peer review — it is the principle method of quality control for scientists. Policies that interfere with the peer review process — such as reciprocal discovery requirements forcing privileged information to be divulged, unwillingness to release data (including bench notes, electronic data, procedural manuals, developmental data, and the like) — are inimical to the scientific method.

In the case described above, the district attorney had ample opportunity to inspect the crime scene and find the evidence and was told that the defense investigator was going to the crime scene. Since one of the fundamental aspects of the criminalist's job is the preservation of evidence, failure by the criminalist to retain the evidence would have been a failure to do a competent job. To recognize evidence (that is, to appreciate the evidentiary value of a physical object at an incident scene), and not take appropriate steps to preserve it, would be failure to perform a basic aspect of the criminalist's job. To do the job properly (which may, in itself, be an ethical mandate), the defense criminalist had no alternative but to collect and preserve the evidence at the scene. Unless a scene is secured for future examination, preservation of evidence at the scene generally requires that the evidence be collected. Generally, the criminalist should preserve any evidence that is perceived as relevant to the case; and such preservation should be directed not only to provide physical security for the evidence, but also to document the circumstances under which the evidence was found, the condition of the evidence when it was found, and other such relevant observations as are necessary to allow the evidence to be utilized to its fullest potential.

Once the evidence has been preserved (the obligation to properly preserve evidence will be discussed elsewhere), what is the obligation of the criminalist to divulge that evidence has been collected? In the case under discussion, was there any obligation to turn the bottle from the crime scene over to the prosecutor? The answer to this question is a legal one — certainly there can be no valid scientific objection to turning the evidence over — but the forensic scientist must make decisions after considering not only the scientific sides of an issue, but also the legal ones. One approach to the legal questions would be to abdicate the decision-making process in favor of the attorney, who is the "client." It is recognized that not all criminalists have an attorney–client relationship with a lawyer. In fact, many criminalists work for an agency that is separate from the lawyers who represent the various parties of interest in litigation. Such agencies may have policies, or be governed by statutory regulations, that control the release of information. With few exceptions — such as investigations with no charged suspects — the work that a criminalist performs is done at the actual or implied request of a party with interests in a matter of litigation. That party may be a defendant or a plaintiff, the people or the state, an administrative body, etc. That party is represented by an attorney. That attorney should be making legal decisions in the case.

The ownership of physical evidence is often proffered as the reason for making the decision to release, not release, or place certain restrictions on the use of physical evidence. One frequently hears the terms *prosecution evidence* or *defense evidence* — not in the context of which party presents the evidence in court, but in the context of which party discovered and collected the evidence. Some legal writers have expressed the view that physical evidence belongs to neither side of the case, but this enlightened view does not generally provide equal access to the evidence for all interested parties.

Because criminalistics is a *forensic* science, a criminalist must be somewhat conversant with the requirements of the law that are relevant to their practice. The criminalist must be generally aware of legal requirements for discovery, disclosure, spoliation of evidence, attorney–client privilege, etc. — and then use that knowledge, along with knowledge and understanding of the relevant principles involved in the process of scientific inquiry, before deciding what to do. In extraordinary circumstances, the criminalist may wish to retain independent counsel, speak formally or informally with the court, or consult with colleagues before deciding on the appropriate course of action. The criminalist might also consult codes of ethics of professional organizations to help determine the best course of action. Above all, the criminalist must recognize the responsibility to not thwart the process of peer review by actions taken with respect to physical evidence. This obligation requires the criminalist to (1) preserve physical evidence so that relevant examinations and tests can be conducted by those who have a legitimate interest in doing so; (2) conserve the evidence during any examinations and tests so that sufficient material remains in as unaltered a condition as possible for further examinations; (3) divulge the existence of evidence that is collected or isolated from other collected evidence during the course of laboratory examination or testing; (4) document the condition of the evidence when collected and during all stages of the examination and testing; (5) report all tests conducted in such a manner that other scientists can understand any changes or alterations that may have been made to the evidence; and (6) not unnecessarily repeat tests or examinations that have already been done.

Potential Ethical Issues

This case illustrates several ethical issues. Should it be an ethical requirement to write a report? The preparation of a report results in something tangible that is "discoverable." Discovery rules often require that reports, if they exist, be provided when requested. However, information not included in reports, either intentionally or inadvertently, may not be discoverable. By preparing a report and forwarding it to the attorney–client, it may become discoverable by opposing counsel. This may prompt the client to not request a report, or it may influence the content of the report.

   Does the criminalist have an ethical responsibility to collect and preserve relevant physical evidence even if the evidence is, or might be, adverse to the interests of the employer? Apparently, there is no legal obligation to collect physical evidence. Certainly no ethical obligation exists to collect everything. But since the essence of the professional responsibility of the criminalist includes the *recognition and preservation* of physical evidence, the failure to carry out this professional responsibility would appear to be unethical. Of course, what constitutes an unethical *failure to recognize* or *failure to preserve* can be the subject of substantial debate. In this case, however, neither the recognition nor the preservation is a technically difficult task — the issue is the responsibility to do so.

Applicable Ethics Code Sections

AAFS

As usual the AAFS code of ethics provides little help. This situation involves neither misrepresentation of the criminalist's qualifications nor the data. The general subject of disclosing test results and physical evidence may, in certain circumstances, be covered by the ethical obligation not to misrepresent data. If, for example, in the above case the criminalist had prepared a report giving his opinion that the bottle broke when it struck the wall, while not revealing in the report that the evidence had been recovered and that tests had been conducted, it could be argued that this is a violation of the AAFS's requirement not to misrepresent data.

ABC

Several sections of the ABC Rules of Professional Conduct appear to leave the criminalist no alternative other than to collect the evidence:

> 3. Treat any object or item of potential evidential value with the care and control necessary to ensure its integrity.

> 4. Ensure that all exhibits in a case receive appropriate technical analysis.

Rule 3 would seem to place a high responsibility on the criminalist to recognize potential physical evidence. Assuming that precognition is not an ethical requirement for ABC certified criminalists, this rule nevertheless requires the criminalist to make a reasonable effort to determine what the issues are in an incident, what potential arguments might be put forth by either side, and what value any objects or observations might be to support or refute those arguments.

Further, in the absence of any law or regulation requiring otherwise, Section 2 of the ABC Rules that requires the criminalist to "treat all information from an agency or client with the confidentiality required" seems to restrict the criminalist to communicate the results of his work only to his client.

CAC

There is no section of the CAC code of ethics that clearly applies to the issue of collection or preservation of evidence. Section I.C states, "… nor will conclusions in case work be based upon such tests and experiments as will not be revealed to the profession." While stated in the context of a prohibition of "secret processes" used in testing, one could argue that, when the object of an experiment or observation is not preserved, then the profession is deprived of the opportunity to review the work that led to the conclusions expressed.

Section IV.D of the CAC code of ethics states, "Generally, the principle of attorney–client relationship is considered to apply to the work of a physical evidence consultant, except in a situation where a miscarriage of justice might occur. Justice should be the guiding principle."

It is not clear exactly when a miscarriage of justice would occur by adherence to the principle of the attorney–client relationship. In the described case, since the evidence was presented in court, the only miscarriage of justice would be a result of the prosecutor's inability to have the evidence independently reviewed and analyzed and an alternative explanation for its condition developed. In the absence of a specific legal requirement that the criminalist advise the prosecutor that the evidence was collected, what miscarriage of justice could have occurred? If the criminalist who collected the evidence misinterpreted the evidence and presented incorrect testimony that was not rebutted because the prosecutor was unable to have the evidence independently reviewed, did a miscarriage of justice occur?

Ethical rules requiring that an action be taken or not taken when a miscarriage of justice might occur and that "justice should be the guiding principle" are rather problematic. When does a miscarriage of justice occur? If a criminalist decides that a miscarriage of justice will occur if he divulges certain information, should he be ethically required not to divulge such information? Frequently a miscarriage of justice is deemed to be synonymous with a trial that results in either the conviction of an innocent person or acquittal of a guilty defendant. But, in general, the criminalist is not and should not be in a position to decide on the guilt or innocence of defendants. Ethical rules should be constructed to prescribe appropriate professional behavior under certain circumstances. Factors to be taken into account during the construction of such ethical rules include concepts of justice, morality, comity, and scientific inquiry.

Criticism of Work Not Done

Facts

In the previous section, we considered the obligation of the defense criminalist to turn evidence over to the prosecutor. In that scenario, after recovering the bottle, the criminalist's examination revealed that the bottle had broken because it was thrown and struck a hard surface. In the original investigative reports, the police officers had observed that the cap of the bottle had been "partially cut apart," presumably (or so the district attorney would argue) to cause the acid to splatter the victim when the bottle was thrown.

It was the defendant's contention that he simply had the bottle in his hand since he had just purchased it to clean some drains in the apartment building he managed. According to the defendant, he instinctively threw the bottle when the victim began to advance toward him in the midst of a heated argument. The defendant alleged he had not altered the bottle in any way before the incident. Clearly, the question of whether the bottle had been altered was relevant to the guilt or innocence of the defendant of the specific intent crime of assault with a caustic substance.

The defense attorney was prepared to make a motion to dismiss the charges based on the failure of the police to preserve the acid bottle, thereby preventing the defendant from presenting evidence that could be clearly exculpatory. The advice of the criminalist retained by the defense was that, from an examination of the bottle, had it been retained, it would probably have been possible to determine if it had been intentionally altered. Before this motion was heard, the bottle was recovered; and examination revealed that, in fact, it had not been altered but had broken as a result of impact when it was thrown. Although it seems that the presentation of this evidence at trial would have likely resulted in an acquittal of the assault with a caustic substance charge, the defense attorney wanted to proceed with the motion to dismiss the charges or at least suppress any evidence of the bottle of acid, based on the failure to preserve the evidence. The criminalist who had recovered the bottle was asked to testify at the motion hearing. The testimony would be restricted to what could have been done had the bottle been recovered.

Possible Actions

The criminalist could testify, answering the questions of the defense attorney who would, presumably, be careful not to ask any questions that would reveal that the bottle had actually been recovered. But how should the criminalist answer a question such as, "If you had the bottle now, could you determine if it had been altered?" Or, "In the absence of the bottle, you cannot tell if it was altered by the defendant or not, can you?" Would it be a better procedure to refer the defense attorney to another criminalist who, unaware of the actual existence of the bottle and assuming that it was no longer in existence, could testify about the way in which the defendant's case was compromised due to the failure of the police to recover the evidence? Is subornation of potentially misleading testimony any less an ethical transgression than actually giving such testimony?

Discussion

One might ask if it is proper for the defense attorney to pursue the motion based on the failure of the police to preserve evidence that the attorney knew was, in fact, available. Whether the attorney is legally or ethically entitled to or prohibited from making such a motion is not particularly relevant to the determination of the proper course of action for the criminalist who is asked to participate in such a motion. If an ethical obligation exists to take or not to take a particular action, that obligation is not changed simply because it does not exist for another person. As a relatively trivial example of this proposition, some codes of ethics for expert witnesses (for example, the CAC code of ethics) prohibit the acceptance of cases on a contingency fee basis. This ethical obligation does not change simply because there is no such prohibition against lawyers. That other experts are not similarly restricted because they have not agreed to a particular code of ethics is also irrelevant. In the particular scenario under consideration, some might feel an ethical responsibility on the part of the criminalist to advise the prosecutor or the court of the existence of the bottle if the defense attorney argues a motion based on the implied assumption that the bottle does not exist. It could be argued that justice would not be served by a case dismissal based on the failure of the police to preserve the evidence when, in fact, the evidence had been preserved by, or at the request of, the lawyer making the motion.

The defense consultant is therefore in the midst of three dilemmas. Is there an obligation to divulge the existence of the evidence if the defense attorney makes an argument that the evidence, in fact, is no longer available? Can the criminalist testify about what *might have* been done with the evidence had it been preserved by the investigating law enforcement agency? Can the criminalist assist the attorney in locating another witness who can testify about what *might have* been done had the bottle been recovered? Even further, the criminalist has obtained evidence that is clearly relevant to the case and has not divulged this fact to the prosecutor. The end result of this activity will be for the judge to be under the impression that the police investigators failed to pick up the evidence (true), that an examination of the evidence might have been able to provide useful information for the defendant (true), but that the item was never picked up and has now been forever lost (false).

The defendant is not required to mount an investigation on his own behalf. But if the defendant chooses to do so, can the results of that investigation be withheld from the prosecution? The answers to these questions lie in applicable laws and are the ethical responsibilities of those who are privy to the defense investigation. Forensic scientists generally consider their ethical and legal obligations fulfilled if a report of their work is provided to their client or employer. It then becomes that person's or agency's responsibility to provide the report to those who are entitled to receive it. While there may be no ethical responsibility to provide the report, or information contained in the report, to anyone other than one's own client or agency, most criminalists would feel uncomfortable about presenting testimony that would infer that something was done or not done when the opposite was actually the case. But is it ethical for a criminalist to speculate about what might be the case when in fact the case is known to be the opposite? At the same time, is it ethically permissible for a criminalist to speculate about something that may have occurred, but he does not know?

Potential Ethical Issues

There are two ethical issues in these types of situations. The first is the criminalist's ethical responsibility to alert the court, either directly or through the attorneys involved in the case, to the existence of physical evidence that might be relevant to the case. The second is the ethical responsibility to not give misleading testimony. One could, of course, hold the position that the criminalist has the responsibility to disclose evidence to both sides of the case. A slight variation on this requirement might be that there is a somewhat different obligation depending on the nature of the criminalist's employment or client in any particular matter. For an employee of a law enforcement agency, the obligation might be controlled by statute, by case law (e.g., *Brady v. Maryland*), or by agency ethical rules. If employed by a government agency that is not a law enforcement agency (a prosecutor's office, a coroner's office, or a publicly funded independent agency), the requirements might be different. Yet different requirements might be applicable to the criminalist working in a private laboratory. Indeed, in a private laboratory the situation becomes quite murky. Are there different obligations to different categories of clients? If retained directly by a defendant, are the obligations different than if retained by the defendant's family or lawyer? Does the private consultant have different obligations depending on whether the client is a law enforcement agency, a prosecutorial agency, a public defender, or a private attorney? Are the obligations dependent upon whether the case is civil, criminal, administrative, or private?

Applicable Ethics Code Sections

CAC

The preamble to the CAC code of ethics states quite plainly:

> In fulfilling this duty, he will use all of the scientific means at his command to ascertain all of the significant physical facts relative to the matters under investigation … . These findings of fact and his conclusions and opinions should then be reported, with all the accuracy and skill of which the criminalist is capable, to the end that all may fully understand and be able to place the findings in their proper relationship to the problem at issue. (Emphasis added.)

The language does not read "to the end that *the client* may fully understand" or "to the end that *all who are entitled* may fully understand." Neither does the language require the criminalist to make sure that everyone receives the report. The language states "all *may* fully understand," clearly implying that such understanding is not mandatory.

Section IV.D of the CAC code states:

> Generally, the principle of "attorney–client" relationship is considered
> to apply to the work of a physical evidence consultant, except in a
> situation where a miscarriage of justice might occur. Justice should be
> the guiding principle.

This section would seem to place the responsibility for disclosure in the
hands of the attorney and restrict the responsibility of the criminalist to
providing the information to the party by whom he is employed or retained.
Of course, the "Justice should be the guiding principle" sentence seems to
imply that there are some circumstances in which the attorney–client privilege must give way to justice. But the attorney–client privilege is not antithetical to, but an integral component of, justice. Clearly, there may be
perceived conflict between the "principle of attorney–client relationship" and
the "guiding principle" of justice. How such a conflict should be resolved in
any particular situation must be considered by an established process for
deciding when an ethical violation has or has not occurred. In making this
judgement it is well to recall the final section of the CAC code of ethics,
Section V.G, which states:

> This Code may be used by any criminalist in justification of his conduct in
> a given case with the understanding that he will have the full support of
> this Association.

AAFS

The AAFS requirement not to misrepresent data could be applicable in the
situation described above or in similar situations. If the report was carefully
worded, or testimony carefully stated so as to neither rely on evidence that
was not divulged nor imply that evidence did not exist which in fact did
exist, then there would seemingly be no "misrepresentation of data upon
which an expert opinion or conclusion is based." It is difficult to imagine,
though, what testimony could be given in the scenario under consideration
that would not give the impression that the evidence had not been recovered.

ABC

The applicable ABC requirements seem to be:

> 7. Ensure that a full and complete disclosure of the findings is made to the
> submitting agency.

> 13. Make efforts to inform the court of the nature and implications of
> pertinent evidence if reasonably assured that this information will not be
> disclosed to the court.

Paragraph 7 requires disclosure only to the submitting agency, while paragraph 13 requires disclosure to the court. There is no recognition in the ABC code of ethics of any concept of attorney–client privilege, nor does there seem to be any recognition of a responsibility to inform the opposing party in litigation of the existence of particular types of evidence. The requirement that the court be informed of *pertinent* (that is, having a clear, decisive relevance to the matter in hand) or *highly relevant* evidence requires the criminalist to make a decision about the nature of the evidence, then somehow convince a court to consider that evidence. This requirement fails to recognize that the vast majority of the time the court does not consider any evidence in the case and that pre-trial dispositions are the rule rather than the exception. Relevant and particularly *highly relevant* evidence not considered by the attorneys while negotiating a disposition of the case is likely never to be considered.

Selective Evidence Examinations

Facts

A criminalist retained by the defense in a criminal case has done a reasonably thorough examination of the evidence, including some evidence obtained, but not analyzed, by the investigating law enforcement agency. This examination of the previously unexamined items results in new evidence developed that is adverse to the defendant's interest. The criminalist's re-examination of the items previously examined by the law enforcement laboratory reveals some errors in the original analysis. The results of the original analysis are incriminating to the defendant, but the re-examination establishes that this evidence is neutral with regard to its impact on the factual issues in the case.

When these findings are reported to the defense attorney, the attorney engages another consultant, advises him of the situation, and tells him that he is being engaged to examine only those items of evidence for which the re-examination resulted in differences from the original analysis. The attorney asks the first consultant to forward to the second only those items of evidence. The consultants realize that the attorney hopes to be able to call the second consultant to testify only about errors made in the original examination of the evidence, and thus avoid putting the original consultant on the stand where the findings that are adverse to the defendant's interest would have to be revealed.

Possible Actions

The first consultant could accommodate the client's wishes and send the evidence to the second consultant. There is no practical way to avoid this happening because once the attorney has decided upon this course of action, the cooperation of the consultant is only a convenience, not a requirement. Is there any ethical reason for the consultant to try to dissuade the attorney from this course of action?

The second consultant can, of course, reject the engagement. Assuming that the second criminalist is aware of the existence of other evidence that might be incriminating for the defendant, is it unethical to examine only the evidence the attorney asks to be analyzed? In general, of course, the second consultant might not be aware of all of the circumstances and might accept the assignment, ignorant of the fact that other incriminating evidence exists that is not being made available. Do criminalists have any ethical responsibility to determine if all of the relevant evidence is examined?

Discussion

A criminalist, whether retained by the prosecution, defense, or law enforcement, is generally requested to examine physical evidence, render a report, and testify in court. Often the evidence submitted for examination or the examinations requested do not represent all of the evidence or examinations available in the case. Unfortunately, in most cases it is not the criminalist but a police investigator or lawyer who obtains the physical evidence, preserves it, and requests that certain analyses be done.

There are many reasons for the selective collection and examination of physical evidence: limited time, facilities, and experience all result in analysis of only a portion of the evidence. In certain instances, only some evidence or examinations will be relevant to the issues as determined by the person or agency submitting the evidence or requesting the examinations. For these valid reasons, in many, if not most cases, the examination of the evidence is more or less limited. Occasionally, the decision to limit the analysis is made in an attempt to ensure that only useful information (information beneficial to one side of a case) is developed. The role of the criminalists in making these kinds of decisions bears consideration.

To make a decision about what evidence is to be analyzed, there are two questions that must be considered. First, what must be done to determine what happened in a particular incident? Second, what things must have happened for the incident to give rise to litigation? These two questions cannot be considered in isolation since, if there is no litigation arising from the incident, the work done may be only of academic interest. Once could, for example, expend a lot of effort in establishing one fact (the identity of a perpetrator, for example) only to discover that the identity of the perpetrator is not really an issue. Rather, the issue is intent, or aggravation, or some other aspect of the legal issues surrounding the case. Issues evolve and cases progress, but knowledge of relevant legal and factual issues allows the forensic scientist to address these issues and perhaps help resolve them.

There are many aspects of the typical case for which some type of scientific evaluation would be appropriate or useful. Unfortunately, the decision of what is to be done is usually made by an investigator or lawyer who is not aware of what might be done — or is sufficiently aware of the process to avoid those things that might be detrimental to his case and his pre-conceived theories. Does the criminalist have an affirmative obligation to make sure that all relevant evidence is examined, and all relevant questions addressed? Is there any obligation on the part of the criminalist other than doing the requested examination and reporting the results to the client or agency requesting the work? The ability of the criminalist to effectively participate in the investigation of an incident is dependent on the extent to which he is afforded the opportunity to comprehensively evaluate the situation and offer advice as to how to proceed. If the criminalist is not able to provide the comprehensive advice and evaluation necessary or is prevented from doing so, the work done on the case will be less than optimal.

The second issue in this scenario is how to demonstrate that conclusions are wrong. In some instances conclusions can be proven wrong based on problems in the original work that was done. In such instances, effective cross-examination can be effective in demonstrating the errors that were made. In many cases, however, the error can only be demonstrated by showing that a re-analysis gave a different result. How to effectively deal with incorrect results when the evidence is incriminating, either at trial or subsequently, is a problem for which there is no easy solution.

Legal writers frequently recommend that the resolution to this dilemma is to have non-testifying experts who can assist the lawyer, be privy to all of the privileged information, participate in legal strategy sessions, determine what evidence needs to be examined or re-examined, and decide what additional investigations are needed. This recommendation understandably results from the nature of litigation with the various privileges and discovery requirements that exist. Many conflicting values must be considered in resolving these issues. Which side has the burden of proof? What constitutes an actual or implied waiver of the right of confidentiality of privileged communications? Is there an ethical obligation for a lawyer to elicit all of the evidence? Is there an ethical obligation for a witness to present all of the evidence, or just that which is elicited by the attorneys?

Potential Ethical Issues

The first and most obvious ethical issue involves failure to examine certain evidence that might be relevant. The criminalist may be unaware that such evidence exists, but the issue of whether efforts should have been made to determine if such was the case can be raised. The second ethical issue has to do with the criminalist engaging in tactics that are designed specifically to assist the defense attorney in presenting his case. In the course of litigation, all attorneys would prefer that only the evidence that benefits their clients is presented, that it is presented in the best possible light, and that evidence that is contrary to their case is discredited in whatever way possible. The obligation of the attorney, therefore, is to the interests of the client he represents. The obligation of the criminalist is not to one side of the case or the other, but to present the scientific evidence in the most convincing possible manner. Advocacy for one litigant or the other is not the role of the criminalist, but advocacy of an opinion derived from a technical study of the evidence is certainly permissible.

Applicable Ethics Code Sections

AAFS

It is difficult to see how the situation described in this dilemma could be resolved by reference to any of the sections of the AAFS code of ethics. There is no specific obligation to present all of the evidence, but only to not misrepresent data when expressing an opinion.

CAC

Section III.G of the CAC code of ethics comes right to the point:

> It is not the object of the criminalist's appearance in court to present only that evidence which supports the view of the side which employs him. He has a moral obligation to see to it that the court understands the evidence as it exists and to present it in an impartial manner.

This ethical requirement means the criminalist who is aware of the situation must refuse to work on the case or refuse to testify. Section I.B further requires that the criminalist "… make adequate examination of his materials, applying those tests essential to proof." Whether this requirement means that the criminalist has to examine evidence that has not been requested would depend on the circumstances of the case. It would clearly seem to be unethical under the rule to fail to examine evidence that is directly related to the issues that the criminalist is addressing. On the other hand, there appears to be no obligation to examine evidence that is not related to those issues that the criminalist is addressing.

Section III.H of the CAC code states, "The criminalist will not by implication, knowingly or intentionally, assist the contestants in a case through such tactics as will implant a false impression in the minds of the jury." If the impression left on the jury is that the original examination results were wrong, therefore the defendant is not guilty, an ethical violation has occurred.

If the impression left on the jury is that some analyses were wrong, then no ethical violation has occurred.

ABC

The ABC Rules of Professional Conduct require the criminalist to "make efforts to inform the court of the nature and implications of pertinent evidence if reasonably assured that this information will not be disclosed to the court" and to "maintain an attitude of independence and impartiality in order to ensure an unbiased analysis of the evidence." These rules parallel the CAC code of ethics and would suggest that selective analysis of the evidence in order to present only that which favors the side by whom the criminalist is employed is unethical. The obligation of the criminalist is to ensure that all of the evidence is being appropriately analyzed. The ABC rules also require that the criminalist "ensure that all exhibits in a case receive appropriate technical analysis."

While there may be some difficulty in informing the court of findings, due to the attorney–client privilege that may require information to be kept confidential, the impact of these ABC rules suggests that selective examination of evidence designed to produce results only favorable to the client, and then presentation of that limited work in court, constitutes a violation of the CAC code of ethics.

Resolution

The resolution in this matter is to convince the defense attorney that, overall, the correct results obtained by the first criminalist retained by the defense are in the client's best interests. Whether the attorney can be convinced is entirely dependent on the particular case. But if all of the evidence can be presented, the ethical issues become moot. If the defense attorney is unwilling to present all of the evidence from his primary consultant, another approach might be to try to restrict the scope of the testimony just to that area that the defense attorney wants and not get into areas that are considered damaging to the defense case. Aside from being a tactically risky maneuver, the criminalist may feel an obligation to testify about all the work that was done. The criminalist should make clear to the attorney that the anticipated testimony cannot be restricted just to those areas the defense attorney might want, but it will include complete disclosure of all relevant findings.

The second defense consultant, retained simply to repeat those analyses that the attorney thinks are favorable to the defense, may not even be aware that he is a pawn in a legal battle. If the nature of the assignment is known, the criminalist could simply refuse to be involved in the case. At times, however, the criminalist may not be aware that other criminalists have worked on the case, and may accept the assignment. Unless the circumstances should have been clearly obvious to the criminalist, to proceed with the assignment would be appropriate.

Identifying Another Examiner's Markings on Evidence

Facts

A thorough laboratory examination has been conducted by a law enforcement laboratory and is submitted to a consultant retained by the defense for re-examination on behalf of the defendant. At trial, a criminalist employed by law enforcement testifies for the prosecution, presenting the evidence in a competent, thorough, and understandable manner to the jury. The defense attorney does not call his consultant as a witness. As sometimes happens, the case results in a hung jury and a mistrial is declared.

In preparation for the second trial, the prosecutor decides to have the evidence re-examined by another consulting criminalist. The results of this second analysis are entirely in agreement with the original analysis conducted by the law enforcement criminalist. During the examination of the evidence, the consultant retained by the prosecutor notes markings on the evidence which he recognizes as those of a professional colleague who, he infers, has examined the evidence on behalf of the defendant. During an initial conversation with the prosecutor, the prosecutor asks the consultant if he recognizes markings on the evidence as those of another consulting criminalist who, according to the prosecutor, had been retained by the defense in the first trial. The consultant recognizes the markings as those of the colleague, and so informs the prosecutor. The prosecutor then informs the consultant that that same question will be asked when the consultant is called to testify at the upcoming trial. It is apparent to the consultant that it is the prosecutor's intention to elicit testimony to imply to the jury that the defense had the evidence re-examined and, by the absence of the defense consultant, it can be inferred that the defense re-examination was in agreement with the original results obtained.

Possible Actions

There are several courses of action available to the prosecution consultant:

1. The consultant may not perceive anything inappropriate about the prosecutor's proposed questions or his answers to them. The consultant may feel that the jury is entitled to know that the evidence was re-examined by a defense consultant, or at least feel that it is not the

criminalist's responsibility to decide what questions are asked and answered in the courtroom. If the question is improper, an objection and a ruling of the court will resolve the matter.

2. If the criminalist is uneasy about the tactics being employed by the prosecutor, the prosecutor should be informed of those feelings of distaste for the subterfuge.

3. If the criminalist was aware of the prosecutor's proposed tactic before undertaking any significant involvement in the case, the assignment could be refused. Note that under a slightly different set of facts the criminalist might be putting continued employment at risk for refusing to work on a particular case.

4. If called as a witness in the case, the prosecution consulting criminalist could refuse to identify any of the markings.

Discussion

There are two issues presented by the situation described above. The first is the right of the defendant to conduct an investigation on his own behalf and not be required to divulge the results of that investigation to the prosecution. It is not too difficult to imagine that if such right was abrogated by prosecutorial tactics, defendants might be reluctant to exercise that right. The second issue is the obligation of a criminalist to remain neutral in a case and not participate in tactics that are inappropriate.

Once a defendant has been charged with a crime, or even when there are only suspicions that have been raised, the defendant may wish to conduct an investigation using resources available. This investigation may pursue a number of avenues. There may be interviews with witnesses who have or have not previously been interviewed by law enforcement investigators. There may be inquiries intended to develop other suspects in the case. There may be interviews with eyewitnesses, alibi witnesses, or witnesses who can address the defendant's state of mind. The defendant may engage investigators of one type or another to inspect the crime scene, examine physical evidence in the custody of law enforcement or other physical evidence collected by the defendant's investigators, or conduct tests or experiments designed to shed light on one or another of the issues with which the defendant is concerned. This investigation may be directed to establishing an alibi for the defendant, establishing a particular defense such as mental incapacity or necessity, gathering information to attack the credibility of witnesses that the prosecution is expected to call, establishing exactly what happened during the incident giving rise to the charges, or addressing any of a variety of other issues that the defendant or the defense attorney feels will be helpful in presenting his case.

If the investigation conducted by the defense includes a thorough review and analysis of the physical evidence available, the consultant retained by the defense to conduct this investigation must be free to do whatever is necessary to complete the assignment. Simply to review the evidence to be presented by the prosecution, the defense consultant needs all of the relevant data and reports. To conduct an independent analysis of the evidence, the defense investigator needs to have access to all of the evidence and the authority to conduct whatever tests are necessary for a thorough investigation. Such access to the analytical data and records, as well as the evidence itself, are necessary for a valid and thorough scientific evaluation of any theory or hypothesis. When legal rules, lawyer tactics, or judicial restraints restrict access to information or evidence, the results of the investigation will be less than optimum.

The second issue involved in this scenario concerns the participation of the forensic scientist in litigation tactics that goes beyond a presentation of the scientist's opinions and conclusions. It is clear from the prosecutor's questions that he intends to involve the criminalist in providing information to the jury that they would probably not get any other way and to which they might not be entitled. It is incumbent on the criminalist to be aware of such courtroom tactics and refuse to be a party to them. By allowing such manipulation, the criminalist contributes to a situation in which a review of the scientific evidence is avoided; or the review is curtailed in order to avoid the possibility that the facts and results of the review will be detrimental to the defendant. Since the process of scientific inquiry requires that such a review be conducted, to contribute to a system in which review is thwarted is contrary to good scientific practice — no matter what the legal rules are.

Applicable Ethics Code Sections

AAFS

No applicable section of the AAFS code of ethics was found. The above scenario addresses the predictable conflict between an ethical responsibility of a forensic scientist and what might be considered a lawyer's prerogative. Establishing an ethical requirement that would serve both purposes — the unfettered access to information and unrestricted ability to conduct the scientific investigation that scientists require, and the various aspects and consequences of disclosure and confidentiality that are the hallmarks of legal procedures — would be difficult This is one of the conflicts inherent in the interface between science and the law.

ABC

A number of the ABC rules require the criminalist to do a complete and thorough job of examination of the evidence. Of course, that is impossible if the relevant information or evidence is not divulged or made available. On the other hand, ABC rule 13 requires that the criminalist "make efforts to inform the court of the nature and implications of pertinent evidence if reasonably assured that this information will not be disclosed to the court." Whether it is even possible for a criminalist to take the initiative to inform the court of the nature and implications of evidence is doubtful. Perhaps the ABC rules anticipate that disclosure of the evidence to an officer of the court (the lawyer) satisfies the requirement. Further, the ways to accomplish this goal are not specified. A literal interpretation of this rule would require that criminalists forward all reports to a judge — but which judge is not specified by the rules.

No ABC rule exists that addresses the issue of the criminalist assisting the prosecutor by inferring that the evidence had already been examined by a criminalist retained by the defense. While this might not be "maintain[ing] an attitude of independence and impartiality" (ABC rule 14), that attitude is only required "in order to ensure an unbiased analysis of the evidence." Generally, the ABC rules are silent on prohibitions against tactical maneuvers, as long as opinions rendered and testimony given are based on appropriate technical analysis.

CAC

The CAC code of ethics addresses the issues of confidentiality and participation in tactical games played by an attorney. Quite simply, the CAC code requires that "… the principle of *attorney–client* relationship is considered to apply to the work of a physical evidence consultant." The CAC code then confounds this statement by adding "… except in a situation where a miscarriage of justice might occur." The confidentiality of the attorney–client relationship is not dependent on a determination of what might or might not be a miscarriage of justice. Justice is, presumably, the end result of a process which, when properly carried out, includes confidentiality of certain information. Informant's name, a witness's medical history, the defendant's criminal history, or PCR primer sequences are matters that may be kept confidential, or at least not divulged to everyone, without compromising the final result of the litigation.

The CAC code also requires that "the criminalist will not by implication, knowingly or intentionally, assist the contestants in a case through such tactics as will implant a false impression in the minds of the jury." Criminalists need to be sufficiently sophisticated in the ways of the courtroom to avoid putting themselves in the position of assisting the contestants in giving the jury false impressions.

Resolution

There is no single convenient and inarguable way in which to proceed in this situation. Some criminalists may feel that it would be entirely appropriate to tell the jury that the initials on the bag are those of the consultant, that the consultant was (or may have been) retained by the defendant, and the failure of the consultant to testify has implications for the jury to decide. Such a criminalist is of the opinion that this is information the jury should know, and that it is only appropriate that the jury be made aware of the previous examination.

For those criminalists who feel less comfortable participating in this tactical maneuver, there are several options. The assignment could be refused. The reluctance to participate in the charade could be made clear to the attorney. While testifying the witness could look forcefully at the other attorney, hoping for an objection. It would be interesting to hear the court and attorneys' reactions to the witness who, when asked, "Do you recognize the markings on this bag of evidence?" would reply, "I'm sorry, but it would be unethical of me to comment on that." In the end, of course, there will be situations where an answer to the question is unavoidable. While the CAC code does not say that the criminalist will avoid assisting the contestants in a case *except when ordered to do so*, it is doubtful that a criminalist would ever be found to be unethical for giving a truthful answer to a question when ordered to do so by the court.

Agency Proposes to Retain an Incompetent or Unethical Criminalist

Facts

A consultant is retained by a district attorney's office to work on a particular aspect of a major case in which the local laboratory, which has worked on other aspects of the case, does not have the necessary expertise. The consultant hired by the district attorney's office has been the subject of allegations which, if true, would cast doubts on the competence or credibility of the consultant. The fact that the consultant is hired is known to the criminalists in the government crime laboratory. Are the criminalists in the local laboratory under an obligation to inform the prosecutor's office the allegations that have been made against the consultant? Are they under any obligation to inform the defense attorneys in the case about the allegations against the prosecution witness?

Possible Actions

The actions the criminalists might take are quite clear: they can either relay the information that they know to the attorneys involved in the case, or they can choose to remain silent. Part of the practical considerations in this case involves the relationship between the laboratory and the prosecutor's office. If the laboratory is operated by the prosecutor's office, the obligations might be different than if the laboratory were operated by an agency with no direct tie to the prosecutor's office. The obligation of a criminalist to an employer may be different than the obligation to an outside agency. If the criminalist decides to inform the prosecutor of the information about the consultant, does the criminalist have an obligation to inform the defense attorney of the same information?

Discussion

Possible resolutions to this dilemma must take into account the criminalists' ethical responsibilities, the formal relationship of the laboratory and the prosecutor's office, and the right of the defendant to confront witnesses. If the information about the consultant is such that the prosecutor would have an obligation to inform the defense attorney, does that obligation extend to the publicly employed criminalist?

Whatever the formal relationship is between the laboratory and the prosecutor's office, in this specific case a relationship — an attorney–client relationship — exists because the laboratory has been engaged by the prosecutor's office to work on certain aspects of the case. This relationship carries certain obligations. Most of these obligations concern the work done by the laboratory and the communication of the results to the prosecutor. But is simply doing the work requested by the prosecutor the extent of the laboratory's, or criminalist's, responsibility? It would not be difficult to understand the frustration of the prosecutor if the consultant's testimony were to be impeached by cross-examination on the issues about which the laboratory was aware, but the prosecutor was not.

Beyond the obligation to the client, does the criminalist who works in a laboratory operated by a law enforcement agency have any obligation to provide information to the defense? A variety of circumstances have to be considered. If the information is simply about the consultant's background, the obligation may be different than if the criminalist believes that the work done by the consultant is or will be incompetent.

The criminalist must evaluate three things in reaching a decision in this situation. How reliable is the information? Are there any constraints on the criminalist that might prevent divulging the information? Are there any requirements to divulge information? Let us assume, for example, that the allegations against the consultant included failure to use appropriate controls in an experiment in a prior case. The allegations resulted in ethics charges brought against the consultant which, after due investigation and hearing, were substantiated. The consultant was reprimanded by his professional organization; and such reprimand, by the organization's policy, was not made public. Can the criminalist divulge the information? What would be the proper course of action if, rather than allegations having been proven, they were simply allegations made by sources the criminalist considers trustworthy?

Ethical Issues

The main ethical issues in this case involve the responsibility of the criminalist to inform the client of relevant information about the case, the responsibility of the criminalist to keep confidential matters of professional ethics that are determined to be confidential, the danger of spreading false innuendos about the consultant, and the various obligations that result from the nature of the criminalist's employment or the nature of the relationship with the prosecutor's office.

In addition to the ethics codes that might be applicable due to the criminalist's membership in a professional organization, the criminalist's employer may have a code of ethics that the criminalist is required to follow. Indeed, these various sets of ethics rules may be mutually contradictory — one requiring, for example, that certain information remain confidential while the other requires that the same information be divulged.

The ethical issue may revolve around the question of the consultant's credibility. Presumably, the prosecutor who has retained the consultant has made a decision that the consultant will make an effective and credible witness. This is a decision that an experienced attorney presumably is able to make. Alternatively, the ethical issue may revolve around the technical aspects of the case. Generally, the attorneys involved in the case are unable to competently or objectively evaluate the work that the consultant has done on the case, especially when that work supports the arguments that the attorney who retained the consultant intends to present. If the criminalist feels that the work was incompetently done, is the obligation different than if the criminalist is aware of matters involving professional discipline?

Applicable Ethics Code Sections

AAFS

There does not appear to be any reasonable interpretation of the AAFS code of ethics that would require any action on the part of the government criminalist in this case. Neither, however, does the AAFS code of ethics offer any support for any decision that the criminalist might make.

CAC

The CAC code of ethics (Section V.E) requires that matters that come before the association during business meetings not be discussed with people who are not members of the association. So if the findings, according to the CAC ethics enforcement policy, were for a private reprimand, the CAC code of ethics would prevent a member from passing the information along to another party.

Another section of the CAC code of ethics states that it is permissible for a criminalist to assist in the cross-examination of another expert as long as it is done "in good faith." If the criminalist then believes that the information he has is reliable, and if he believes that the information is relevant to the issues in the case, he would seemingly be ethically permitted to provide the information so the prosecutor could be prepared, if necessary. The preamble to the CAC code might be applicable in this situation. There is an ongoing debate as to whether the preamble is part of the ethics code. Some feel that the requirements for ethical conduct are those that are explicitly stated in the numbered sections of the code, while others feel that the language in the preamble is as much a part of the code of ethics as the numbered sections.

The preamble says, "The failure to meet or maintain certain of these standards will justifiably cast doubt upon an individual's fitness for this type of work." Interestingly, the CAC code makes no specific requirement that anyone other than the professional organization be advised in the event of unethical conduct of a member. While there are certain restrictions on what may be divulged, there are no explicit guidelines about what should be divulged.

ABC

The ABC code of ethics requires the criminalist to "ensure that techniques and methods which are known to be inaccurate and/or unreliable are not utilized." Note that this requirement is not restricted to the work that the criminalist does, but extends beyond that. The extent to which the criminalist is required by this rule to ensure that unreliable techniques are not used is not specified in this section.

The introductory paragraph to the ABC Rules of Professional Conduct states, "These rules describe conduct in the profession of forensic science (criminalistics) and are meant to encompass not only work done by Applicants, Affiliates and Diplomates, but to the extent possible, work supervised by them as well." In this case the work may not be supervised by the criminalist, so perhaps the section does not apply and the obligation is therefore removed. But even if the obligation is removed, could this section be used by the criminalist as justification for informing the prosecutor or the defense attorney that he believes the work done by the consultant may be "inaccurate or unreliable"?

Resolution

As with most ethical dilemmas, it is not possible to say that there is a single correct answer in this situation. In the first place, the nature of the allegations and how they became known to the criminalist are critical in deciding a proper course of action. In one situation the allegations may be true and of a very serious nature that would cast significant doubts on the accuracy or reliability of the work. But if these allegations are only known to the criminalist through a mechanism, such as being privy to an ethics investigation, that may not ethically be divulged, the final decision may be different than in some other circumstance. For example, if the criminalist overhears a conversation at a professional meeting where colleagues are alleging that the consultant is incompetent, the decision of the criminalist might well be something different.

Whatever decision the criminalist makes, whether it is ultimately determined to be a decision contrary to or in compliance with applicable ethical rules, the issue is not one that can be answered by reference to a fundamental moral principle. The decision may be a difficult one, made solely on the basis of an attempt to abide by an ethical requirement. Whether the decision is ultimately determined to be correct (i.e., ethical) or incorrect (i.e., unethical), any objection to the course of action taken must be minimal.

Attempting To Avoid the Rigors of Cross-Examination

Facts

In a recent case in which the defense attorney was prepared to undertake a thorough cross-examination of the criminalist, the criminalist employed a tactic that, while perhaps not intended to do so, intimidated the attorney. The witness came into court with his 4-year-old daughter, who was dressed in her best Sunday school clothes. He sat his daughter down in the front row of the courtroom gallery, where she primly sat with her gaze affectionately fastened on her father as he was sworn in and took the witness stand.

Possible Actions

The witness, faced with the unpleasant reality of an aggressive or oppressive cross-examination, has few options. Part of the obligation that comes with the privilege of expressing an opinion from the witness stand is to defend that opinion, to defend the work that led to it, and to defend against attacks designed to diminish the value of the opinion. The process of advocacy which is the basis of the justice system is not taught in most college or university science curricula. It is, for many forensic scientists, an uncomfortable part of the job.

Discussion

The presence of the cherubic little girl certainly had an intimidating effect on the defense attorney. How could he engage in vigorous cross-examination of the witness, the purpose of which is, at least in part, to attack the credibility of the witness, with this darling little girl sitting in the front row? Surely the jurors would not take kindly to an attorney who would commence such an assault on someone in front of his adoring child. If he were to engage in such vigorous cross-examination, the jury would feel such an outpouring of sympathy for the witness and antipathy for the lawyer that the effect would be opposite of what the lawyer intended.

It is doubtful that a criminalist would actually take a child to court in an effort to curtail cross-examination, and it is further doubtful that an attorney would be intimidated by such a tactic. Nevertheless, attempts to avoid cross-examination are not uncommon. Laboratory notes are left in the laboratory rather than brought to court; photographs are not taken; reports are written in a terse and perfunctory manner; or witnesses fail to acknowledge use of literature that they should be familiar with. All of these tactics may be done in an effort to minimize cross-examination.

When testifying in court, the criminalist is faced with a difficult task. The technical evidence and issues must be explained fully and carefully so that a relatively naïve jury can understand the nature and implications of the evidence; the questions posed by counsel must be clear, and their implications understood by the witness, so as to avoid misleading the jury; and the criminalist must allow counsel an opportunity to thoroughly explore not only the opinion of the witness but also the justification that the witness has for the opinion and the qualifications of the witness to express that opinion. The witness must also allow counsel an opportunity to explore any possible bias that the witness may have. All of these are legitimate functions within the advocacy system. That is not to say, however, that the legitimate actions that lawyers are expected to take while representing their clients are always palatable to the person on the witness stand.

In addition to legitimate questions designed to fully explore the witness's opinion, lawyers are often allowed to ask questions that, while serving no legitimate purpose in furthering an understanding of the issues in the trial, must nevertheless be answered by the witness. The traditional advice given to expert witnesses in books is that the purpose of these questions is to try to provoke the witness so that in some fashion his credibility will be lessened in the eyes of the jury. In this time of increased scrutiny of scientific evidence, it is not unusual to be asked about college grades, details of college course content, on-the-job training course content, the witness's performance in those courses, testimony given in past cases, performance on proficiency tests, performance on certification examinations, and statements made at professional meetings or even informally to colleagues. It is not unusual for the lawyer to relate a telephone conversation with the witness and imply or directly state that the witness made a comment during that conversation that the witness does not recall.

All witnesses, not just expert witnesses, are faced with questions that may appear to be meaningless, misleading, unintelligible, or just plain dumb. As expert witnesses, though, criminalists (and other forensic scientists) undoubtedly hear more than their fair share of such questions. Sometimes such questions are designed to intimidate, embarrass, or confuse the witness. Other times the questions are designed to mislead or confuse the jury. Yet other times the questions are designed to elicit some response from opposing counsel. And, at times, the questions are simply inarticulately stated, based on a misunderstanding or ignorance of the subject matter. Most lawyers, however, have developed a knack for making even the dumbest of questions sound plausible, leaving it to the witness to respond appropriately.

One of the favorite lunchroom and cocktail party pastimes of criminalists (indeed, it has recently become a regular feature of the *CAC News*, a publication of the California Association of Criminalists) is to relate "war stories" describing the clever and subtle tactics they have used in the past to deal with attorneys who have asked embarrassing, insulting, difficult, sarcastic, or personal questions of the type that all expert witnesses have come to know and love. It is a perfectly acceptable part of the "theater of the courtroom" to devise mechanisms to deal with these types of questions while recognizing that it is the right, indeed perhaps the obligation, of the attorney to ask these questions — just as it is the obligation of the witness to answer them. The witness has no right to avoid answering the question — it is his obligation to answer the questions with "the truth, the whole truth, and nothing but the truth." Avoiding the question with a witty riposte or other clever tactic is an inappropriate response to the obligation the witness has accepted as part of the job.

Beyond answering the question, the witness has a further obligation to make sure that the answer given is responsive to the question asked. For any of the reasons described above, the question asked may be difficult for the witness to understand. Just because the witness does not understand the question, though, does not mean the jury will appreciate the problems with the question that are confounding the witness as he attempts to craft an understandable answer to the question. To respond to a confusing question with the standard, "I don't understand the question," is likely to convince the jury that the witness is avoiding answering an embarrassing question or does not know the answer to a complex question. If the "I don't understand the question" response is given to avoid the necessity of giving an embarrassing answer or answering "I don't know," the witness is not fulfilling the oath that has been taken. If the question appears to be ambiguous or to omit information necessary to give the answer, the witness should reply to the question either by explaining specifically why the question cannot be answered, restating the question in the process of giving the answer, or some other technique that clarifies it not only for the judge or jury but also for a person reading the transcript of the witness's opinion.

Applicable Ethics Code Sections

AAFS

No section of the AAFS code of ethics directly relates to this situation. It is conceivable, depending on the details of the circumstances, that Sections 1, 2, or 3 could be considered applicable. If by some technique the witness were to avoid answering the questions that were embarrassing or for some other reason deemed objectionable, it might be argued that the witness has been unethical by "… material misrepresentation of education, training, experience or area of expertise." By failing to respond to questions about the nature of the analysis, the data produced, etc., the witness might have violated the ethics provision against "… material misrepresentation of data upon which an expert opinion or conclusion is based."

CAC

The CAC code requires that "the criminalist will answer all questions put to him in a clear, straightforward manner," and, further, that the criminalist will not "assist … counsel through such tactics as will implant a false impression in the minds of the jury." Tactics designed to thwart the ability of the attorney to ask questions, or to avoid giving answers to those questions, are considered unethical.

ABC

The ABC code of ethics does not have any directly applicable section. Section 10, regarding testimony, and Section 13, regarding impartiality, would seemingly require the criminalist to do nothing that would result in misleading testimony.

Resolution

No real resolution exists for the dilemma of trying to answer difficult, improper, misleading, or confusing questions. Jurisdictions and judges differ in their reactions and tolerances to the interactions between witnesses, including expert witnesses, and lawyers. The expert witness's obligation, however, is to give a full and complete presentation of the opinion and the reasons for that opinion. The lawyer's job is to ask questions that allow the witness to fulfill that obligation. Tactics on the part of either the witness or the lawyer that tend to obscure the testimony, limit the full disclosure of the basis for the testimony, or confuse or obscure the implications of the testimony are inappropriate and, under some circumstances, may be unethical or illegal.

Evidence Is Discovered by a Defense Criminalist

Facts

A criminalist is retained by the defense in a case in which the defendant is charged with attempted murder. The defendant, placed at the scene by a reliable eyewitness, is accused of firing a gun and wounding the victim in the chest. Crime scene examination reveals a spent bullet in a location that is unlikely, given the trajectory from the defendant's position to the victim. The class characteristics of the bullet suggest that it could have been fired from a particular make and model handgun that the defendant had purchased, but which was not recovered during the investigation of the shooting incident. Ammunition of the same type as the bullet recovered at the scene was found in the defendant's residence. Thus, the physical evidence shows a bullet from the scene, not connected by any evidence to the victim, which could have been from the ammunition in the defendant's possession and could have been fired from the gun that the defendant had purchased. The reconstruction, however, suggests that if the defendant did fire his weapon, it was not toward the victim but in a different direction (where the bullet was found).

The evidence is obtained by the defense for re-examination. The evidence obtained includes the fired bullet from the scene, the ammunition recovered from the defendant's residence, and the clothing of the victim. In examining the bullet, the criminalist retained by the defense finds a fiber embedded in the nose of the bullet that is indistinguishable from the colored synthetic fibers of the victim's shirt. For characterization and comparison, the fiber from the bullet is removed and mounted on a microscope slide. Thus, the defense has developed the only evidence linking the *bullet* to the victim. The evidence is now to be returned to the investigating agency to be used at trial. What should be done with the "incriminating fiber"?

Possible Actions

1. Throw the fiber away — it cannot be proven to be from the victim's sweater; based on the scenario described, it is not from the victim and is therefore irrelevant to the case. The prosecution has examined the bullet and has not reported about or removed the fiber, so perhaps it is just contamination.
2. Retain the slide with the fiber in case the fiber for some reason becomes important in the litigation. The criminalist can safely preserve the evidence and make it available when requested or required to do so, and the chances of it getting lost during inspection of the evidence at trial, for example, will be eliminated.

3. The slide bearing the fiber could be packaged together with the bullet and returned to the agency. The defendant has no right to expect that the criminalist retained to examine the evidence on his behalf will not turn over to the prosecution any evidence that is found during the course of the investigation. After all, guilty defendants have no right to expect that the results of investigations conducted on their behalf will be confidential; innocent defendants could suffer no harm from evidence being turned over.

4. The incriminating fiber could be returned to its original location on the bullet, then the bullet returned. The evidence is returned in the same condition, or as close to that as possible, as it was received. The evidence was photographically documented before it was removed from the bullet, when it was mounted on the slide for microscopic examination, and after it was removed from the bullet. If the prosecution should undertake another examination, they should be able to discover the evidence that they should have found in the first place; if no further examination is done, the evidence is in its original condition and should stay that way.

Discussion

The consideration of these alternatives requires reviewing legal and scientific requirements and values. First let us consider the rights of the defendant in this matter.

The right of the defendant to investigate the case against him is fundamental. The right to do so without the fear of the results being used against him is fundamental to the exercise of the right. Some would assert that no such right exists, but the law clearly allows the defendant to conduct an independent investigation. That the results of such investigation should be privileged is not in dispute, although there may be disagreement about when the results need to be made available to opposing counsel in particular circumstances. This is not some legal loophole invented by clever attorneys as a method to allow their guilty clients to avoid conviction. Rather, the ability to confidentially review the evidence is the fundamental way in which the evidence used to convict is tested. This is especially true of physical evidence, for which other methods of evaluating the evidence — cross-examination, for example — may not be particularly effective.

A guilty defendant would not ask for the evidence to be re-examined if the results were to be turned over to the prosecution. A defense attorney would not risk the chance that incriminating evidence would be turned over to the prosecution. Even an innocent defendant could not run the risk of an independent analysis of the evidence if the results of such examination were automatically discoverable. What would happen if the examination was faulty, and the results were incriminating?

One alternative approach in this case might simply be to turn the fiber over to the defense attorney. Whether the attorney has a duty in such circumstances to turn the evidence over to the prosecution is a matter of the law and legal ethics. The ethical responsibility of the criminalist is to preserve the evidence. This obligation includes making sure that evidence is retained in a competent manner. One should not assume that an attorney will have the knowledge or the facilities to preserve evidence, nor should one assume that the attorney has, or perceives, the same ethical responsibility as the criminalist. The responsibility of the criminalist is to preserve the evidence — which includes the responsibility to minimize the chances that the evidence would be inadvertently, or intentionally, lost or destroyed.

Some assert that a criminalist has a responsibility to take whatever actions are necessary "in the interests of justice." But what are these interests of justice? Are they to ensure that all possible evidence that can be used against an accused is presented? Are they to ensure that all actions taken are those required to be taken?

With these factors in mind, each of the four alternatives for disposition of the evidence will be considered:

1. *Throw it away* — the initial reaction to this alternative is to dismiss it immediately. Every criminalist feels that throwing away obviously significant evidence is improper. It can be argued, however, that the prosecution did not discover the evidence. Since it was discovered by the defense, it cannot be used against the defendant, and there would be no harm in discarding it. Certainly, if the evidence is discarded, it will never again be available. It does not seem reasonable, however, that the discovery of physical evidence is a race to see who finds it first, so that the side who discovers it first can take whatever action is appropriate to further the interests of that side's case. The criminalist should not decide, unilaterally, that the evidence should be discarded.

2. *Retain it* — assuming that the defense criminalist will not be called as a witness, this alternative is tantamount to alternative 1 but avoids the problem of actually destroying the evidence. If called as a witness (and the argument of who can, cannot, should, or should not call the defense expert is avoided here) the witness would probably have to admit to the existence of the fiber — especially if directly asked a question such as, "Did you find any evidence linking the bullet to the victim?" To answer "Yes, but I threw it away" would be at the least embarrassing and at the extreme would subject the witness to a charge of obstructing justice or destruction of evidence. Therefore, retaining the fiber appears to be an attractive alternative. But, what if the

prosecution laboratory were asked, at the last minute, to re-examine the bullet? They might find the fiber on the re-examination if it is there, but cannot if the fiber is retained by the defense. But — the argument can go — the prosecution already had their opportunity, and they do not get a second chance. But the examination may not have been requested the first time. Although this argument can go back and forth *ad nauseum*, the essential question is whether the defendant has the right to retain evidence without informing the prosecutor, therefore effectively preventing the prosecution from discovering the evidence.

The answer to this question may or may not be available in applicable statutes or case law. It is entirely possible, however, that the situation is sufficiently unique that the answer is not clear, and different answers would be obtained from different lawyers who might be consulted. The defense attorney might advise that discarding the fiber, or keeping it, is the proper course of action. The prosecutor, if asked, would probably assert that it is the duty of the criminalist to return the fiber, possibly even to advise the prosecutor of its existence. Even though retaining the fiber without informing opposing counsel may not be effectively much different than discarding it, it seems a better alternative than simply discarding it.

3. *Return the slide containing the mounted fiber* — this is another alternative that, at first glance, appears to be a good one. A little reflection, however, leads to obvious difficulties. This alternative would surely bring the evidence to the prosecutor's attention. The defendant's investigation could, then, be used against him. This is fundamentally contrary to the tenet of our legal system that the prosecution must prove its case and the defendant is not required to provide the ammunition for his own demise. One might argue that the proper role of the criminalist, no matter by whom he is employed, is to do whatever can be done to make sure the guilty are convicted and the innocent are not. An alternative view is that the proper role of the criminalist is to promote the interests of justice. Justice is the result of the adversarial process that is governed by a set of rules ("due process") which may not, in every case, result in the conviction of the guilty and the acquittal of the innocent.

It requires only brief consideration to conclude that a defendant must be able to investigate his case with absolute assurance that the results of his investigation cannot be used against him unless the defendant chooses to present the evidence. If this were not the case, no defendant would want to conduct an investigation because of the risk of developing adverse evidence. The adversary process would be an empty one, indeed, if independent investigation could not be conducted.

It seems, therefore, that the third alternative, while initially appearing very attractive, must be rejected on the grounds that it compromises the right of the defendant to conduct an independent and confidential investigation. One variation of the alternative to return the evidence on the slide would be to return the evidence separately, perhaps to the court, so that the prosecution would not have access to it without a hearing. As a practical matter, however, this alternative seems unlikely to be used. Most courts do not accept evidence outside of the trial process, and the prosecution or investigation agency probably will not accept evidence that is not identified for them.

4. *Replace the fiber where it was found* — this alternative runs a risk of losing the fiber in the transfer process or in subsequent handling by individuals unaware of the existence of the fiber. The criminalist has a responsibility to preserve evidence. That responsibility includes protecting the evidence against loss or damage. Such responsibility would, it seems, require the criminalist to secure the fiber in an appropriate evidence container, especially once the fiber had been removed from the original bullet substrate. The manipulation involved in replacing the fiber where it was originally found, much less the chances that the fiber will become dislodged and lost in subsequent evidence handling, would seem to preclude the replacement option. Further, as a practical matter, the chances are that the evidence will not be re-examined and the fiber therefore will not be found, so alternative 1 or 2 is just as reasonable.

Applicable Ethics Code Sections

AAFS

No section of the AAFS code of ethics is explicitly applicable. One might, however, rely on the language which prohibits "… providing any material misrepresentation of data." Arguably, this could be construed to mean that any alteration of evidence that is concealed is unethical. It seems, however, to stretch the language of the AAFS ethic to its limit or beyond.

ABC

An applicable ABC Rule of Professional Conduct is "… treat any object or item of potential evidential value with the care and control necessary to ensure its integrity." If, in this context, this rule is taken to mean physical integrity, then perhaps removing and failing to return the fiber, or returning it separately so as to obscure its origin, might be considered a violation of the rule. Sometimes, however, when evidence is recognized, certain steps must be taken to ensure its preservation. Arguably, in this case, removal and separately packaging the fiber were necessary to ensure its preservation.

CAC

Like the AAFS and ABC, the CAC code of ethics does not have any section that unambiguously addresses this specific issue.

Resolution

There can be no right or wrong answer in this situation; there are just better or worse resolutions. All of the alternatives have pros and cons that reasonable people may argue. Of the alternatives listed above, alternative 4, replacing the fiber in its original location, appears the most reasonable. This alternative has the advantage of not frustrating any efforts made by the prosecution to discover the evidence. It has a distinct disadvantage, however, of putting the existence of the evidence at some risk. A slight variation of the alternatives listed above would be to either keep the evidence (alternative 1) or return the slide with the original evidence (alternative 2), but to inform the defense attorney, preferably in writing, of the action being taken. The attorney then could take appropriate action to prevent the use of the evidence and/or advise the prosecutor of its existence, and the matter could be resolved by the court.

Ethical Issues Involving Technical Competence

6

Issues of technical competence have always been troublesome since there is no general agreement on what criminalists need to know to do their job. There is no uniform college or university curriculum, there are no universally applicable licensing or certification requirements, there are no universally accepted employment criteria, and there are no professional criteria for on-the-job training. This situation will, perhaps, change in the future as the activities of organizations such as the various Scientific Working Groups (… in Materials, or SWGMAT; … in DNA, or SWGDAM; and others) establish training and educational guidelines and as professional organizations (ABC, AFTE) establish certification programs. Even with these developments, the judgment of when, if ever, technical deficiencies reach the point of unethical conduct will continue to be a problem.

Wrong Gun Identified

Facts

In a murder case the fatal bullet recovered from the body of the victim was booked into the property room without having been examined. A search warrant later served on a suspect resulted in the seizure of a Colt Trooper .357 Magnum revolver and some unfired .357 Magnum ammunition. The crime lab was requested to examine the fatal bullet and compare it with the gun and ammunition recovered from the suspect.

All of the evidence was examined by the criminalist; the gun was test fired and a report was written that, in essence, offered the following conclusions:

1. The fatal bullet was too damaged to permit comparison with the recovered weapon.
2. The fatal bullet was fired from a weapon with 6 left rifling.
3. The class characteristics of the fatal bullet are "peculiar" to Colt revolvers.

At trial the criminalist's testimony was essentially the same as his report. He left the impression that he had found the class characteristics of the Colt and the fatal bullet to be the same, and that he was unable to make a positive identification only because of the damage to the fatal bullet.

Examination of the evidence by a defense consultant revealed that the fired bullet had been fired through a barrel rifled 6 left and that the recovered Colt was rifled 6 right. This information was reported to the defense attorney.

Possible Actions

The criminalist who conducted the original examination was incorrect in concluding that the Colt revolver was rifled with a left-hand twist. This error could be easily addressed by pointing out the error to the criminalist, who would then issue a corrected report to resolve the matter. The defense consultant, discovering the error and discovering the fact that the murder bullet could not have been fired from the defendant's weapon, had several courses of action available. The course that was chosen, to advise the defense attorney, was certainly the least the consultant had to do. Presumably, if the prosecution expert had been asked to re-examine the gun he would have recognized the error in his original examination and issued a correction. The defense criminalist might also have advised the criminalist's supervisor of the apparently inadequate or incompetent examination that had been conducted. The criminalist might have advised the court, the prosecutor, and the agency who had submitted the evidence to the lab of the error. And, finally, the defense criminalist might be required to bring ethics charges against the prosecution criminalist.

The defense attorney who had retained the consultant, however, was not hopeful that such resolution of the problem would be of any significant advantage to the defendant; so the consulting criminalist was instructed to keep the results of the examination confidential so the original witness could be confronted with his mistaken analysis during the course of cross-examination. The consulting criminalist was asked to assist the defense attorney in preparation of cross-examination that would force the first criminalist to recognize that the Colt revolver was actually rifled with right-hand rifling and admit the error in the report. This was intended to be an exercise conducted in open court, in front of the jury, to maximize the dramatic and tactical value of the criminalist's mistake.

Discussion

The situation involves two somewhat unusual ethical issues. First is the question of whether competence is an ethical issue. The second involves the relationship between professional colleagues. While both of these issues seem to involve only the criminalists, the determination of the appropriate course of action involves interactions with the attorneys. This situation holds the potential for a conflict in the ethical requirements for the criminalist and the tactical or ethical problems facing the lawyers.

This case requires a consideration of whether an erroneous conclusion or observation is the result of unethical conduct. Surely there are situations in which a criminalist may reach a wrong conclusion with no hint of any unethical conduct in the sequence of events leading to the error. Mistakes can result from unethical conduct. Failure to conduct a thorough examination, failure to understand the basic principles of the relevant science, and reliance on poor samples may all be considered unethical and may lead to erroneous results. Of course, any of these ethical transgressions can occur and not lead to a wrong answer. It is not, then, getting the right answer that is central to unethical conduct. Unethical conduct is more a result of the failure of the criminalist to follow a specific process in arriving at conclusions that are expressed in a report or in testimony.

The process that criminalists are expected to follow is one that is generally referred to as the *scientific method*. The scientific method has no universally accepted definition (or else it would be convenient to say that criminalists are unethical if they fail to follow the scientific method). Among their other functions, codes of ethics are intended to specify the steps that a practitioner in any field must follow. The code of ethics should be an accepted protocol by which a practitioner can judge whether the procedures followed in a particular professional assignment fall within those acceptable guidelines. So while a code of ethics for criminalists is not expected to define the scientific method, the code should provide guidelines for the practitioner in defining what must be done, at least minimally, to ensure that the scientific method has been followed in any particular case or assignment.

Potential Ethical Issues

Ethical issues in this case involve not only the competence or care with which the original examination was conducted but also the ethical responsibilities of the defense consultant. Inspection of a revolver to determine the rifling direction is certainly something that every criminalist should be able to do. Perhaps the criminalist testifying for the prosecution failed to conduct the examination and jumped to the conclusion that, since the revolver was manufactured by Colt, it must have been rifled with a left-hand twist. This is a reasonable assumption that at times may be useful, but it turned out to be faulty in this case. Alternatively, perhaps the criminalist did not have the necessary skill or knowledge to determine the direction of twist of the weapon, or perhaps he just made a mistake. Whatever the reason for the incorrect characterization of the revolver rifling, most criminalists would agree that this is an error that could have been easily avoided by an adequate examination of the evidence.

Applicable Ethics Code Sections

AAFS

The key issue in the AAFS code of ethics is the misrepresentation of data. Misrepresentation would seem to require (1) intent and (2) data. If there are no data — if the weapon were not even examined — then perhaps there would be no ethical violation. While the AAFS ethics code might excuse simple mistakes, it is difficult to imagine that it could overlook the failure of a criminalist to do the basic examinations necessary to gather the relevant data. Perhaps this case would establish that failing to obtain data, then representing that such data had been obtained, is an ethical violation. By expressing the opinion that the rifling on the recovered bullet and the weapon match, the criminalist certainly infers that data supporting that conclusion were obtained. If no such examination were conducted and no data were obtained, misrepresentation would exist. If, however, the data were incompetently collected or were misinterpreted when collected, perhaps this would be merely a case of incompetence. Does this level of incompetence rise to the level of an ethics violation? What are the criteria for making that determination?

No requirement exists in the AAFS code of ethics that would require any particular action on the part of the criminalist who discovered the error. The Academy code places no ethical requirement on Academy members with respect to their interactions with colleagues, nor with their interactions with the justice system.

ABC

The ABC rule applicable to the original examiner is quite clear: "4. Ensure that all exhibits in a case receive appropriate technical analysis." Obviously, failing to determine that the weapon is rifled in a different direction than that shown by the bullet supposedly fired from the weapon is proof that an "appropriate technical analysis" was not done. There seems to be no leeway in this requirement for error or incompetence.

The only sections of the ABC rules that mention relationships with peers state that ABC Diplomates and Fellows shall "16. Regard and respect their peers with the same standards that they hold for themselves" and "18. Find it appropriate to report to the Board, any violation of these Rules of

Professional Conduct by another Applicant or Diplomate." These sections do not seem to require action on the part of the consulting criminalist with respect to the case being tried but do require that a report be made to the ABC Board of Directors.

CAC

Many sections of the CAC code of ethics can be applied to the actions of the criminalist who conducted the original examination as well as the criminalist who consulted for the defense. From the above facts it is apparent that the original examiner had every opportunity to determine the difference in the rifling between the fatal bullet and the suspect's gun. (Clearly, if this determination were made but not reported, it would constitute an ethical violation as well as a violation of law.) Is the fact that the rifling difference was not noted during the original examination a violation of the criminalist's responsibility to "use all of the scientific means at his command," to "make adequate examination of his materials," or to use "experimental controls"?

The CAC code of ethics includes a requirement that differences of opinion between criminalists should be resolved prior to trial. However, the CAC code, as well as the law, maintain that the attorney–client privilege exists between the criminalist and his lawyer–client. The defense lawyer might feel that he would lose a tactical advantage by having this matter resolved prior to trial, since he could use the error to impeach the prosecution expert or embarrass the prosecutor's case. Without permission of the defense attorney to do so, the ability of the consulting criminalist to bring the error to the attention of the original examiner is severely restricted.

The CAC code of ethics states, "… where a difference of opinion arises, however, as to the significance of the evidence or to test results, it is in the interest of the profession that every effort be made by both analysts to resolve their conflict before the case goes to trial." Clearly, it is generally in the best interest of the profession to avoid exposing incompetence or shoddy work to the glaring light of publicity. The theater of the courtroom, however, is where such issues are often resolved — or at least presented. Attempts to utilize extra-legal procedures to resolve such disputes run the risk of failing to adequately consider all aspects of the question. Differences of opinion on matters involving science are not usually resolved by private agreements between the scientists holding differing views. Such disagreements are best resolved by public debate of the alternative views. This is the method most likely to provide a thoughtful and intelligent resolution.

Some would argue that the consideration of scientific disputes by judges or juries not versed in the applicable sciences is not liable to result in the best decision. It is probably true that serious consideration needs to be given to the question of whether or not the courtroom, or the procedures currently utilized in the courtroom, are optimal for the resolution of scientific or technical differences of opinion. Whether a private agreement between two scientists with differing opinions is the best way to resolve such disputes is an alternative that could be considered.

Resolution

The appropriate action to take within the context of the case depends primarily on the manner in which the client wants the matter resolved. Even though it would seem that the original examiner would quickly revise his opinion once the error was pointed out, one cannot always assume such would be the case. When the issues are less clear-cut, such a resolution might not always be so easy to achieve. And, in general, one must question whether differences of opinion should be settled by private discussions between the disagreeing experts, or by presentations made to jurors by both sides and letting the jury decide. After all, the reason we have trials is to settle differences of opinion between two parties. If that difference of opinion has to do with a piece of physical evidence, should the process be any different?

While there may be an ethical requirement to try to resolve a difference of opinion outside of the courtroom, there is a legal and ethical requirement to maintain the attorney–client privilege. In the absence of a release from the confidentiality of the attorney–client privilege, the criminalist has no alternative but to make certain that the results are known only to the client.

The requirements to report unethical behavior to the professional organization applies to *any* violation on the part of a Diplomate of the ABC and to "serious or repeated" violations on the part of a member of the CAC. The ABC requirement seems inflexible — if a violation is thought to exist, it must be reported. The CAC code provides a little more discretion to the consultant. The consultant can decide whether the ethical violation was serious. A mistake made due to an inadequate examination of the evidence might be less serious than a mistake made due to a failure to do the examination at all.

Attacking Incorrect or Incompetent Work

Facts

In reviewing a case that has been worked by a criminalist employed in a law enforcement laboratory, a consulting criminalist finds what he believes to be major discrepancies between the conclusions expressed in the report of the prosecution criminalist and the data as reflected in the laboratory records that were obtained by virtue of a discovery order. In some cases, the data in the laboratory notes are not included in the report. For example, in the examination of a semen stain, the presence of genetic markers noted in laboratory data are not reported, and the typing results of that stain are said to be inconclusive. In other instances, there are no data in the notes regarding the examination of certain items of evidence, yet such examinations are described in the laboratory report. After reviewing the notes of the prosecution criminalist, the consultant concludes that, at the very least, the prosecution criminalist failed to keep adequate and accurate records of the work he did in the laboratory. In addition, there is some indication that some of the work included in the report was, in fact, never done.

After reviewing the reports and notes of the prosecution criminalist, and re-examining the same evidence, the consultant concludes that the findings of the prosecution criminalist are not only incorrect — but they are incorrect due to a basic lack of understanding of the principles and laboratory procedures involved in the examination of this type of physical evidence. In addition to the presence of data in the laboratory notes that were not reflected in the written report, there is also strong indication that analyses reflected in the report were not done. The re-analysis of the physical evidence results in data that are highly incriminating for the defendant who has retained the consulting criminalist.

As a result of the consultant's findings, the defense attorney decides not to call the consultant as a witness, but to call the prosecution criminalist as a witness since the findings in the prosecution criminalist's report are more favorable to the defense. The defense attorney clearly intends to use what the consultant feels is incorrect and misleading evidence from the prosecution criminalist in an attempt to win an acquittal for his client. Does the consulting criminalist have any responsibility to take any action in this situation?

Possible Actions

1. Do nothing. Once the consulting criminalist has completed the requested analyses of the physical evidence and provided the defense attorney with a review of the other criminalist's work (in other words, completed the requested work on the case) there is no further obligation.
2. Alert the prosecutor to the situation, without providing specific information. This action would allow the prosecutor to request a second opinion on the case.
3. Prepare a report detailing the problems with the original analysis and the results of the re-analysis. Send that to the defense attorney, prosecutor, or perhaps the judge. In some jurisdictions such a report, if provided to the defense attorney, must also be made available to the prosecution. In most jurisdictions, however, and in the practice of most defense attorneys, such a report would not be divulged to the

prosecution. Simply sending the report to the defense attorney would, in all likelihood, be equivalent to option 1 above.

4. Contact the criminalist and, if necessary, the laboratory supervisor to request that the work be redone and an amended report issued.

Discussion

It is clear that the criminalist doing the original work has been unethical; data developed during the examination have not been reported, reports have been written without supporting data, and, apparently, the criminalist is not qualified to do the work. But what of the defense consultant? The defense consultant has an obligation to honor the privilege that exists between the defense attorney and the defendant, which extends to the criminalist, and to protect the confidentiality of the work that has been done on behalf of the defendant. Perhaps there is no further obligation on the part of the defense consultant.

Many would feel, and some ethics requirements would suggest that, knowing a miscarriage of justice is likely to result (e.g., a guilty defendant will be freed), the defense consultant has some obligation to make the true facts of the case known. This ethical requirement, if it exists, must be balanced against the legal requirement of maintaining the confidentiality of privileged communications. The development and implementation of a code of ethics must take into account legal obligations. It would seem to be illogical to establish an ethical requirement that is contrary to a legal requirement. If a legal requirement of confidentiality exists, then one would assume that an ethical requirement to act "in the interests of justice" would be to take *no* action in this particular circumstance. Of course, the criminalist contemplating such an action should be certain that the legal obligation actually does exist. There may be situations, for example, in which the criminalist is required to divulge information.

Going beyond this particular case, does the defense consultant have an obligation to inform anyone about the apparent deficiencies in the work of the prosecution criminalist? Presumably, the criminalist who did the original work is now working on other cases and making the same errors of omission and commission. Apparently, these errors are not being caught by any process of review within the laboratory (maybe there is no process of review, perhaps the review process is not designed to detect the errors that were made, or perhaps the review process itself is faulty). Does the defense consultant have an obligation to call these problems to the attention of the top management in the criminalist's agency — or should he even go beyond that? Some reluctance may exist on the part of laboratory management to take decisive action. In such a situation, what alternatives are available and what actions can the consultant take?

Applicable Ethics Code Sections

AAFS

The AAFS code of ethics makes misrepresentation of data a violation. But what constitutes misrepresentation? Can data be omitted from reports and disregarded in conclusions because the analyst feels that the data are, for some reason, invalid or misrepresentative? If the criminalist is unaware of the significance of the data due to lack of understanding of the science underlying the analysis, is failing to report or failing to consider the data a violation of this AAFS ethical requirement?. The criminalist who did the original analysis seems likely to be in violation of the requirement to not misrepresent data, but this may be an issue that can only be decided by some process of peer review of the circumstances and data in the case.

But what of the ethical obligations of the defense consultant? Nothing in the AAFS code of ethics would require the consultant to take any action. Neither is there any support in the code of ethics for any actions the defense consultant might take. While a code of ethics cannot anticipate and prescribe appropriate action for every conceivable situation, it would be of some benefit for a member of a profession to follow an ethical code that provides guidance in predictably troubling situations. One of the advantages of having a code of ethics that is written by a peer group of practitioners is that they can see certain potentially troubling situations and attempt to craft rules that would provide guidance to their peers in such situations.

ABC

A number of the ABC Rules of Professional Conduct are applicable to the first criminalist in this scenario. Sections 4, 5, 6, 7, and 8, and possibly 5, may apply.

Section 13 of the ABC Rules of Professional Conduct requires the ABC certified criminalist to "… (m)ake efforts to inform the court of the nature and implications of pertinent evidence if reasonably assured that this information will not be [otherwise] disclosed to the court." No specific provision in the ABC code of ethics permits the criminalist to honor an attorney–client or other privilege that may exist. We must therefore conclude that failure to advise the court of the results of the examinations is a violation of the ABC Rules of Professional Conduct, or that legal requirements, when in conflict with ethical obligations, will prevail. A consultant charged with violating this provision of the ABC code of ethics might argue that the requirement to "… make efforts to inform the court…" is met if the information is provided to the defense attorney, who is an officer of the court. Such an argument, however, does not seem be consistent with the spirit of Section 13 of the ABC rules. This is an example of an ethical rule that is in direct conflict with existing law.

CAC

The ethical violations of the first criminalist under the CAC code of ethics are many. The preamble to the CAC code of ethics states, "These findings of fact and his conclusions and opinions should then be reported, with all the accuracy and skill of which the criminalist is capable, to the end that all may fully understand and be able to place the findings in their proper relationship to the problem at issue." CAC code of ethics Sections I.B and II.A may be specifically applicable, as may others sections in Part II of the CAC code. Which sections are most applicable will depend on the specific circumstances of the case.

Unlike the ABC, the CAC code of ethics in Section IV.D specifically recognizes that the attorney–client relationship exists between an attorney and the criminalist retained by that attorney. If that privileged relationship permits or requires the criminalist to maintain the confidentiality of work done for that attorney, then the criminalist is on ethically solid ground in not releasing that information *except*, according to the CAC code, "… in a situation where a miscarriage of justice might occur. Justice should be the guiding principle." Presumably, one of the interests of justice is that the guilty are convicted and the innocent go free. But there are other competing interests of justice that must be considered. One of these interests is the privilege of confidentiality that exists among the various participants in the case. Other interests include the right of the defendant to investigate the case without fear that his investigation will be used against him, and the obligation of the prosecution to prove the case against the accused beyond a reasonable doubt and to a moral certainty. Obviously, different people may have different opinions as to which interest of justice takes precedence. The resolution of these issues may vary in different jurisdictions or circumstances.

Resolution

The ability to conduct an investigation, including a review and re-analysis of the evidence, is the primary method of quality control of the legal system. Traditionally this has been accomplished by interviewing witnesses and then cross-examining them. Such an approach is of limited utility in the case of physical evidence and professional witnesses. If a defendant or his attorney believes that the results of an examination of physical evidence will be provided to the prosecutor, such requests for re-analysis will be made only in the most unusual circumstances. Some legal writers have even alleged that to conduct such a re-examination would constitute professional malpractice on the part of the attorney if there were even a *potential* obligation to reveal the results to the prosecution.

A balance of conflicting interests appears to require the criminalist to communicate his findings to his client, the defense attorney — and, as distasteful as it might seem to some, not volunteer the information to other parties. To attempt to prevent further repetition of the same errors, the consulting criminalist might consider speaking vaguely and without specifics either to the criminalist or to a supervisor in hopes that the problems are appropriately addressed internally.

Whether the consultant has an obligation to report a potential ethics violation to the appropriate professional organization depends entirely on the circumstances of the case and the details of what was or was not done. Confounding this situation, of course, is the same confidentiality issue. An ethics investigation, and particularly a hearing and resolution of the matter, cannot be done confidentially or even anonymously. While it might be possible to pursue the matter by redacting all information that would allow the case to be specifically identified, it is unlikely that this would be successful. In some circumstances it might be possible to deal only with the shortcomings of the original analysis without divulging the data from the re-analysis. In general, however, proof of the problems with the original analysis is only possible by re-analysis. How to conduct an ethics investigation in such a circumstance is not clear.

Ambiguous Blood Stain Analysis

Facts

The body of a young woman was found in a secluded area. Autopsy examination revealed she had been severely beaten. Investigation revealed that she had been seen the evening of the reported disappearance with two young men whose identities were soon established. Based on this information, the police obtained a search warrant and searched the residences of the suspects. In the bedroom closet of Suspect 1, hanging on a hook, was a pair of blue overalls. Blood samples from each of the suspects were also obtained.

The overalls were submitted to the laboratory with a request to examine them for blood and to compare any blood found with the blood samples from the two suspects and the victim.

Ultimately, three different PGM tests were performed. The results, as reported by the analyst, are listed in Table 6.1. The rationale for each run is given in the paragraphs following the chart.

Initially the laboratory screened the reference samples using ABO and PGM to see whether the three individuals could be separated using these genetic markers. Results of the PGM testing are listed in the row labeled *First run.*

Subsequently, examination of the overalls revealed a small blood stain on the front of the bib portion. Based on the results of the first tests, the criminalist decided to do PGM subtyping of the stain and the reference samples. The results of this analysis are shown in the chart as *Second run.*

Table 6.1 PGM Results[a]

Run Sample	Suspect 1	Suspect 2	Victim	Overalls	Standard	Standard
First run	1-1	2-1	2-1	Not done	2+2–	1+1–
Second run	1+	1+	Overloaded	2+1+	2+2–	No reaction
Third run	1–1–	2–1+	2+1+	Not done	2+2–	1+1–

[a] A note is required on PGM nomenclature. Original research on the PGM enzyme system revealed two alleles, 1 and 2. Genotypes detected from these two alleles were 1-1, 2-1, or 2-2. Later research showed that both alleles could be further differentiated into + and – variants. Thus individuals who were a 1-1 by conventional testing could be divided into 1+1+, 1+1–, and 1–1– subtypes. Similarly, the 2 allele can be divided into 2+ and 2–. A person who is a conventional 2-1 must have *both* a 2+ or 2– *and* a 1+ or 1–.

A discrepancy was noted in the PGM type between the first conventional run and the second subtyping run for Suspect 2. Specifically, the conventional PGM showed a type 2-1, while the second subtyping test gave a type 1+. Either the first test should have given a type 1-1, or the second typing should have had a 2 allele in it. Two other problems can be seen with this run. The victim's type could not be determined because it was overloaded; and, most crucially, one of the standards did not give a readable type. Because of these problems and discrepancies, a third determination was done. Results are listed in the chart as *Third run.*

These results were consistent with the first run and inconsistent with the second run. The overall evaluation is that the second run was misinterpreted due to the failure of at least one of the standards and/or analyst experience and competence. Since it is clear that some samples have been mistyped, none of the types can be considered correct without further confirmation. Significantly, the evidence was run only on the second determination. The inference is strong that this typing result is unreliable.

The report that was issued stated that the victim was PGM type 2+1+, and Suspect 1 was 1–1–. The stain on the overalls was 2+1+ and was, therefore, compatible with the victim's blood but not compatible with the suspect's blood.

It is the stated policy of the laboratory that all reports are subject to management review, specifically directed to ensuring that any conclusions expressed in the report are supported by data in the analyst's notes.

A criminalist is retained by the defense attorney to review the work done in this case and advise the attorney on how to proceed.

Possible Actions

The most obvious course of action, and the one recommended if not mandated by the CAC code of ethics, would be to retain a criminalist to re-analyze the evidence, after which the two criminalists can discuss the best interpretation of the data produced in all of the analyses. Some of the analyses may be ignored, by mutual agreement of the criminalists; other analyses may be given more or less weight as they deem appropriate, given everything they wish to consider. In the end a consensus between the two criminalists will be reached and presented to the concerned parties. While this procedure may at first seem to be the best way to proceed, there are practical problems from both the legal and the scientific perspectives. From the legal perspective, the lawyers involved may not want to enter in to such a discussion and may claim that the information that their respective experts have is privileged and cannot be shared with the other expert. In a criminal case, the prosecutor might not be able to make a claim of privilege, but the defense attorney certainly could make the claim.

From the scientific perspective, such disputes are not normally settled by private discussions between two scientists. The scientific dispute is normally settled by a process of peer review, either by publication of opposing view-points in peer-reviewed literature or some other process by which the views of both sides are presented, and a group of peers explicitly or implicitly decides on the correct interpretation of the data. To substitute this peer review process with what amounts to a private agreement between two scientists runs the risk of allowing personalities or self-interest to replace the peer review process.

Another alternative available to the defense consultant includes simply advising the attorney about the problems with the analyses and suggesting cross-examination questions designed to demonstrate the problems with the analyses to the jury. This approach avoids the problem of having the re-analyses redone and developing incriminating evidence and also avoids the possibility that the evidence developed by the re-examination would be excul-patory. Alternatively, the defense attorney could request re-analyses and call his consultant as a witness if the results are favorable, or not call him if the results are incriminating. In most jurisdictions the results of the analyses would not be available to the prosecution, but the implications of the absence of the defense consultant from the defendant's witness list would not be lost on the prosecutor. Whether that could be mentioned to the jury depends on the court and the cleverness of the prosecutor.

Another possible action would be to approach the original criminalist's supervisor and express the concerns with the analyses or interpretation of the data. Given that the supervisor will have already reviewed and approved the report, such action appears futile, but this approach might be useful under some circumstances. Presumably, the supervisor, if convinced of the problems with the report, could ask that the analyses be redone by the same or a different analyst, could ask that the report be rewritten, or could take whatever action might be helpful.

Discussion

A recurrent theme in discussions about ethics among forensic scientists is the relationship of competence to ethics. Some hold that there is no connection between ethics and competence. Those holding this view claim that there is no ethical requirement for a criminalist to be competent; to recognize his own limitations of insufficient training, experience, or knowledge; or to competently perform examinations. Those holding this view equate ethical conduct with conduct reflecting good intentions on the part of the worker; and unless there is some malevolent motive on the part of the scientist, no ethical violation occurs. Others hold the view that there is an ethical responsibility to be technically competent and to follow technically appropriate procedures in the examination and analysis of evidence and in other aspects of the practice of criminalistics. These people generally admit to the reality that there are degrees of competence and that not everyone is expected to be the Michelangelo of forensic science. On the other hand, there is a certain baseline level of competence that every criminalist is expected to understand; and there are certain procedures and protocols that are so fundamental to the practice of criminalistics that failure to follow them is evidence of gross incompetence or malfeasance, which is unethical.

One of the practical difficulties in evaluating competence is the lack of a common educational background among all practitioners. In many professions, where generally similar educational and training requirements are in place for all members of the profession, the determination of what rises to a minimum level of competence is relatively easy to define. However, in the practice of forensic science, the disparate educational and experiential backgrounds of workers in the field make determination of a baseline level of competence relatively difficult. Many criminalists express the view that it is the responsibility of the employer to provide the necessary training and to determine competence. Combining the lack of common educational background with the view that the employer bears the responsibility for training and evaluation of competence allows criminalists to reject the assertion that they have personal responsibility for their own competence. If there is no personal responsibility, of course, how can there be any type of ethical violation as a result of incompetence?

To hold that unethical conduct cannot result from incompetent or inadequate work, and that any unethical behavior must arise from some essentially immoral or illegal activity on the part of the practitioner, practically eliminates a large part of the value of a code of ethics. If evidence analysis does not follow some minimal level of competence and thoroughness, if reports are not written without some minimal level of accuracy and completeness, if testimony is not given with some minimal level of accuracy and objectivity, are there any meaningful standards of professional conduct for which a criminalist can be held accountable?

The scenario presented above introduces the subject of ethics for supervisors. The codes of ethics for organizations such as CAC and ABC do not explicitly address the issue of ethics for laboratory supervisors and managers — individuals who are not directly involved with the work in a specific case, but may have various responsibilities such as supervising the work, assigning cases to various bench workers, reviewing and countersigning reports, allocating resources for training and equipment, etc. While this book does not attempt to address issues involved in personnel management, resource allocation, or similar management issues, the involvement of supervisors in reviewing and approving work must be considered. When a manager or supervisor assigns work, monitors that work as it is in progress, reviews the work, and countersigns the report, the manager becomes an integral part of the final product of the laboratory. In that role, there must be certain expectations of conduct on the part of the manager. The American Society of Crime Laboratory Directors (ASCLD) has developed a code of ethics for its members that is applicable to laboratory managers and supervisors. (No distinction is made in this discussion between a laboratory manager and a laboratory supervisor. This discussion is limited to issues directly surrounding the activities of the organization that result in reports, opinions, or testimonies about specific circumstances or incidents.)

By specific reference in the ASCLD code of ethics, supervisors are ethically responsible for the requirements in the ASCLD *Laboratory Management Guidelines*. These guidelines, in a number of places, directly charge the supervisor with ensuring that laboratory processes are carried out in a competent manner. For example:

ETHICS
Laboratory managers must strive to ensure that forensic science is conducted in accordance with sound scientific principles and within the framework of the statutory requirements to which forensic professionals are responsible.

Potential Ethical Issues

A number of potential ethical issues arise from the scenario presented above. These include:

1. Do the data justify the conclusions as expressed in the report? Should the analyst have recognized the problem in the second set of PGM determinations and repeated all of the analyses from that particular run? Are there problems with the data that should have alerted either the criminalist or the supervisor that additional work was required? Does the failure to perform or demand any additional work rise to the level of unethical behavior for the criminalist or any supervisors directly involved in reviewing this work?

2. Should the criminalist's supervisor have caught the discrepancy between the data and the report? Is competence part of ethical behavior, whether at the bench or as a supervisor?
3. Is the failure to do a species determination, whether by oversight or design, acceptable practice? If not, is it unethical?
4. Can a criminalist who has re-examined evidence for the defense, and who has found some of the evidence damaging to the defendant, testify about the improper conclusions expressed in the laboratory report without having to testify about the damaging evidence he has found?

Applicable Ethics Code Sections

This scenario presents a number of issues. Perhaps the most perplexing problem is whether there is evidence of incompetence in the data that are presented. It is possible, of course, that the report was issued with full knowledge on the part of the criminalist or the supervisor of the problematic nature of the data. However, since the results implicated the defendant in the crime under investigation, a conscious decision was made to avoid any further tests that might change the result from one which is arguably favorable to the prosecution to one which is not. While such motives on the part of the criminalist would be virtually impossible to establish or prove, such actions would clearly be unethical under a variety of sections of any of the codes of ethics that are applicable — and possibly illegal. It is not assumed in this discussion that such clear malfeasance has occurred. It is rather assumed that the actions taken by both the criminalist and the supervisor are based on their failure to appreciate any difficulties in interpretation of, or discrepancies in, the data.

It is certainly possible that any competent forensic serologist looking at the actual analytical gels from these analyses would conclude that the data are exactly as presented in the report and that there is no reason to question the results. It also seems reasonable to consider the possibility that the 1+ allele detected in the analysis of the stain from the overalls is suspect since the 1+ allele from other samples in that same run are apparently incorrect. For the sake of the following discussion, we will assume that forensic serologists would agree that the results of the second run are suspect, especially in light of the results of the third run. Based on this general agreement, we will assume that we would expect a competent criminalist to recognize this problematic analysis and take steps to resolve any discrepancies or ambiguities in the data before issuing a report. We will also assume that there is general agreement that a competent review of the data and other case material (such as actual analytical gels if such a procedure is part of the laboratory policy) by the criminalist's supervisor would have resulted in a determination of the problems with the data and suggestions for further analyses to try to resolve any ambiguities. If the problems were not recognized either by the criminalist or the supervisor, or additional work was not suggested by the supervisor, is there an ethical violation on the part of either?

CAC

Section I.B of the CAC code of ethics states:

> The true scientist will make adequate examination of his materials, applying those tests essential to proof.

This section of the CAC code of ethics would apparently require the criminalist to understand what tests are necessary to establish proof of a proposition and, conversely, to understand when those essential tests have not been done. The determination of essential tests is, of course, subject to various opinions of different people. Must a PGM sub-type gel have a known standard detected for each of the unknown alleles detected on samples on that gel? If one allele in one sample on a gel is incorrectly characterized, should it be assumed that the same allele in other samples on the gel may have been incorrectly characterized? These questions can probably only be answered by reference to the original analytical material.

> II.D Where possible, the conclusions reached as a result of analytical tests are properly verified by re-testing or the application of additional techniques.

> II.E Where test results are inconclusive or indefinite, any conclusions drawn shall be fully explained.

These sections are certainly applicable in the event the criminalist recognizes that the results are *inconclusive or indefinite* but do not require *re-testing or the application of additional techniques* — especially if there is limited material. If the criminalist does not appreciate that there are any problems with the data, then no unethical behavior has occurred (unless it is held that lacking the competence necessary to appreciate the discrepancy is unethical).

Codes of ethics must be explored in somewhat greater detail to determine if technical competence is an ethical requirement. The CAC code states:

> I.F The progressive worker will keep abreast of new developments in scientific methods and in all cases view them with an open mind. This is not to say that he need not be critical of untried or unproved methods, but he will recognize superior methods, if and when they are introduced.

II.H Scientific method demands that the individual be aware of his own limitations and refuse to extend himself beyond them. It is both proper and advisable that the scientific worker seek knowledge in new fields; he will not, however, be hasty to apply such knowledge before he has had adequate training and experience.

Taken together, these two sections of the CAC code imply that a criminalist must be sufficiently knowledgeable to use new and better methods when they are available, have the technical knowledge to evaluate the limitations of methods in use, and make efforts to stay abreast of new developments as they might affect the analysis of evidence in a particular case. The language in both of these sections of the CAC code, however, seems to be more applicable to situations in which criminalists are utilizing new procedures that may not be sufficiently developed or established to warrant their use. Whether this directive would require a criminalist to stay abreast of new developments in the field is not specifically addressed.

The responsibility of the supervisor under the CAC code of ethics seems essentially equivalent to that of the criminalist doing the analysis. If the supervisor recognizes that the test results are *inconclusive or indefinite*, then there should be some explanation of the conclusions stated. If the supervisor does not recognize that the data are *inconclusive or indefinite*, then the ethical responsibility for technical competence on the part of the supervisor becomes the issue. This requirement for the supervisor is not specifically mentioned in the CAC code of ethics, so the same requirements that exist for the bench-level criminalist presumably exist for the supervisor. The CAC code does not specifically address that issue.

A rather specific detail, which touches on the issue of technical competence as well as other ethical requirements, deals with whether in this case the garment needs to be tested for the presence of human blood. Since none of the tests performed specifically identify the blood stain as human, should a human species test have been performed? Part of this question is purely technical — *Can blood stains from other animals give results for PGM and Es-D typing which are human specific?* If the answer to this question is either affirmative or unknown, then the human species test is necessary. If the answer to this question is negative, then perhaps the failure to conduct such a test, or the failure to recognize that such a test should have been conducted, is unethical.

The next question concerns how to address this issue in court. An alert defense attorney might notice the problems with the data, or a consultant for the defense might point out the deficiencies in the work. Assume that, in order to try to resolve the ambiguity in the data, additional examinations are conducted by the defense, and it is found that, indeed, the conclusions are correct. The defense consultant believes that, even though the conclusions expressed by the prosecution expert are correct, the data produced by the prosecution expert do not justify those conclusions. Is it appropriate in these circumstances for the defense consultant to be called as a witness and to testify as to the problems with the data? Would it be appropriate for the defense consultant to assist the defense attorney in cross-examination of the prosecution witness to bring out the shortcomings in the analysis? Would it be appropriate for the defense consultant to refer the defense attorney to another consultant for the purpose of preparing the cross-examination of the prosecution witness?

Relevant sections of the CAC code are:

III.G It is not the object of the criminalist's appearance in court to present only that evidence which supports the view of the side which employs him. He has a moral obligation to see to it that the court understands the evidence as it exists and to present it in an impartial manner.

III.H The criminalist will not by implication, knowingly or intentionally, assist the contestants in a case through such tactics as will implant a false impression in the minds of the jury.

These sections would seem to indicate that the criminalist can neither offer testimony critical of the other expert's work if the answer is known to be correct, nor assist the attorney in attempting to demonstrate that through cross-examination.

If the discrepancy between the data and the conclusions expressed in the report is not noticed by the criminalist's supervisor, and the defense attorney is precluded from calling his own witness because the re-analysis is less favorable to the defendant, what mechanism does the profession of criminalistics have to ensure quality control? It is frequently asserted by criminalists that the ultimate in quality control is the necessity of responding to a vigorous cross-examination. Indeed, the CAC code provides that:

IV.E. It shall be ethical for one of this profession to serve an attorney in a advisory capacity regarding the interrogation of another expert who may be presenting testimony. This service must be performed in good faith and not maliciously. Its purpose is to prevent incompetent testimony but not to thwart justice.

Is it incompetent to provide testimony that gives a correct answer based on a faulty premise or inadequate data? Is assisting an attorney in demonstrating that fact an attempt to "thwart justice"?

ABC

The ABC Rules of Professional Conduct state an applicable requirement succinctly:

> 4. Ensure that all exhibits in a case receive appropriate technical analysis.

This statement does not appear to allow any leeway for limitations on the part of the examiner, but simply provides for some differences of opinion, perhaps, on the definition of the word *appropriate*. The ABC rules are of marginal help in determining what is appropriate. The only applicable section states:

> 5. Ensure that appropriate standards and controls to conduct examinations and analyses are utilized.

Again, the use of the word *appropriate* in this requirement means that the specific circumstances will have to be reviewed by a panel charged with that responsibility; and a decision must be reached as to what is appropriate in the specific circumstances.

There is nothing in the ABC rules to specifically address the ethical responsibilities of supervisors. Presumably, Sections 4 and 5 quoted above would apply to the supervisor who reviews the work; the same considerations would apply as to whether the work done, or the controls used, were appropriate. The decision would have to be made in the same way for the supervisor and the criminalist who performed the original work.

Was the failure to do the species test *appropriate*? Since the ABC rules provide little guidance as to what is appropriate, that determination is left to a group or committee to judge, given the specific facts of the case. The determination of *appropriate* or *adequate* tests, standards, and controls is not a straightforward issue. Every piece of physical evidence is different, and every fact situation is different; what is appropriate or adequate in one case may be wholly inappropriate or inadequate in another case. Further, there are few universally accepted standards for the practice of criminalistics. Documents developed by the various Scientific Working Groups (SWGs) sponsored by the Federal Bureau of Investigation or other federal law enforcement agencies have promulgated some guidelines. The American Society for Testing and Materials (ASTM), through Committee E30 on Forensic Science, has originated some standard methods or procedural guides and has adapted SWG documents to ASTM purposes. A further complication is the absence of any universally agreed upon educational curriculum for criminalists. Although some of the SWG standards specify minimum educational levels for different specialists, these requirements are very broad and do not require training or education specifically directed to the forensic science aspects of the work.

There is little in the ABC rules addressing the issue of ethical testimony or the ethics of assisting counsel in cross-examination of another expert. The ABC does require the criminalist to:

13. Make efforts to inform the court of the nature and implications of pertinent evidence if reasonably assured that this information will not be disclosed to the court.

This section could require the criminalist to withhold testimony critical of work done if the reported results appear to be correct. There would be no ethical restriction, apparently, on one criminalist helping develop cross-examination designed to show that the conclusions expressed are not based on sound or adequate data.

AAFS

The AAFS rules, as usual, are not explicitly applicable to these circumstances. Rule 2 states:

Every member of the AAFS shall refrain from providing any material mis-representation of data upon which an expert opinion or conclusion is based.

This rule could apply if the testimony indicated that the conclusions reached by the first criminalist were incorrect when the defense consultant knew from the re-analysis that the conclusions were, in fact, correct. It is possible that testimony could be carefully given without implication other than the fact that, in the consultant's opinion, the original data were prob-lematic and did not warrant the conclusions as originally stated. The defense attorney, with the evidence presented by his consultant, may argue that the conclusions expressed by the original criminalist were incorrect. Does the use of the evidence provided by the defense consultant to make such a misleading argument result in any ethics violation on the part of the con-sulting criminalist? Presumably, the defense attorney knew that the result was correct in the view of the consultant that he retained.

ASCLD

The American Society of Crime Laboratory Directors explicitly recognizes the responsibility of its members to support and encourage ethical behavior on the part of the staff of the laboratories in which its members work:

Therefore, as members of the AMERICAN SOCIETY OF CRIME LABORATORY DIRECTORS, we will strive to foster an atmosphere within our laboratories which will actively encourage our employees to understand and follow ethical practices.

The precise ethical standards that the employees are encouraged to follow, however, are not stated. At a minimum, employees are presumably encouraged to follow the ethical practices that are part of any professional organizations to which they belong. There may also be employer or agency ethical standards that are applicable to the laboratory staff and which the laboratory management should encourage its staff to follow.

Members of ASCLD are expected to:

> ... discharge our responsibilities toward the public, our employers, our employees and the profession of forensic science in accordance with the ASCLD *Guidelines for Forensic Laboratory Management Practices*.

A review of the *ASCLD Guidelines for Forensic Laboratory Management Practices* shows limited discussion of requirements designed to ensure adequacy or competence in the performance of laboratory tasks:

> WORK QUALITY
> A quality assurance program must be established. Laboratory managers and supervisors must accept responsibility for evidence integrity and security; validated, reliable methods; casework documentation and reporting; case review; testimony monitoring; and proficiency testing.
>
> SUPERVISION
> Laboratory managers must provide staff with adequate supervisory review to ensure the quality of the work product. Supervisors must be held accountable for the performance of their staff and the enforcement of clear and enforceable organizational and ethical standards.

The second ethical statement would imply that supervisors are responsible for the performance of their staff, whether in technical competence or ethical practices. The ethical standards that supervisors should enforce are not specified.

Resolution

Assuming that a pre-trial resolution of the differences of opinion is not possible, there are two options open to the defense. The first is to present a witness to criticize the work that was done. The second is to redo the work, cross-examine the prosecution criminalist (the right of cross-examination is assured in any case), and try to show that the conclusions are, in some way, suspect. The tactical problem with the first alternative is that the defense attorney never knows for sure what the correct answer is, and it might be exculpatory. Further, cross-examination of the defense witness would establish that the evidence had never been retested, and such revelation would not be beneficial to the defense. If, on the other hand, the work was redone and the original conclusions proven to be correct, there are two consequences: the defense attorney effectively loses the services of his consultant since he cannot, according to the CAC code of ethics, even give advice on cross-examination, and the poor quality of work done by the original criminalist is accepted without criticism.

The only alternative that seems to address the poor quality of the original work is to bring the matter to the attention of the employer of the original criminalist and to the attention of the relevant professional organization. The employer may be reluctant to take any action; the professional organization may find itself hampered by lack of cooperation, questions of confidentiality, or claims of inability to participate in any investigation if the case is still in litigation.

The difficulty of addressing these issues demonstrates a deficiency within the profession of criminalistics — there is no clear method for resolving disputes or addressing substandard work outside the arena of the courtroom, which is not the best place to resolve such differences.

Preservation of Test Results

Facts

Preservation of evidence is one of the primary functions of a criminalist. This is usually thought of in terms of work done at a crime scene, or evidence collected from other items in the laboratory. As the following example illustrates, evidence produced during analyses may also give rise to issues of appropriate evidence preservation. Crossover electrophoreses (CEP) is a well-established technique for the determination of the species origin of a blood tain. For the criminalist, one of the advantages of this test is that it allows the preservation of the results of the test. Indeed, when properly done, the gel is dried and then stained to visualize the precipitin bands that are formed when an antigen–antibody reaction occurs. Once the gel has been dried and stained, preservation is simple: the gel is placed in an envelope. In the situation upon which this scenario is based, the criminalist not only failed to stain the gel — he did not know that the proper procedure was to dry and stain the gel. The focus of this scenario is the responsibility of the criminalist to preserve the evidence — the CEP gel — upon which the opinions are based.

Possible Actions

If the criminalist was not aware that the gel could be preserved, then the decision to discard it may simply be a question of the criminalist's knowledge of the procedure. If, however, the criminalist was aware of the fact that the gel could be preserved, then a decision to discard it would be problematic. Criminalists do many tests while working in a laboratory. The results of these tests are preserved in a variety of ways — instrumental data may be recorded electronically or on paper records; visual data may be documented in written notes or photograph records; certain types of tests result in tangible objects that can be saved (thin layer chromatography plates, Southern blot membranes, Greiss or Rhodizonate test papers, etc.). The decision to preserve or not preserve the results of laboratory examinations should be made on the basis of whether what is saved is sufficient to allow an independent review of the work that was done and the conclusions that were reached. A secondary goal of evidence preservation is to allow a re-examination or re-analysis of the evidence.

Discussion

The definition of *criminalistics* adopted by the California Association of Criminalists, and often reprinted in various tests and other sources, states, in part, "Criminalistics is that profession … dedicated to the … preservation of physical evidence." While it is inherently one of our professional responsibilities to preserve physical evidence, the courts have made it clear that this is also a legal responsibility on the part of law enforcement agencies. The obligation extends to forensic laboratories that undertake work on behalf of law enforcement or prosecutorial agencies. As a result of the *People* v. *Nation* case, law enforcement is required to preserve evidence, but only in those cases in which the evidence has potentially exculpatory value. The *Nation* case was used for many years as justification for *not* preserving evidence in cases where the defendant could not show a reasonable likelihood that, had the evidence been preserved, an examination of that evidence might have provided exculpatory evidence.

The defendant in the *Nation* case, after serving nearly 20 years in jail, was exonerated by a DNA test. Since such tests were not available when the case was originally appealed, the defendant at that time could not make the argument that the evidence was potentially exculpatory. Years later, when DNA testing procedures had been developed, evidence was discovered that had not been discarded that had biological evidence which could be genetically profiled using PCR procedures. This case illustrates the risk inherent in the proposition that there is no testing that could be done that would result in exculpatory evidence. Prediction of the future is not a skill noticeably present in either forensic scientists or lawyers.

The preservation of evidence takes three forms — preservation of evidence observed at an incident scene, preservation for subsequent re-examination of evidence utilized in laboratory examination, and preservation of the results or data from laboratory examinations. Each of these topics bears further discussion; but whatever course of action is taken when an evidence preservation issue arises must be based on the principle that the validity of any scientific opinion is only as good as its ability to be reviewed, tested, and assessed by other scientists. It is the obligation of the forensic scientists to preserve the evidence that allows those review functions to take place.

The most challenging part of evidence preservation occurs at an incident scene. It is ironic that this critical part of the work of the forensic scientist is most often left to police officers or evidence technicians. It is not that these individuals are incapable of preserving the evidence — for the most part they are. If the preservation of evidence were simply a matter of picking things up and putting them in containers, the preservation tasks could be given to people with minimal training. But before evidence is preserved, it must be recognized. Indeed, the recognition of physical evidence must be considered one of the basic functions of the forensic scientist. It is not enough to look down and see a drop of blood or a fired cartridge case and know to place the cartridge case in an envelope or absorb the blood on a moistened swab and ensure that it dries before it is packaged. Preservation of the evidence at an incident scene applies not only to that which is obviously relevant at the time the scene is being processed. One must consider how the evidence could become relevant to future investigative issues and also the capabilities and limitations of the evidence and test procedures. One must have sufficient knowledge to anticipate future issues and preserve relevant items or observations from the scene.

Several examples show how evidence can be inadequately preserved. At a scene with many shoe impressions, only certain impressions were photographed. At the edge of these photographs were other shoe impressions that were not specifically photographed. Some of the impressions, but not all, were photographed with a scale in place. Apparently, the crime scene photographer decided that only certain of the impressions were important enough to photograph with a scale. None of the photographs was taken with a camera set up directly above or with the plane of the film parallel to the plane of the impression. Determining dimensions of the impressions was therefore difficult. Finally, the orientation of the impressions was not noted. It was not possible to determine if the impressions were made when the perpetrator approached or departed from the crime scene.

A similar situation frequently occurs when blood stains are cut from items submitted to the laboratory, or from objects at a scene, without any record of the nature of the stain. As techniques to individualize evidence become more common, we can expect to see more physical evidence collected that can be linked to a specific source. While in many cases establishing such a link is all that is necessary to establish the guilt of the accused, in some cases alternative explanations will certainly be proposed. In a case in California,

finding the defendant's fingerprint on a murder weapon was legally insufficient evidence to convict him of the murder because, several months prior
to the murder, the victim had purchased the murder weapon from a retail
establishment — and the object may have been handled by the defendant
prior to the purchase. Would the outcome of the case have been any different
if the crime scene investigators had made observations or collected evidence
that might have established that the fingerprint could not have survived, or
that the fingerprint was in a position consistent with the use of the object as
a weapon in the assault on the victim?

The case just discussed leads us to the second evidence preservation
topic — preservation of evidence in the laboratory. If the location of the
latent print had been documented — preferably by photography before the
lift was taken — it might have been possible to show that the fingerprint was
from use of the object as the weapon in the assault. This is usually much
more difficult than showing that the fingerprint is from a particular individual, but the determination that the evidence is related to the incident provides
the crucial link between the suspect, the physical evidence, and the incident.
The necessary link between the item of physical evidence and the incident
investigated is often overlooked in the evidence recognition and preservation
process. Without preserving the evidence of that link, however, the relevance
of the evidence is compromised. The mere presence of an object associated
with an individual at an incident scene does not provide evidence that associates that individual with the incident.

The preservation of observations on which conclusions are based is
another aspect of evidence preservation that poses some interesting dilemmas. The ongoing debate about the use of microcrystal tests for the identification of illegal drugs is based, at least in part, on the difficulty of
preserving the data (the crystal form and habit) for review. Other debates
concerning the preservation of data include the preservation of electronic
data upon which conclusions in DNA and toxicology analyses are based.
Some forensic scientists maintain that their opinions are based on the data;
once their opinions have been reached, the data upon which they are based
become irrelevant. Nothing could be further from the truth — once conclusions have been reached, the data that underlie those conclusions
become the very basis of the peer review necessary to give those conclusions
scientific credibility. It is not enough to preserve evidence for re-analysis.
Especially if the re-analysis were to show some discrepancy with the original
conclusions, review of the data upon which those conclusions were based
may be the only recourse to resolving differences of opinion. In general, if
the data from which conclusions were drawn are not preserved, the basis
for resolving disputes or establishing the accuracy of the original conclusions no longer exists.

The responsibility for preservation of a portion of the evidence for subsequent re-analysis is a responsibility that is drummed into every forensic scientist. Most criminalists realize that this responsibility includes not only preservation of a portion of whatever was used for any analysis that consumes the evidence, but also the responsibility to preserve that evidence in a manner so that re-analysis is possible. Labile evidence — such as biological material, arson debris, or trace evidence that may either change or be lost if not properly preserved — is most vulnerable to improper preservation. Generally, criminalists recognize their responsibilities to preserve such evidence in a manner that minimizes change. A more problematic issue is the responsibility to preserve the evidence in such a way that other possible types of examinations can be conducted. For example, the preservation of latent fingerprints on evidence is frequently overlooked in cases in which a fingerprint examination was not originally requested. When the requested examinations are conducted, fingerprints present may be obliterated or new fingerprints added, with confusion resulting. Another example is the preservation of the physical appearance of a blood stain, or the geometry of a blood spatter pattern, in cases in which genetic typing of blood stains is requested. In both of these cases, and many other similar cases, subsequent developments in the investigation or interests of defendants may produce an interest in aspects of the evidence that were either not considered or considered unimportant by the original investigators or criminalists.

It is, of course, impossible to consider all possible contingencies in the examination of physical evidence. The criminalist does, however, have a responsibility to understand the significance of the physical evidence to an investigation and what could be learned from various analyses or examinations of that evidence. It is not enough simply to do a competent job in conducting an examination requested by an investigator or attorney. The criminalist must accept the role of a scientific advisor in the investigation and do what is necessary to ensure that all available avenues of the scientific investigation are pursued. This obligation begins at the incident scene and continues through with the recognition and preservation of the evidence, both in the field and in the laboratory.

Clearly there is a professional, legal, and scientific responsibility on the part of forensic scientists to preserve evidence. To a scientist, it should be apparent that this is a necessary part of the job, since only when evidence is properly preserved can the results of analyses be verified. This verification provides the quality control in science. Many scientists have unlimited amounts of equivalent material for analysis, so experiments designed to validate their hypotheses can readily be conducted by other scientists. The sample that a criminalist works with, however, is the result of a single event that happened in the past and can never be exactly repeated. For this reason criminalists must be inclusive in the recognition and preservation of evidence at incident scenes, sparing in their consumption of the evidence during analyses, and meticulous in the documentation and preservation of the results of the analyses.

Potential Ethical Issues

If there is an ethical responsibility to preserve evidence, that responsibility takes different forms at an incident scene and in the laboratory. Evidence preservation in the laboratory, in the sense of preserving portions of the sample for re-analysis, is straightforward; and few criminalists would dispute their responsibility to do so. There might be some discussion over the appropriate procedure in the event that the entire sample is consumed by the analysis. Some might argue that in such cases all interested parties should be advised that the sample may be consumed by the analysis and that such analysis is deferred pending agreement by all parties of how to proceed. Whether such notification is the responsibility of the criminalist is another issue. Some maintain that advising their client is their only responsibility, and others hold that they have a responsibility to ensure that all interested parties are informed. Another difficult situation occurs when the identity of the potentially interested party is not known. In "suspectless" cases, important evidence may be consumed in an attempt to develop investigative leads. In cases where evidence will be consumed in the analysis, criminalists have a responsibility to ensure that the analyses conducted are likely to produce useful information. Two situations are often encountered. Often an analysis that gives apparently unacceptable results will be repeated, perhaps with some slight variation, in order to try to get an answer that makes sense. It is generally pointless to keep repeating the same analysis over and over — maybe the unexpected answer is the right one, or perhaps the sample is incapable of analysis using a particular technique. In any case, simply repeating an analysis is pointless unless some defect in the original analysis can be found. In other situations, limited sample sizes may preclude more than one analysis. In such a situation the responsibility of the criminalist is to determine how the analysis can be conducted while still allowing independent peer review. Documentation of the analysis by photography or videography, detailed notations, and careful preservation of resulting data are critical to allowing the peer review process.

Applicable Ethics Code Sections

The problem posed at the beginning of this section was the failure of a criminalist to dry, stain, and preserve a cross-over electrophoresis gel used for species determination of a blood stain. The discussion included the responsibility of preserving evidence at an incident scene as well as preserving a sufficient amount of evidence for re-analysis. Each of these requirements may pose different ethical issues, but the focus here is on two: the ethical consequences of the criminalist's lack of understanding of the proper procedures for performing the test and the ethical consequences of failure to preserve the CEP gel.

CAC

Section I.F of the CAC code of ethics requires the criminalist to "... keep abreast of new developments," and Section II.A requires the criminalist to "... use proven methods ... where it is practical to do so." Failing to understand that the test is best performed by drying the gel and staining it, after which it can be easily preserved, seems to demonstrate a failure to meet these ethical requirements.

Does Section II.H of the code of ethics, which "... requires (that) the individual be aware of his own limitations" mean that, before an analysis is attempted, the criminalist should be familiar with the technique? Is the process of saving CEP gels one that everyone using CEP should be familiar with? If, in giving testimony, a criminalist asserts that there is no known technique by which CEP gels can be preserved, is this evidence of a failure of the criminalist to *be aware of his own limitations* or to *seek knowledge in new fields*? If the criminalist does not know whether or not CEP gel can be preserved, is the individual *aware of his own limitations*, or is this evidence that the criminalist has attempted to *apply such knowledge before he has had adequate training and experience*? Is it the criminalist's responsibility to define *adequate training and experience*? Or is this the responsibility of the laboratory supervisor? How do we evaluate what a criminalist is ethically required to know — or is a criminalist not required by the code of ethics to know anything about criminalistics?

Under the CAC code of ethics, then, two separate issues must be addressed. First is the issue of whether the criminalist is expected to know that CEP gel can be preserved. Is the method of doing CEP analysis above reproach if the method does not include preservation of the gel? The second issue is whether the criminalist is ethically required to preserve the gel. The criminalist's opinion is based on the characteristics observed in the gel. Does proper laboratory procedure require documentation of observations and data to the extent possible? If there is sufficient sample remaining for independent re-analysis, are the requirements for preservation of the gel different than if the analysis consumed all of the sample? If an analysis consumes all of a sample, are the requirements for documentation more rigid? Are sample preservation issues dependent on legal requirements? Some legal decisions mandate saving material of negligible or limited value for any subsequent analysis (breathalyzer ampoules, for example). Does a legal requirement to save such a sample mean there is also an ethical requirement? On the other hand, there is generally no legal obligation to collect evidence at an incident scene. In the absence of a legal obligation to collect evidence, can there be an ethical obligation to do so?

These same questions can be generalized to other types of evidence and other situations. Are all of the shoe impressions at a crime scene to be preserved? Do they all need to be cast as well as photographed? Do Greiss or Sodium Rhodizonate overlays need to be photographed *and* preserved, photographed *or* preserved, or neither? Many directives influence the manner in which the criminalist's job is performed — technical necessity, scientific methodology, practical reality, managerial edict, legal mandate, and ethical guidelines. These various directives are not necessarily without conflict. Guidelines for making these decisions can be established in a code of ethics, but precise rules for implementation of those guidelines need to be established within the circumstances of a particular set of facts. The final judgment in most ethics issues is left to the collective wisdom of professional peers who apply the ethical guidelines and their own professional judgment to the fact situation.

ABC

The ABC Rules of Professional Conduct require the criminalist to "ensure that all exhibits in a case receive appropriate technical analysis." Further, the ABC code requires the criminalist to "ensure that work notes on all items, examinations, results and findings are made at the time that they are done, and appropriately preserved." The crux of the problem in the example discussed is the criminalist's lack of knowledge about how the test is best performed. Whether his apparent ignorance is to be held against him in an ethics hearing is something that the people sitting in judgment must determine. The use of the word *appropriate* in this context can only mean that a judgment decision has to be made. That decision must be made by the criminalist's peers because no one else is in a position to establish standards of professional conduct.

What if the judgment of one's peers turns out to be different than the judgment of other people — lawyers, judges, supervisors, or employers? Each of these groups that may pass judgment on a particular action has its own rules, procedures, and sanctions. It is not necessarily true that each group has the same set of rules.

AAFS

The AAFS code of ethics does not contain any applicable provisions that deal with the issue of competency of the analyst or the analyst's failure to follow appropriate procedures in a laboratory. It is, of course, always possible to allege that an activity was not "in the best interest of the Academy" or to claim that there was "material misrepresentation of data." It is always in the best interests of any organization for its members to adhere to its established standards. If such standards are established on an *ad hoc* basis each time an issue is raised, adherence to such standards is difficult. Further, such standards as "best interests" do not provide the practitioner with any particular guidance.

Appendices

APPENDIX 1: Code of Ethics and Conduct of the American Academy of Forensic Science

1. Every member of the American Academy of Forensic Science shall refrain from exercising personal or professional conduct adverse to the best interests and purposes of the Academy.
2. Every member of the AAFS shall refrain from providing any material misrepresentation of education, training, experience, or area of expertise. Misrepresentation of one or more criteria for membership in the AAFS shall constitute a violation of this section of the code.
3. Every member of the AAFS shall refrain from providing any material misrepresentation of data upon which an expert opinion or conclusion is based.
4. Every member of the AAFS shall refrain from issuing public statements which appear to represent the position of the Academy without specific authority first obtained from the Board of Directors.

The Code of Ethics of the
California Association of Criminalists

Adopted May 17, 1957

Revised April 11, 1958, and May 17, 1985 (Section V.F)

Preamble

This Code is intended as a guide to the ethical conduct of individual workers
in the field of criminalistics. It is not to be construed that these principles are
immutable laws nor that they are all-inclusive. Instead, they represent general
standards which each worker should strive to meet. It is to be realized that each
individual case may vary, just as does the evidence with which the criminalist
is concerned, and no set of guides or rules will precisely fit every occasion. At
the same time the fundamentals set forth in this Code are to be regarded as
indicating, to a considerable extent, the conduct requirements expected of
members of the profession and of this Association. The failure to meet or
maintain certain of these standards will justifiably cast doubt upon an individual's fitness for this type of work. Serious or repeated infractions of these
principles may be regarded as inconsistent with membership in the Association.

Criminalistics is that professional occupation concerned with the scientific analysis and examination of physical evidence, its interpretation, and its
presentation in court. It involves the application of principles, techniques
and methods of the physical sciences, and has as its primary objective a
determination of physical facts which may be significant in legal cases.

It is the duty of any person practicing the profession of criminalistics to
serve the interests of justice to the best of his ability at all times. In fulfilling
this duty, he will use all of the scientific means at his command to ascertain
all of the significant physical facts relative to the matters under investigation.
Having made factual determinations, the criminalist must then interpret and
evaluate his findings. In this he will be guided by experience and knowledge
which, coupled with a serious consideration of his analytical findings and
the application of sound judgment, may enable him to arrive at opinions

125

and conclusions pertaining to the matters under study. These findings of fact and his conclusions and opinions should then be reported, with all the accuracy and skill of which the criminalist is capable, to the end that all may fully understand and be able to place the findings in their proper relationship to the problem at issue.

In carrying out these functions, the criminalist will be guided by those practices and procedures which are generally recognized within the profession to be consistent with a high level of professional ethics. The motives, methods, and actions of the criminalist shall at all times be above reproach, in good taste, and consistent with proper moral conduct.

I.   Ethics Relating to Scientific Method:

   A. The criminalist has a truly scientific spirit and should be inquiring, progressive, logical, and unbiased.

   B. The true scientist will make adequate examination of his materials, applying those tests essential to proof. He will not, merely for the sake of bolstering his conclusions, utilize unwarranted and superfluous tests in an attempt to give apparent greater weight to his results.

   C. The modern scientific mind is an open one incompatible with secrecy of method. Scientific analyses will not be conducted by "secret processes," nor will conclusions in case work be based upon such tests and experiments as will not be revealed to the profession.

   D. A proper scientific method demands reliability of validity in the materials analyzed. Conclusions will not be drawn from materials which themselves appear unrepresentative, atypical, or unreliable.

   E. A truly scientific method requires that no generally discredited or unreliable procedure be utilized in the analysis.

   F. The progressive worker will keep abreast of new developments in scientific methods and in all cases view them with an open mind. This is not to say that he need not be critical of untried or unproved methods, but he will recognize superior methods, if and when, they are introduced.

II. Ethics Relating to Opinions and Conclusions:

   A. Valid conclusions call for the application of proven methods. Where it is practical to do so, the competent criminalist will apply such methods throughout. This does not demand the application of "standard test procedures," but, where practical, use should be made of those methods developed and recognized by this or other professional societies.

B. Tests are designed to disclose true facts and all interpretations shall be consistent with that purpose and will not be knowingly distorted.

C. Where appropriate to the correct interpretation of a test, experimental controls shall be made for verification.

D. Where possible, the conclusions reached as a result of analytical tests are properly verified by re-testing or the application of additional techniques.

E. Where test results are inconclusive or indefinite, any conclusions drawn shall be fully explained.

F. The scientific mind is unbiased and refuses to be swayed by evidence or matters outside the specific materials under consideration. It is immune to suggestion, pressures, and coercions inconsistent with the evidence at hand, being interested only in ascertaining facts.

G. The criminalist will be alert to recognize the significance of a test result as it may relate to the investigative aspects of a case. In this respect he will, however, scrupulously avoid confusing scientific fact with investigative theory in his interpretations.

H. Scientific method demands that the individual be aware of his own limitations and refuse to extend himself beyond them. It is both proper and advisable that the scientific worker seek knowledge in new fields; he will not, however, be hasty to apply such knowledge before he has had adequate training and experience.

I. Where test results are capable of being interpreted to the advantage either side of a case, the criminalist will not choose that interpretation favoring the side by which he is employed merely as a means of justifying his employment.

J. It is both wise and proper that the criminalist be aware of the various possible implications of his opinions and conclusions and be prepared to weigh them, if called upon to do so. In any such case, however, he will clearly distinguish between that which may be regarded as scientifically demonstrated fact and that which is speculative.

III. Ethical Aspects of Court Presentation:

A. The expert witness is one who has substantially greater knowledge of a given subject or science than has the average person. An expert opinion is properly defined as "the formal opinion of an expert." Ordinary opinion consists of one's thoughts or beliefs on matters, generally unsupported by detailed analysis of the subject under consideration. Expert opinion is also defined as the considered opinion of an expert, or a formal judgment. It is to be understood that an "expert opinion" is an opinion derived only from a formal consideration of a subject within the expert's knowledge and experience.

B. The ethical expert does not take advantage of his privilege to express opinions by offering opinions on matters within his field of qualification which he has not given formal consideration.

C. Regardless of legal definitions, the criminalist will realize that there are degrees of certainty represented under the single term of "expert opinion." He will not take advantage of the general privilege to assign greater significance to an interpretation than is justified by the available data.

D. Where circumstances indicate it to be proper, the expert will not hesitate to indicate that while he has an opinion, derived of study and judgment within his field, the opinion may lack the certainty of other opinions he might offer. By this or other means, he takes care to leave no false impressions in the minds of the jurors or the court.

E. In all respects, the criminalist will avoid the use of terms and opinions which will be assigned greater weight than are due them. Where an opinion requires qualification or explanation, it is not only proper but incumbent upon the witness to offer such qualification.

F. The expert witness should keep in mind that the lay juror is apt to assign greater or less significance to ordinary words of a scientist than to the same words when used by a lay witness. The criminalist, therefore, will avoid such terms as may be misconstrued or misunderstood.

G. It is not the object of the criminalist's appearance in court to present only that evidence which supports the view of the side which employs him. He has a moral obligation to see to it that the court understands the evidence as it exists and to present it in an impartial manner.

H. The criminalist will not by implication, knowingly or intentionally, assist the contestants in a case through such tactics as will implant a false impression in the minds of the jury.

I. The criminalist, testifying as an expert witness, will make every effort to use understandable language in his explanations and demonstrations in order that the jury will obtain a true and valid concept of the testimony. The use of unclear, misleading, circuitous, or ambiguous language with a view of confusing an issue in the minds of the court or jury is unethical.

J. The criminalist will answer all questions put to him in a clear, straightforward manner and refuse to extend himself beyond his field of competence.

K. Where the expert must prepare photographs or offer oral "background information" to the jury in respect to a specific type of analytic method, this information shall be reliable and valid, typifying the usual or normal basis for the method. The instructional material shall be of that level which will provide the jury with a proper basis for evaluating the subsequent evidence presentations, and not such as would provide them with a lower standard than the science demands.

L. Any and all photographic displays shall be made according to acceptable practice, and shall not be intentionally altered or distorted with a view to misleading the court or jury.

M. By way of conveying information to the court, it is appropriate that any of a variety of demonstrative materials and methods be utilized by the expert witness. Such methods and materials shall not, however, be unduly sensational.

IV. Ethics Relating to the General Practice of Criminalistics:

A. Where the criminalist engages in private practice, it is appropriate that he set a reasonable fee for his services.

B. No services shall ever be rendered on a contingency fee basis.

C. It shall be regarded as ethical for one criminalist to re-examine evidence materials previously submitted to or examined by another. Where a difference of opinion arises, however, as to the significance of the evidence or to test results, it is in the interest of the profession that every effort be made by both analysts to resolve their conflict before the case goes to trial.

D. Generally, the principle of "attorney–client" relationship is considered to apply to the work of a physical evidence consultant, except in a situation where a miscarriage of justice might occur. Justice should be the guiding principle.

E. It shall be ethical for one of this profession to serve an attorney in an advisory capacity regarding the interrogation of another expert who may be presenting testimony. This service must be performed in good faith and not maliciously. Its purpose is to prevent incompetent testimony but not to thwart justice.

V. Ethical Responsibilities to the Profession:

In order to advance the profession of criminalistics, to promote the purposes for which the Association was formed, and encourage harmonious relationships between all criminalists of the State, each criminalist has an obligation to conduct himself according to certain principles. These principles are no less matters of ethics than those outlined above. They differ primarily in being for the benefit of the profession rather than specific obligations to society. They, therefore, concern individuals and departments in their relationship with one another, business policies, and similar matters.

A. It is in the interest of the profession that information concerning any new discoveries, developments, or techniques applicable to the field of criminalistics be made available to criminalists generally. A reasonable attempt should be made by any criminalist having knowledge of such developments to publicize or otherwise inform the profession of them.

B. Consistent with this and like objectives, it is expected that the attention of the profession will be directed toward any tests or methods in use which appear invalid or unreliable in order that they may be properly investigated.

C. In the interest of the profession, the individual criminalist should refrain from seeking publicity for himself or his accomplishments on specific cases. The preparation of papers for publication in appropriate media, however, is considered proper.

D. The criminalist shall discourage the association of his name with developments, publications, or organizations in which he has played no significant part, merely as a means of gaining personal publicity or prestige.

E. The C.A.C. has been organized primarily to encourage a free exchange of ideas and information between members. It is, therefore, incumbent upon each member to treat with due respect those statements and offerings made by his associates. It is appropriate that no member shall unnecessarily repeat statements or beliefs of another as expressed at C.A.C. seminars.

F. It shall be ethical and proper for one criminalist to bring to the attention of the Association a violation of any of these ethical principles. Indeed, it shall be mandatory where it appears that a serious infraction or repeated violations have been committed and where other appropriate corrective measures (if pursued) have failed.

G. This Code may be used by any criminalist in justification of his conduct in a given case with the understanding that he will have the full support of this Association.

APPENDIX 3: The Code of Ethics Enforcement of the California Association of Criminalists

I. Statement of Principles

It shall be the duty and responsibility of the California Association of Criminalists (hereafter "CAC") to supervise, investigate, enforce its members' adherence to the Code of Ethics. Such enforcement shall be fair and impartial, and shall be conducted in accordance with the procedures specified in Section II.

II. The Allegation and its Investigation

A. The Allegation:

1. An allegation of ethical violation (hereafter "allegation") must be submitted in writing to the President. An allegation sent to an officer or member other than the President shall be forwarded immediately to the President and shall not be officially deemed received by the CAC until it is received by the President. ("President," as used herein, shall mean that person then serving as President or such person who shall assume the duties of the President in his absence.)
2. An allegation may be submitted by any person, whether or not a member of the CAC.
3. An allegation, while it need not be in any particular format, must refer to facts and circumstances as specifically as possible, and if the Accuser is a CAC member, to the section or wording of the CAC Code of Ethics which has been violated (as interpreted by the Accuser) and his reasons for concluding that a violation was committed.
4. It shall be proper for the President to contact the Accuser in order to clarify an allegation.
5. If an allegation does not, in the President's opinion, constitute a potential ethical violation, he may discontinue its further consideration, provided that he first obtains the written concurrence of the President-Elect and the chairman of the Ethics Committee in such discontinuation. The person making this allegation shall be advised in writing (by certified mail-return receipt requested) within 30 days of the discontinuation and the reason(s) therefor.

6. Within 15 days from receipt of the Notice of Discontinuation, the Accuser may send to the President a written, signed request for appeal from this decision. This appeal shall be heard by the Board of Directors (hereafter "Board") within 30 days following receipt of it. The following procedures shall be followed during this thirty-day period.

   (a) The President shall convene the Board in order to consider the propriety of the allegation and accompanying Notice of Discontinuation; for the purposes of this paragraph, the President may "Convene" the Board by poll, in such manner as he deems appropriate.

   (b) Board members must vote on the Notice of Discontinuation by responding in writing to the President. If two thirds of the total membership of the Board vote to overrule the Notice of Discontinuation, the allegation shall be forwarded to the Ethics Committee for investigation. A vote of less than two thirds of the total Board membership is a denial of the appeal.

   (c) The President shall advise the Accuser in writing (by certified mail-return receipt requested) of the Board's decision. There shall be no right of appeal or of reconsideration by any person whomsoever from this decision.

B. Referral to the Ethics Committee:

1. The President shall forward (by certified mail-return receipt requested) the allegation to the Chairman of the Ethics Committee for investigation within 30 days of receipt provided that a Notice of Discontinuation has not been issued. If a Notice of Discontinuation has been issued and successfully appealed, the President shall forward the allegation to the Chairman of the Ethics Committee within seventy-five days of receipt.

2. Upon receiving an allegation, the Chairman shall send (by certified mail-return receipt requested) a "Notice of Referral" to the President, the Accuser, and the person against whom the allegation has been made (hereafter "Accused"). The Notice need not be in any particular format, but shall contain the following: (1) the entire text of the allegation; (2) indication that the allegation is under "investigation" by the Ethics Committee; (3) the apparent Ethics Code section(s) involved; (4) an invitation to the Accused to provide the Ethics Committee with any written statement or other documentation which the Accused might deem appropriate and a specification of the date (which shall be no later than 90 days from the date of the Notice, subject to the provisions of Paragraph II.C.4) by when the Chairman shall forward the Report of Investigation to the President.

3. If at any time following the issuance of the Notice of Referral, an Accused resigns from the membership, the President shall forthwith issue an "Order of Exclusion", which shall bar the Accused from membership in the CAC until said Order is rescinded thereafter by 75% vote of the Board, and all proceedings or investigations then being conducted with reference to the Accused shall be suspended. Upon notification of the Order of Exclusion, the Ethics Committee will prepare and submit a signed Interim Report of Investigation to the President. Should the Accused be reinstated to membership, all proceedings then being conducted with reference to the Accused shall proceed forward from that point at which they were suspended. The Interim Report of Investigation will meet with the format guidelines stated in Section II.D.1.

C. Investigation by the Ethics Committee:

1. The investigation shall be one of fact-finding, not advocacy. The investigation shall be as thorough, objective and comprehensive as possible. During the investigation, the Ethics Committee may investigate any potential ethical violations which come to its attention.
2. It shall be proper for the Ethics Committee to change the section of the Code of Ethics which the Accused is accused of violating or to bring additional charges based upon considerations of the same or other events encountered during the investigation, whether or not such other events were originally contained in the allegation. Any such changes in the charges require that an amended Notice of Referral be sent, within seven days of the decision to effect such changes, to the President, the Accuser, and the Accused.
3. Determination of the manner of investigation and of investigative assignments within the Ethics Committee shall be the responsibility of the Chairman.
4. The Chairman shall provide the President with the "Report of Investigation" no later than 90 days after the date of the Notice of Referral, except that the Chairman shall receive a 60-day extension by sending a Notice of Extension to the President and the accused. The Notice of Extension shall specify the new date when the Report of Investigation shall be forwarded to the President. Further extension may be granted thereafter by the President, at his discretion, but only for good cause.
5. While an allegation is under investigation by the Ethics Committee, the allegation shall not be discussed by the President or by members of the Ethics Committee except as their official duties might require.
6. In no event shall an investigation be discontinued by changes in the membership of the Ethics Committee or the identity of the Chairman.

Once an investigation has commenced, the term of any Ethics Committee member whose term has expired may be extended by the Chairman until the submission of the Report of Investigation. If the Chairman's term expires, he shall, with his consent, be appointed "Investigating Officer" by the President and shall have, for such investigation, all the duties and powers of chairman; if he declines, his powers and duties shall be assumed by the new Chairman.

7. No members of the Ethics Committee shall serve in that capacity in any matter pertaining to an accusation of ethical violations when the Accused or the Accuser is employed in the same laboratory as that member. In the event that a member of the Committee is disqualified from serving by the provisions of this paragraph, the President shall appoint another individual to the Committee to serve in all aspects of Committee activities pertaining to the relevant individual. The regularly appointed member shall continue to serve on the Committee in other matters. The provisions of this paragraph shall not serve to disqualify any member who shares a common employer with the Accused, but whose place of employment is in a different laboratory from that of the Accused.

8. When a request is made by the Ethics Committee, acting in its official fact-finding capacity, it shall be the duty of every member to assist the Committee to the extent that the member is reasonably able to do so.

D. Report of Investigation:

1. The report need not be in any particular format, but shall contain the following in separate sections: 1) a summary of each purported ethical violation (with specific reference to applicable Code of Ethics sections) investigated; 2) facts in support of each allegation; 3) facts in contravention of each allegation; 4) a listing of the names of all persons contacted by the Ethics Committee (including addresses and telephone numbers); 5) a listing of and copies of supporting documents (if any) possessed by the Ethics Committee; 6) a listing and location of other documents (if any) referred to by the Committee during its investigation; and 7) a chronology of events such as interviews, continuances (with the reason(s) why), the receipt and distribution of documents, etc.

2. The report of Investigation shall be comprehensive and shall contain all relevant facts and topics discovered by the Ethics Committee, notwithstanding the extent to which, if at all, such facts or topics were addressed in the allegation.

3. The Report of Investigation shall contain a recommendation(s) to the Board regarding whether or not a basis for consideration of Ethics

violation exists. In addition, the Report shall include a recommended sanction in instances where a basis for consideration does exist.

4. Statements from persons interviewed by the Ethics Committee should be in the form of "Declarations" whenever possible. Declarations add importance to the statements made and help pinpoint issues. In addition, there is no personal liability for a person who in good faith testifies under the penalty of perjury to something he/she believes is true. Further questions to Declaration authors, by the Board or Accused, should also be answered through the use of Declarations.

5. The Report of Investigation shall be sent to the President within the time limits heretofore specified and shall be signed by the Chairman. At the same time, a copy of the Report shall be sent to the Accused (by certified mail-return receipt requested). Copies of the Report shall be sent by the President to all members of the Board of Directors.

III. Powers and Procedures of Enforcement of Ethics by the Board

A. Board Consideration of Report of Investigation:

1. Within the first 30-day period following receipt of the Report of Investigation, questions may be directed by Board members, through the President, to the Chairman of the Ethics Committee. Written responses to such questions shall appear as addenda to the Report of Investigation. A copy of this addenda will be sent by the Ethics Committee Chairman to the accused and to each Board Member at the closure of the 30-day period. Within 90 days following receipt of the Report of Investigation, the President shall convene the Board in Executive session (closed to non-Board members except the Ethics Committee) in order to consider the Report and any addenda. For the purposes of this paragraph, the President may "convene" the Board by poll or in such manner as he deems appropriate.

2. After consideration of the Report, the Board in its sole discretion by a vote of its membership, shall determine the action to be taken.

   (a) If the Board, by a two thirds vote, determines that a basis for consideration of ethics violation exists, it shall issue a "Notice of Ethics Hearing," signed by the President, to the "Accused" (by certified mail-return receipt requested). The Notice of Ethics Hearing shall specify the time, date and place of hearing, shall include a copy of Paragraphs III.A.3 and III.B of the Article and shall itemize the acts or omissions for which the accused is to be held to account. In addition, it shall issue a Notice of Ethics Hearing to the membership, which Notice shall specify only the time, date and place of hearing. The date of the Ethics Hearing shall not be sooner than 60 days nor later than 120 days from the date of the Notice. However, the President may grant such earlier or later date as he deems appropriate upon written request therefor from the Accused (provided that no later date shall be greater than 180 days from the date of the Notice) or such later date as he deems appropriate upon written notice therefor from the Chairman (provided that no later date shall be greater than 180 days from the date of the Notice).

(b) If a two thirds vote is not obtained, the Board thus determines that a basis for consideration of ethics violation does not exist. It shall then issue a "Notice of Dismissal of the Allegation" signed by the President, to the Accused and the Accuser, and further consideration of the allegations shall terminate forthwith. There shall be no right of appeal or of reconsideration by any person whomsoever from this decision.

(c) The Board of Directors can also elect to take a course of action other than that described above in III.A.2a and 2b. It may use the discretion given to it (via a motion made and passed at the May 17, 1985 Business Meeting, Oakland, CA) that parallels the discretion individual members have pursuant to Ethics Code Section V.F (revised May, 1985). The Board of Directors may therefore, evaluate the Report of Investigation and determine by a two thirds vote that the incident(s) reported on has (have) been dealt with in a constructive manner and as such causes it not to require the application of additional procedures of the Enforcement of the Code of Ethics. It shall then issue a "Notice of Procedural Termination of the Allegation" signed by the President, to the Accused and further consideration of the Allegations shall terminate forthwith. There shall be no right of appeal or of reconsideration by any person whomsoever from this decision.

3. At any time at least 14 days prior to the date of the hearing, upon written request to the Chairman of the Ethics Committee, the Accused shall be supplied with copies of the names (and last known address and telephone number) of all persons contacted by the Ethics Committee during the investigation, copies of all documents (including affidavits or declarations) obtained by the Ethics Committee during the investigation, copies of all documents (including affidavits or declarations) obtained by the Ethics Committee during the investigation, and a specification of the last known location of all other documents or things examined by the Ethics Committee during its investigation that have not already been provided as attachments to the Report of Investigation.

Such written request shall be honored by the Chairman within 10 days from the receipt thereof. Requests for discovery shall be honored, in a spirit of openness and fairness, whenever practical to do so.

B. Ethics Hearing:

1. The Hearing shall be conducted by no less than two thirds of the entire membership of the Board exclusive of the President who presides over the hearing.
2. Members of the CAC may attend the Hearing except as otherwise stated herein. Such attendance shall be that of an observer, not a participant.
3. The Hearing shall be conducted in accordance with the following rules:
    (a) The Accused may be represented by one counsel of his choice, which counsel may be a member of the State Bar of California. Questions of witnesses and statements to the Board may be made by either the Accused or his counsel, but not by both. Unless the President specifically so allows, the designation of the Accused or counsel shall be made by the Accused at the beginning of the hearing upon request from the President. Requests made by the Accused during the hearing to change attorneys or questioning rights shall be considered by the President.
    (b) The evidence developed in the Report of Investigation shall be presented by such person ("Moderator") who is designated to do so by the President; a member of the Ethics Committee shall be so designated and the President is encouraged, but not required, to so designate the person who signed the Report of Investigation.
    (c) The Accused may summon and present evidence in his own behalf after the Moderator has concluded his presentation of evidence. Upon the written request given in the same manner specified in "Discovery" (Paragraph III.A.3), the Moderator shall cooperate with the Accused in arranging for the appearance at the hearing of any witness contacted by the Ethics Committee when it is practical to do so and when it creates no extreme hardship on any other person.
    (d) Evidence considered by the Board must be relevant; it may be real, testimonial and documentary. Written declarations, if given under penalty of perjury, may be received and considered with the same force and effect as if given orally under oath at the Hearing. Oral testimony shall be given under oath. Real and documentary evidence shall be required to be authenticated by the person who presents such evidence.

(e) The admissibility of evidence shall be determined solely by the President, whose determination may be guided but shall not be governed by the Evidence Code of the State of California. The President may, in his discretion, exclude relevant evidence or prevent questioning which is cumulative, unduly prejudicial to the Accused, misleading or dilatory. It shall be proper for the moderator to advocate the propriety of the investigation by the Ethics Committee.

(f) Both the Moderator and the Accused shall have the right to examine and cross-examine the evidence of the other, subject to the restrictions stated herein. The Moderator may call the Accused as a witness, provided that the Accused has not already testified orally in his own behalf and further provided that the Accused has concluded his presentation, if any, of evidence pursuant to Paragraph III.B.3c herein.

(g) Both the Moderator and the Accused, in that order, shall have the right to present a summation, or closing argument, for a reasonable length of time which shall be generally specified, in advance, by the President; the Moderator shall have a right to present a rebuttal argument for a length of time no greater than one-half of the time of the Accused's summation.

(h) The President shall exclusively determine the format and conduct of the hearing, including, but not limited to, number and duration of recesses, presence of spectators and witnesses, decorum, times of adjournment, marking of the exhibits, ruling on objections, etc. However, the President shall not adjourn the proceedings during normal business hours except to accommodate Sunday and legal holidays or for such period as that to which both the Moderator and the Accused may agree.

4. The Ethics Hearing shall be divided Into an "Accusation Phase" and a "Sanction Phase."

(a) During the Accusation Phase, the Board shall consider all properly admitted evidence and, having so considered, shall determine if one or more ethical violations have been demonstrated by clear and convincing proof. It shall determine each such ethical violation by a number of votes no less than two thirds of the entire then-serving membership of the Board, Exclusive of the President, who shall not be empowered to vote.

(b) If there is no such determination of ethical violation, the Hearing shall be terminated by order of the President and the President shall issue and sign a "Notice of Exoneration" to the Accused and the Accuser, and further consideration of the allegation, and investigation thereof, shall cease forthwith. This Notice shall be sent within 14 days by certified mail-return receipt requested. The Notice of Exoneration, while it need not be in any particular format, must contain a complete and detailed description of the allegation. There shall be no right of appeal or of reconsideration by any person whomsoever from this decision.

(c) If the Board does determine that one or more ethical violations have been committed by the Accused, then it shall forthwith convene the Sanction Phase. During the Sanction Phase, the Board may also consider such additional evidence as the Moderator or the Accused may wish to present, subject to the Hearing rules aforestated, concerning the Accused's prior acts, professional background, character, or mitigating circumstances which may be instructive to the Board in determining any appropriate sanction; the Moderator is discouraged from doing so unless such evidence is first offered by the Accused. Upon request of the Accused, all members who are present at the hearing pursuant to Paragraph III.B.2. shall be excluded during the Sanction Phase.

5. Determination and Notification of Sanctions:
   (a) The Board will determine, based on the ethical violation proven and other evidence as presented pursuant to paragraph III.8.4.C, which of the following sanctions shall be imposed:
       (1) Letter of Reprimand.
       (2) Suspension of the rights and privileges of Membership in the Association for a period of time determined by the Board.
       (3) Expulsion of the Member from the Association.
   (b) The sanction shall be determined by two thirds of the entire membership of the Board, but, if two thirds of the Board do not approve sanction (2) or (3), sanction (1) shall be imposed.
   (c) Within ten days following the determination of sanctions, the Board shall send (by certified mail-return receipt requested) a "Finding of Ethical Violation and Specification of Sanctions," signed by the President, to the Accused. Said Finding shall state the ethical violation(s) determined and shall specify all terms and conditions imposed on the Accused by the sanctions; it shall also state, verbatim, the provisions of Paragraph IV.A.1 and 2 pertaining to the Accused's right of appeal from the Finding.
   (d) The Board's finding(s) of ethical violation and determination of sanctions shall be final; there shall be no right of appeal or of reconsideration, except as stated in Paragraph IV.A.1 and 2.

6. Sanctions will go into effect after 35 days if no appeal is filed. If an appeal is filed, the sanctions shall be stayed until the disposition of the appeal hearing.

C. Notification of Results to Membership:

1. Following the disposition of the case by the Board or the membership (in the event of an appeal), a summary of the facts and sanctions, if any, in each case will be prepared by the Board and distributed to the membership. Specific names, places and like identifying information will not be included, except at the written request of the Accused, in the summary of a case where either the Board determines that an ethics violation has not occurred or where the matter is Procedurally Terminated, but shall be so included where the Board or membership has determined that an ethics violation has occurred.

IV. Procedures for Appeal and Hearing of Appeal

A. Appeal from Ethics Hearing:

1. Within 35 days from the date of the Finding, the Accused may send to the President, a written, signed request for appeal from all, or any part of, the Finding. The request for appeal need not be in any particular form, but must specify exactly from what findings or sanctions the appeal is made, if it is not made from all findings or sanctions; absent such specificity, the appeal shall be treated as an appeal from all findings or sanctions.
2. No person other than the Accused shall have a right of appeal from, and no person shall have a right of request for reconsideration of, the Finding. The Accused shall have no right of appeal if, at the time of requesting said appeal, he is not a member of, or has resigned from, the CAC.
3. The appeal shall be heard by the general membership of the CAC. As used herein, "general membership" shall include only those who are entitled to vote in an election of officers of the CAC.
4. Within 30 days following receipt of the Accused's request for appeal, the President shall specify the time, date and place for the hearing of the appeal. The appeal shall be heard no later than the next regularly scheduled business meeting of the general membership; however, if the President received the Accused's notice of appeal within 60 days prior to said next regularly scheduled business meeting, he may in his sole discretion, postpone the hearing of the appeal until the regularly scheduled business meeting next thereafter.

B.   The Hearing of the Appeal:

1. The President shall appoint a Hearing Officer, who shall not be a member of the Board, the Moderator, the Chairman or the Investigating Officer. The Hearing Officer shall preside over the hearing of the appeal.

2. The hearing of the appeal shall be governed by the same rules as specified in Paragraph III.B.3 above, except that "Hearing Officer" shall be substituted therein for "President."

3. Each general member present shall be provided with a copy of the Finding, except that any violation or sanction therein from which appeal is not made shall be deleted. Each member shall be provided with a list of all allegations which are the subject of the appeal.

4. Each general member present shall be provided with a copy of the Report of Investigation.

5. Questions from the general membership shall be permitted and are to be submitted in writing to and specifically authorized by the Hearing Officer.

6. Each general member present shall have one vote.

7. After all evidence has been received, the Hearing Officer shall declare the appeal closed.

8. Following the closing of the appeal and as to each allegation specified pursuant to Paragraph IV.8.3, each general member shall, by written vote, answer the following: "Did the Accused violate the Code of Ethics as alleged in Allegation No._____? Yes_____ No_____." If the "Yes" votes exceed two thirds of the votes cast thereon, the Hearing Officer shall announce that an "Ethical Violation has been proved as to Allegation No._____." If not, he shall announce that an "Ethical Violation has not been proven as to Allegation No._____" and further consideration thereof shall cease, except as stated in Paragraph IV.B.9.

9. Immediately following the announcement of the Hearing Officer and prior to the commencement of the provisions of Paragraph IV.8.10, any member may request a recount, which must be honored. A second recount will be made only if there is a disparity between the original count and the recount.

10. Following the Finding of any or all allegations and following the completion of procedures authorized pursuant to Paragraph IV.B.9, if applicable, the Hearing Officer shall announce the sanctions which were determined by the Board. Thereafter, each general member shall, by written vote, answer the following: "Shall the sanctions imposed upon the Accused by the Board of Directors of the CAC be sustained? Yes_____ No_____."

(a) If the "Yes" votes exceed two thirds of the votes cast thereon, the sanctions shall become final and the Hearing Officer shall issue and sign a "Finding of Ethical Violation and Specification of Sanctions" in the manner described in Paragraph III.B.5.C, except that it shall contain no reference to Paragraphs IV.A.1 and 2.

(b) If the "Yes" votes do not exceed two thirds, the Hearing officer shall request and compile nominations of sanctions from the general membership as they are defined in Paragraph III.B.5.a. If there are more than two nominations, each such nomination shall be thereafter voted upon by show of hands as counted by the Hearing Officer and/or such other single person as he may designate. If there are only two nominations or following the determination of the two nominations which receive the greatest number of hands shown in the manner specified herein, said two nominations shall be identified to the general membership who shall then vote between the two of them in writing. Of the two, the one receiving more than two thirds of the votes cast shall become final and the Hearing Officer and Board shall treat it thereafter in the manner specified in Paragraph IV.8.10.a. In no case shall the sanction be less than a "Letter of Reprimand" written by the President.

(c) Any vote conducted pursuant to this Paragraph 10 shall be subject to the provisions of Paragraph IV.B.9.

11. The findings and sanctions, if any, by the general membership shall be final and shall not be subject to reconsideration.

APPENDIX 4:   American Academy of Forensic Sciences Good Forensic Practice Guidelines

1. Forensic scientists generally should follow the standards of their respective disciplines. They should apply with care any assessment methods, technical skill, scientific and other areas of specialized knowledge to legal issues and questions. They should always strive to do high quality work.
2. Forensic scientists should strive to keep current and maintain competence in their scientific discipline. Although competence at minimum should be a goal, forensic scientists should strive for excellence.
3. Forensic scientists should demonstrate honesty and should strive for objectivity, by examining scientific questions from all reasonable perspectives and by actively seeking all relevant obtainable data that could distinguish between plausible alternative possibilities.
4. Forensic scientists should strive to be free from any conflicts of interest. They should possess an independence that would protect their objectivity. Any potential conflicts of interest should be disclosed. Work on related cases should be avoided or discontinued if objectivity may be compromised.
5. Forensic scientists should undertake cases and give opinions only in their areas of expertise, attained through education, training, and experience.
6. Forensic scientists should attempt to identify, deter, and help eliminate unethical behavior by other forensic scientists through methods such as discussion with a colleague, education, and, if unsuccessful, by filing an ethics complaint.
7. It is essential to recognize that honest differences of opinion exist and do not imply unethical behavior by either attorneys seeking out experts with favorable opinions. Forensic scientists should not be blamed unfairly for unpopular verdicts, honest differences of opinion, or the vagaries of the legal system.
8. Passions against an opposing disagreeing expert, or personal animosity, should not constitute the basis for an ethics complaint. Ethics complaints must be made in good faith. If based primarily on passion, such ethics complaints themselves are inappropriate.

9. Forensic scientists should present their opinions of fact in concise understandable language, but care must be taken since such efforts can result in oversimplification and loss of some precision. In their efforts to communicate effectively, forensic scientists should strive to be as accurate as possible and avoid distortion. Every reasonable effort should be made to ensure that others (including attorneys) do not distort the forensic scientist's opinions.

10. Forensic scientists should strive to instill the highest ethical and scientific standards in their students and colleagues through such means as teaching, supervision, setting a good example, publications, and presentations at meetings.

11. Forensic scientists should strive for excellence and the highest degree of integrity. Forensic opinions should not be based on undisciplined bias, personal advantage, or a desire to please an employer or an attorney.

12. When forensic scientists are asked and appropriately expected to express opinions on a legal issue, they should make every effort to become familiar with the applicable legal criteria in the pertinent jurisdiction. They should take care to reach only those legal conclusions that result from proper application of the data to that legal issue.

13. Unlike attorneys, forensic scientists are not adversaries. They take an oath in court to tell the whole truth. They should make every effort to uphold that oath.

14. When a forensic scientist accepts any privileged information from an attorney, care should be taken to ensure that all such information is kept confidential and does not reach the opposing side. After accepting such information, forensic scientists should not provide their services to the opposing side unless legally ordered to do so. Forensic scientists should alert attorneys not to make payment or provide privileged information, if they wish to retain the option to be employed by the opposing side.

The AMERICAN SOCIETY OF CRIME LABORATORY DIRECTORS recognizes the existence of ethics issues arising from activities unique to managers, such as hiring, training, and supervising subordinates; establishing procedures for evidence handling and analysis; and providing quality assurance. These management responsibilities may have a profound effect on the integrity and quality of the work product of a crime laboratory, yet are not generally addressed in the ethics codes of other forensic science associations.

Therefore, as members of the AMERICAN SOCIETY OF CRIME LABORATORY DIRECTORS, we will strive to foster an atmosphere within our laboratories which will actively encourage our employees to understand and follow ethical practices. Further, we shall endeavor to discharge our responsibilities toward the public, our employers, our employees, and the profession of forensic science in accordance with the *ASCLD Guidelines for Forensic Laboratory Management Practices*.

Guidelines for Forensic Laboratory Management Practices

Introduction

The American Society of Crime Laboratory Directors is a professional organization of managers and supervisors employed in forensic laboratories. We are the holders of a public trust because a portion of the vital affairs of other people has been placed into our hands by virtue of the role of our laboratories in the criminal justice system. The typical users of forensic laboratory services are not in a position to judge the quality of our work product or management for themselves. They must rely on the expertise of individual professional practitioners and the standard of practice maintained by the profession as a whole.

The purpose of this document is to provide guidelines for the conduct of managers and supervisors of forensic laboratories so as to safeguard the integrity and objectives of the profession. These are not immutable laws nor are they all inclusive. Instead, they represent general standards which each manager and supervisor should strive to meet.

Laboratory managers must exercise individual judgment in complying with the general guidelines in this document. The guiding principle should be that the end does not justify the means; the means must always be in keeping with the law and with good scientific practice.

Adopted 1987, Revised 1994

Responsibility to the Employer

Employers rarely have the ability to judge the quality and productivity of their forensic laboratory. Therefore, the employer relies upon the forensic manager to develop and maintain an efficient, high quality forensic laboratory.

Managerial Competence

Laboratory managers should display competence in direction of such activities as long range planning, management of change, group decision making, and sound fiscal practices. The role(s) and responsibilities of laboratory members must be clearly defined.

Integrity

Laboratory managers must be honest and truthful with their peers, supervisors and subordinates. They must also be trustworthy and honest when representing their laboratories to outside organizations.

Quality

Laboratory managers are responsible for implementing quality assurance procedures which effectively monitor and verify the quality of the work product of their laboratories.

Efficiency

Laboratory managers should ensure that laboratory services are provided in a manner which maximizes organizational efficiency and ensures an economical expenditure of resources and personnel.

Productivity

Laboratory managers should establish reasonable goals for the production of casework in a timely fashion. Highest priority should be given to cases which have a potentially productive outcome and which could, if successfully concluded, have an effective impact on the enforcement or adjudication process.

Meeting Organizational Expectations

Laboratory managers must implement and enforce the policies and rules of their employers and should establish internal procedures designed to meet the needs of their organizations.

Health and Safety

Laboratory managers are responsible for planning and maintaining systems that reasonably assure safety in the laboratory. Such systems should include mechanisms for input by members of the laboratory, maintenance of records of injuries and routine safety inspections.

Security

Laboratory managers are responsible for planning and maintaining the security of the laboratory. Security measures should include control of access both during and after normal business hours.

Management Information Systems

Laboratory managers are responsible for developing management information systems. These systems should provide information that assists managers and the parent organization in decision making processes.

Responsibility to the Employee

Laboratory managers understand that the quality of the work generated by a laboratory is directly related to the performance of the staff. To that end the laboratory manager has important responsibilities to obtain the best performance from the laboratory's employees.

Qualifications

Laboratory managers must hire employees of sufficient academic qualifications or experience to provide them with the fundamental scientific principles for work in a forensic laboratory. The laboratory manager must be assured that employees are honest, forthright, and ethical in their personal and professional life.

Training

Laboratory managers are obligated to provide training in the principles of forensic science. Training must include handling and preserving the integrity of physical evidence. Before casework is done, specific training within that functional area shall be provided. Laboratory managers must be assured that the employee fully understands the principles, applications, and limitations of methods, procedures, and equipment they use before beginning case work.

Maintaining Employee's Competency

Laboratory managers must monitor the skills of employees on a continuing basis through the use of proficiency testing, report review, and evaluation of testimony.

Staff Development

Laboratory managers should foster the development of the staff for greater job responsibility by supporting internal and external training, providing sufficient library resources to permit employees to keep abreast of changing and emerging trends in forensic science, and encouraging them to do so.

Environment

Laboratory managers are obligated to provide a safe and functional work environment with adequate space to support all the work activities of the employee. Facilities must be adequate so that evidence under the laboratory's control is protected from contamination, tampering, or theft.

Communication

Laboratory managers should take steps to ensure that the employees understand and support the objectives and values of the laboratory. Pathways of communication should exist within the organization so that the ideas of the employees are considered when policies and procedures of the laboratory are developed or revised. Communication should include staff meetings as well as written and oral dialogue.

Supervision

Laboratory managers must provide staff with adequate supervisory review to ensure the quality of the work product. Supervisors must be held accountable for the performance of their staff and the enforcement of clear and enforceable organizational and ethical standards. Employees should be held to realistic performance goals which take into account reasonable workload standards.

Supervisors should ensure that employees are not unduly pressured to perform substandard work through case load pressure or unnecessary outside influence. The laboratory should have in place a performance evaluation process.

Fiscal

Laboratory managers should strive to provide adequate budgetary support. Laboratory managers should provide employees with appropriate, safe, well maintained, and calibrated equipment to permit them to perform their job functions at maximum efficiency.

Responsibility to the Public

Laboratory managers hold a unique role in the balance of scientific principles, requirements of the criminal justice system, and the effects on the lives of individuals. The decisions and judgments that are made in the laboratory must fairly represent all interests with which they have been entrusted. Users of forensic laboratory services must rely on the reputation of the laboratory, the abilities of its analysts, and the standards of the profession.

Conflict of Interest

Laboratory managers and employees of forensic laboratories must avoid any activity, interest, or association that interferes or appears to interfere with their independent exercise of professional judgment.

Response to Public Needs

Forensic laboratories should be responsive to public input and consider the impact of actions and case priorities on the public.

Professional Staffing

Forensic laboratories must hire and retain qualified personnel who have the integrity necessary to the practice of forensic science. Verification of academic, work experience, and professional association credentials is essential.

Recommendations and References

Professional recommendations of laboratories and/or analysts should be given only when there is knowledge and an endorsement of the quality of the work and the competence of the laboratory/analyst. Referrals of clients to other professional colleagues carry a lesser degree of endorsement and are appropriate when a laboratory is unable to perform the work requested.

Legal Compliance

Laboratory managers shall establish operational procedures in order to meet constitutional and statutory requirements as well as principles of sound scientific practice.

Fiscal Responsibility

Public laboratories should be managed to minimize waste and promote cost effectiveness. Strict inventory controls and equipment maintenance schedules should be followed.

Accountability

Laboratory managers must be accountable for decisions and actions. These decisions and actions should be supported by appropriate documentation and be open to legitimate scrutiny.

Disclosure and Discovery

Laboratory records must be open for reasonable access when legitimate requests are made by officers of the court. When release of information is authorized by management, all employees must avoid misrepresentations and/or obstructions.

Work Quality

A quality assurance program must be established. Laboratory managers and supervisors must accept responsibility for evidence integrity and security; validated, reliable methods; casework documentation and reporting; case review; testimony monitoring; and proficiency testing.

Responsibility to the Profession

Laboratory managers face the challenge of promoting professionalism through the objective assessment of individual ability and overall work quality in forensic sciences. Another challenge is dissemination of information in a profession where change is the norm.

Accreditation

The Laboratory Accreditation Board (ASCLD/LAB) provides managers with objective standards by which the quality of work produced in forensic laboratories can be judged. Participation in such a program is important to demonstrate to the public and to users of laboratory services the laboratory's concern for and commitment to quality.

Peer Certification

Laboratory managers should support peer certification programs which promote professionalism and provide objective standards that help judge the quality of an employee's work. Meaningful information on strengths and weaknesses of an individual, based on an impartial examination and other factors considered to be important by peers, will add to an employee's abilities and confidence. This results in a more complete professional.

Peer Organizations

Laboratory managers should participate in professional organizations. They should encourage employee participation in professional societies and technical working groups which promote the timely exchange of information among peers. These societies prove their worth to forensic science, benefiting both the employee and employer, through basic training as well as continuing education opportunities. Personal contacts with other agencies and laboratories with similar interests are also beneficial for professional growth.

Research

When resources permit, laboratory managers should support research in forensic laboratories. Research and thorough, systematic study of special problems are needed to help advance the frontiers of applied science. Interaction and cooperation with college and university faculty and students can be extremely beneficial to forensic science. These researchers also gain satisfaction knowing their work can tremendously impact the effectiveness of a forensic laboratory.

Ethics

Professional ethics provide the basis for the examination of evidence and the reporting of analytical results by blending the scientific principles and the statutory requirements into guidelines for professional behavior. Laboratory managers must strive to ensure that forensic science is conducted in accordance with sound scientific principles and within the framework of the statutory requirements to which forensic professionals are responsible.

APPENDIX 6: American Board of Criminalistics Code of Ethics

These rules describe conduct in the profession of forensic science (criminalistics) and are meant to encompass not only work done by Applicants, Affiliates, and Diplomates, but to the extent possible, work supervised by them as well. They meet general acceptance by peers in that profession. They specify conduct that must be followed in order to apply for, receive, and maintain the certification status provided for by the American Board of Criminalistics.

Applicants and Diplomates of the ABC shall:

1. Comply with the by-laws and regulations of the ABC.
2. Treat all information from an agency or client with the confidentiality required.
3. Treat any object or item of potential evidential value with the care and control necessary to ensure its integrity.
4. Ensure that all exhibits in a case receive appropriate technical analysis.
5. Ensure that appropriate standards and controls to conduct examinations and analyses are utilized.
6. Ensure that techniques and methods which are known to be inaccurate and/or unreliable are not utilized.
7. Ensure that a full and complete disclosure of the findings is made to the submitting agency.
8. Ensure that work notes on all items, examinations, results, and findings are made at the time that they are done, and appropriately preserved.
9. Render opinions and conclusions strictly in accordance with the evidence in the case (hypothetical or real) and only to the extent justified by that evidence.
10. Testify in a clear, straightforward manner and refuse to extend themselves beyond their field of competence, phrasing their testimony in such a manner so that the results are not misinterpreted.
11. Not exaggerate, embellish, or otherwise misrepresent qualifications, when testifying.
12. Consent to, if it is requested and allowed, interviews with counsel for both sides prior to trial.

13. Make efforts to inform the court of the nature and implications of pertinent evidence if reasonably assured that this information will not be disclosed to the court.
14. Maintain an attitude of independence and impartiality in order to ensure an unbiased analysis of the evidence.
15. Carry out the duties of the profession in such a manner so as to inspire the confidence of the public.
16. Regard and respect their peers with the same standards that they hold for themselves.
17. Set a reasonable fee for services if it is appropriate do so; however, no services shall ever be rendered on a contingency fee basis.
18. Find it appropriate to report to the Board any violation of these Rules of Professional Conduct by another applicant or Diplomate.

In England, the Council for the Registration of Forensic Practitioners (CFRP) has established a code of conduct which all who apply for registration by the Council must agree to follow. While under initial funding from the Home Office, the CFRP ultimately intends to become an independent body supported solely by the practitioners whom it registers.

1. Recognise that your overriding duty is to the court and to the administration of justice: it is your duty to present your findings and evidence, whether written or oral, in a fair and impartial manner.
2. Act with honesty, integrity, objectivity, and impartiality: you will not discriminate on grounds of race, beliefs, gender, language, sexual orientation, social status, age, lifestyle, or political persuasion.
3. Comply with the code of conduct of any professional body of which you are a member.
4. Provide expert advice and evidence only within the limits of your professional competence and only when fit to do so.
5. Inform a suitable person or authority, in confidence where appropriate, if you have good grounds for believing there is a situation which may result in a miscarriage of justice.
6. Take all reasonable steps to maintain and develop your professional competence, taking account of material research and developments within the relevant field and practising techniques of quality assurance.
7. Declare to your client, patient, or employer, if you have one, any prior involvement or personal interest which gives, or may give, rise to a conflict of interest, real or perceived; and act in such a case only with their explicit written consent.
8. Take all reasonable steps to ensure access to all available evidential materials which are relevant to the examinations requested; to establish, so far as reasonably practicable, whether any may have been compromised before coming into your possession; and to ensure their integrity and security are maintained whilst in your possession.
9. Accept responsibility for all work done under your supervision, direct or indirect.

10. Conduct all work in accordance with the established principles of your profession, using methods of proven validity and appropriate equipment and materials.

11. Make and retain full, contemporaneous, clear, and accurate records of the examinations you conduct, your methods, and your results, in sufficient detail for another forensic practitioner competent in the same area of work to review your work independently.

12. Report clearly, comprehensively, and impartially, setting out or stating:
    a. your terms of reference and the source of your instructions;
    b. the material upon which you based your investigation and conclusions;
    c. summaries of your and your team's work results and conclusions;
    d. any ways in which your investigations or conclusions were limited by external factors, especially if your access to relevant material was restricted; or if you believe unreasonable limitations on your time, or on the human, physical or financial resources available to you, have significantly compromised the quality of your work;
    e. that you have carried out your work and prepared your report in accordance with this Code.

13. Reconsider and, if necessary, be prepared to change your conclusions, opinions, or advice and to reinterpret your findings in the light of new information or new developments in the relevant field; and take the initiative in informing your client or employer promptly of any such change.

14. Preserve confidentiality unless:
    a. the client or patient explicitly authorises you to disclose something;
    b. a court or tribunal orders disclosure;
    c. the law obliges disclosure; or
    d. your overriding duty to the court and the administration of justice demands disclosure.

15. Preserve legal professional privilege: only the client may waive this. It protects communications, oral and written, between professional legal advisers and their clients; and between those advisers and expert witnesses in connection with, or in contemplation of, legal proceedings and for the purpose of those proceedings.

SUPREME COURT OF THE UNITED STATES

WILLIAM DAUBERT, ET UX., ETC., ET AL., PETITIONERS

v.

MERRELL DOW PHARMACEUTICALS, INC.

No. 92–102

ON WRIT OF CERTIORARI TO THE
UNITED STATES COURT OF APPEALS FOR THE NINTH CIRCUIT

[June 28, 1993]

JUSTICE BLACKMUN delivered the opinion of the Court.

In this case we are called upon to determine the standard for admitting expert scientific testimony in a federal trial.

I

Petitioners Jason Daubert and Eric Schuller are minor children born with serious birth defects. They and their parents sued respondent in California state court, alleging that the birth defects had been caused by the mothers' ingestion of Bendectin, a prescription anti-nausea drug marketed by respondent. Respondent removed the suits to federal court on diversity grounds.

After extensive discovery, respondent moved for summary judgment, contending that Bendectin does not cause birth defects in humans and that petitioners would be unable to come forward with any admissible evidence that it does. In support of its motion, respondent submitted an affidavit of Steven H. Lamm, physician and epidemiologist, who is a well-credentialed expert on the risks from exposure to various chemical substances.[1] Doctor Lamm stated that he had reviewed all the literature on Bendectin and human birth defects—more than 30 published studies involving over 130,000 patients. No study had found Bendectin to be a human teratogen (*i.e.,* a substance capable of causing malformations in fetuses). On the basis of this review, Doctor Lamm concluded that maternal use of Bendectin during the first trimester of pregnancy has not been shown to be a risk factor for human birth defects.

Petitioners did not (and do not) contest this characterization of the published record regarding Bendectin. Instead, they responded to respondent's motion with the testimony of eight experts of their own, each of whom also possessed impressive credentials.[2] These experts had concluded that Bendectin can cause birth defects. Their conclusions were based upon *in vitro* (test tube) and *in vivo* (live) animal studies that found a link between Bendectin and malformations; pharmacological studies of the chemical structure of Bendectin that purported to show similarities between the structure of the drug and that of other substances known to cause birth defects; and the "reanalysis" of previously published epidemiological (human statistical) studies.

[1] Doctor Lamm received his master's and doctor of medicine degrees from the University of Southern California. He has served as a consultant in birth-defect epidemiology for the National Center for Health Statistics and has published numerous articles on the magnitude of risk from exposure to various chemical and biological substances. App. 34–44.

[2] For example, Shanna Helen Swan, who received a master's degree in biostatics from Columbia University and a doctorate in statistics from the University of California at Berkeley, is chief of the section of the California Department of Health and Services that determines causes of birth defects, and has served as a consultant to the World Health Organization, the Food and Drug Administration, and the National Institutes of Health. App. 113–114, 131–132. Stewart A. Newman, who received his master's and a doctorate in chemistry from Columbia University and the University of Chicago, respectively, is a professor at New York Medical College and has spent over a decade studying the effect of chemicals on limb development. App. 54–56. The credentials of the others are similarly impressive. See App. 61–66, 73–80, 148–153, 187–192, and Attachment to Petitioners' Opposition to Summary Judgment, Tabs 12, 20, 21, 26, 31, 32.

The District Court granted respondent's motion for summary judgment. The court stated that scientific evidence is admissible only if the principle upon which it is based is "'sufficiently established to have general acceptance in the field to which it belongs.'" 727 F. Supp. 570, 572 (SD Cal. 1989), quoting *United States* v. *Kilgus*, 571 F.2d 508, 510 (CA9 1978). The court concluded that petitioners' evidence did not meet this standard. Given the vast body of epidemiological data concerning Bendectin, the court held, expert opinion which is not based on epidemiological evidence is not admissible to establish causation. 727 F. Supp., at 575. Thus, the animal-cell studies, live-animal studies, and chemical-structure analyses on which petitioners had relied could not raise by themselves a reasonably disputable jury issue regarding causation. *Ibid.* Petitioners' epidemiological analyses, based as they were on recalculations of data in previously published studies that had found no causal link between the drug and birth defects, were ruled to be inadmissible because they had not been published or subjected to peer review. *Ibid.*

The United States Court of Appeals for the Ninth Circuit affirmed. 951 F.2d 1128 (1991). Citing *Frye* v. *United States*, 54 App. D.C. 46, 47, 293 F. 1013, 1014 (1923), the court stated that expert opinion based on a scientific technique is inadmissible unless the technique is "generally accepted" as reliable in the relevant scientific community. 951 F.2d, at 1129–1130. The court declared that expert opinion based on a methodology that diverges "significantly from the procedures accepted by recognized authorities in the field ... cannot be shown to be 'generally accepted as a reliable technique.'" *Ibid.*, at 1130, quoting *United States* v. *Solomon*, 753 F.2d 1522, 1526 (CA9 1985).

The court emphasized that other Courts of Appeals considering the risks of Bendectin had refused to admit reanalyses of epidemiological studies that had been neither published nor subjected to peer review. 951 F.2d, at 1130–1131. Those courts had found unpublished reanalyses "particularly problematic in light of the massive weight of the original published studies supporting [respondent's] position, all of which had undergone full scrutiny from the scientific community." *Ibid.*, at 1130. Contending that reanalysis is generally accepted by the scientific community only when it is subjected to verification and scrutiny by others in the field, the Court of Appeals rejected petitioners' reanalyses as "unpublished, not subjected to the normal peer review process and generated solely for use in litigation." *Ibid.*, at 1131. The court concluded that petitioners' evidence provided an insufficient foundation to allow admission of expert testimony that Bendectin caused their injuries and, accordingly, that petitioners could not satisfy their burden of proving causation at trial.

We granted certiorari, __ U. S. __ (1992), in light of sharp divisions among the courts regarding the proper standard for the admission of

expert testimony. Compare, *e.g., United States* v. *Shorter*, 257 U.S. App.
D.C. 358, 363–364, 809 F.2d 54, 59–60 (applying the "general acceptance"
standard), cert. denied, 484 U.S. 817 (1987), with *DeLuca* v. *Merrell Dow
Pharmaceuticals, Inc.*, 911 F.2d 941, 955 (CA3 1990) (rejecting the "general
acceptance" standard).

II

A

In the 70 years since its formulation in the *Frye* case, the "general acceptance" test has been the dominant standard for determining the admissibility
of novel scientific evidence at trial. See E. Green and C. Nesson, *Problems,
Cases, and Materials on Evidence*, 649 (1983). Although under increasing
attack of late, the rule continues to be followed by a majority of courts,
including the Ninth Circuit.[3]

The *Frye* test has its origin in a short and citation-free 1923 decision
concerning the admissibility of evidence derived from a systolic blood pressure deception test, a crude precursor to the polygraph machine. In what has
become a famous (perhaps infamous) passage, the then Court of Appeals for
the District of Columbia described the device and its operation and declared:

"Just when a scientific principle or discovery crosses the line between the
experimental and demonstrable stages is difficult to define. Somewhere in
this twilight zone the evidential force of the principle must be recognized,
and while courts will go a long way in admitting expert testimony deduced
from a well-recognized scientific principle or discovery, *the thing from which
the deduction is made must be sufficiently established to have gained general
acceptance in the particular field in which it belongs.*" 54 App. D.C., at 47,
293 F., at 1014 (emphasis added).

Because the deception test had "not yet gained such standing and scientific recognition among physiological and psychological authorities as would
justify the courts in admitting expert testimony deduced from the discovery,
development, and experiments thus far made," evidence of its results was
ruled inadmissible. *Ibid.*

The merits of the *Frye* test have been much debated, and scholarship on
its proper scope and application is legion.[4] Petitioners' primary attack, however, is not on the content but on the continuing authority of the rule. They
contend that the *Frye* test was superseded by the adoption of the Federal
Rules of Evidence.[5] We agree.

---

[3] For a catalogue of the many cases on either side of this controversy, see P. Gianelli and
E. Imwinkelried, *Scientific Evidence* §1–5, pp. 10–14 (1986 & Supp. 1991).

We interpret the legislatively-enacted Federal Rules of Evidence as we would any statute. *Beech Aircraft Corp.* v. *Rainey*, 488 U.S. 153, 163 (1988). Rule 402 provides the baseline:

"All relevant evidence is admissible, except as otherwise provided by the Constitution of the United States, by Act of Congress, by these rules, or by other rules prescribed by the Supreme Court pursuant to statutory authority. Evidence which is not relevant is not admissible."

"Relevant evidence" is defined as that which has "any tendency to make the existence of any fact that is of consequence to the determination of the action more probable or less probable than it would be without the evidence." Rule 401. The Rule's basic standard of relevance thus is a liberal one.

Frye, of course, predated the Rules by half a century. In *United States* v. *Abel*, 469 U.S. 45 (1984), we considered the pertinence of background common law in interpreting the Rules of Evidence. We noted that the Rules occupy the field, *Ibid.*, at 49, but, quoting Professor Cleary, the Reporter explained that the common law nevertheless could serve as an aid to their application:

"In principle, under the Federal Rules no common law of evidence remains. 'All relevant evidence is admissible, except as otherwise provided ... .' In reality, of course, the body of common law knowledge

---

[4] See, e.g., Green, Expert Witnesses and Sufficiency of Evidence in Toxic Substances Litigation: The Legacy of Agent Orange and Bendectin Litigation, 86 *Nw. U. L. Rev.*, 643 (1992) (hereinafter Green); Becker and Orenstein, The Federal Rules of Evidence After Sixteen Years—The Effect of "Plain Meaning" Jurisprudence, the Need for an Advisory Committee on the Rules of Evidence, and Suggestions for Selective Revision of the Rules, 60 *Geo. Wash. L. Rev.*, 857, 876–885 (1992); Hanson, James Alphonso Frye is Sixty-Five Years Old; Should He Retire?, 16 *W. St. U. L. Rev.*, 357 (1989); Black, A Unified Theory of Scientific Evidence, 56 *Ford. L. Rev.*, 595 (1988); Imwinkelried, The "Bases" of Expert Testimony: The Syllogistic Structure of Scientific Testimony, 67 *N.C. L. Rev.*, 1 (1988); Proposals for a Model Rule on the Admissibility of Scientific Evidence, 26 *Jurimetrics J.*, 235 (1986); Gianelli, The Admissibility of Novel Scientific Evidence: Frye v. United States, A Half-Century Later, 80 *Colum. L. Rev.*, 1197 (1980); The Supreme Court, 1986 Term, 101 *Harv. L. Rev.*, 7, 119, 125–127 (1987).
Indeed, the debates over *Frye* are such a well-established part of the academic landscape that a distinct term — "*Frye–ologist*" — has been advanced to describe those who take part. See Behringer, Introduction, Proposals for a Model Rule on the Admissibility of Scientific Evidence, 26 *Jurimetrics J.*, at 239, quoting Lacey, Scientific Evidence, 24 *Jurimetrics J.*, 254, 264 (1984).
[5] Like the question of *Frye's* merit, the dispute over its survival has divided courts and commentators. Compare, e.g., *United States* v. *Williams*, 583 F.2d 1194 (CA2 1978), cert. denied, 439 U.S. 1117 (1979) (*Frye* is superseded by the Rules of Evidence), with *Christopherson* v. *Allied-Signal Corp.*, 939 F.2d 1106, 1111, 1115–1116 (CA5 1991) (en banc) (*Frye* and the Rules coexist), cert. denied, __ U.S. __ (1992), 3 J. Weinstein and M. Berger, *Weinstein's Evidence*, ¶702[03], pp. 702–36 to 702–37 (1988) (hereinafter Weinstein and Berger) (*Frye* is dead), and M. Graham, *Handbook of Federal Evidence* §703.2 (2d ed. 1991) (*Frye* lives). See generally P. Gianelli and E. Imwinkelried, Scientific Evidence §1–5, pp. 28–29 (1986 & Supp. 1991) (citing authorities).

continues to exist, though in the somewhat altered form of a source of guidance in the exercise of delegated powers." *Ibid.*, at 51–52.

We found the common-law precept at issue in the *Abel* case entirely consistent with Rule 402's general requirement of admissibility, and considered it unlikely that the drafters had intended to change the rule. *Ibid.*, at 50–51. In *Bourjaily* v. *United States*, 483 U.S. 171 (1987), on the other hand, the Court was unable to find a particular common-law doctrine in the Rules, and so held it superseded.

Here there is a specific Rule that speaks to the contested issue. Rule 702, governing expert testimony, provides:

"If scientific, technical, or other specialized knowledge will assist the trier of fact to understand the evidence or to determine a fact in issue, a witness qualified as an expert by knowledge, skill, experience, training, or education, may testify thereto in the form of an opinion or otherwise."

Nothing in the text of this Rule establishes "general acceptance" as an absolute prerequisite to admissibility. Nor does respondent present any clear indication that Rule 702 or the Rules as a whole were intended to incorporate a "general acceptance" standard. The drafting history makes no mention of *Frye*, and a rigid "general acceptance" requirement would be at odds with the "liberal thrust" of the Federal Rules and their "general approach of relaxing the traditional barriers to 'opinion' testimony." *Beech Aircraft Corp.* v. *Rainey*, 488 U.S., at 169 (citing Rules 701 to 705). See also Weinstein, Rule 702 of the Federal Rules of Evidence Is Sound; It Should Not Be Amended, 138 *F.R.D.* 631, 631 (1991) ("The Rules were designed to depend primarily upon lawyer-adversaries and sensible triers of fact to evaluate conflicts"). Given the Rules' permissive backdrop and their inclusion of a specific rule on expert testimony that does not mention "general acceptance," the assertion that the Rules somehow assimilated *Frye* is unconvincing. *Frye* made "general acceptance" the exclusive test for admitting expert scientific testimony. That austere standard, absent from and incompatible with the Federal Rules of Evidence, should not be applied in federal trials.[6]

That the *Frye* test was displaced by the Rules of Evidence does not mean, however, that the Rules themselves place no limits on the admissibility of purportedly scientific evidence.[7] Nor is the trial judge disabled from screening such evidence. To the contrary, under the Rules the trial judge must ensure

[6] Because we hold that *Frye* has been superseded and base the discussion that follows on the content of the congressionally-enacted Federal Rules of Evidence, we do not address petitioners' argument that application of the *Frye* rule in this diversity case, as the application of a judge-made rule affecting substantive rights, would violate the doctrine of *Erie R. Co.* v. *Tompkins*, 304 U.S. 64 (1938).

[7] THE CHIEF JUSTICE "do[es] not doubt that Rule 702 confides to the judge some gatekeeping responsibility," *post*, at 4, but would neither say how it does so, nor explain what that role entails. We believe the better course is to note the nature and source of the duty.

that any and all scientific testimony or evidence admitted is not only relevant, but reliable.

The primary locus of this obligation is Rule 702, which clearly contemplates some degree of regulation of the subjects and theories about which an expert may testify. "*If scientific,* technical, or other specialized *knowledge will assist the trier of fact* to understand the evidence or to determine a fact in issue" an expert "may testify *thereto.*" The subject of an expert's testimony must be "scientific ... knowledge."[8] The adjective "scientific" implies a grounding in the methods and procedures of science. Similarly, the word "knowledge" connotes more than subjective belief or unsupported speculation. The term "applies to any body of known facts or to any body of ideas inferred from such facts or accepted as truths on good grounds." *Webster's Third New International Dictionary,* 1252 (1986). Of course, it would be unreasonable to conclude that the subject of scientific testimony must be "known" to a certainty; arguably, there are no certainties in science. See, *e.g.,* Brief for Nicolaas Bloembergen et al. as *Amici Curiae,* 9 ("Indeed, scientists do not assert that they know what is immutably 'true'—they are committed to searching for new, temporary theories to explain, as best they can, phenomena"); Brief for American Association for the Advancement of Science and the National Academy of Sciences as *Amici Curiae,* 7–8 ("Science is not an encyclopedic body of knowledge about the universe. Instead, it represents a *process* for proposing and refining theoretical explanations about the world that are subject to further testing and refinement") (emphasis in original). But, in order to qualify as "scientific knowledge," an inference or assertion must be derived by the scientific method. Proposed testimony must be supported by appropriate validation—*i.e.,* "good grounds," based on what is known. In short, the requirement that an expert's testimony pertain to "scientific knowledge" establishes a standard of evidentiary reliability.[9]

---

[8] Rule 702 also applies to "technical, or other specialized knowledge." Our discussion is limited to the scientific context because that is the nature of the expertise offered here.

[9] We note that scientists typically distinguish between "validity" (does the principle support what it purports to show?) and "reliability" (does application of the principle produce consistent results?). See Black, A Unified Theory of Scientific Evidence, 56 *Ford. L. Rev.,* 595, 599 (1988). Although "the difference between accuracy, validity, and reliability may be such that each is distinct from the other by no more than a hen's kick," Starrs, *Frye* v. *United States* Restructured and Revitalized: A Proposal to Amend Federal Evidence Rule 702, 26 *Jurimetrics J.* 249, 256 (1986), our reference here is to *evidentiary* reliability—that is, trustworthiness. Cf., e.g., Advisory Committee's Notes on Fed. Rule Evid. 602 ("'[T]he rule requiring that a witness who testifies to a fact which can be perceived by the senses must have had an opportunity to observe, and must have actually observed the fact' is a 'most pervasive manifestation' of the common law insistence upon 'the most reliable sources of information.'" (citation omitted)); Advisory Committee's Notes on Art. VIII of the Rules of Evidence (hearsay exceptions will be recognized only "under circumstances supposed to furnish guarantees of trustworthiness"). In a case involving scientific evidence, *evidentiary reliability* will be based upon *scientific validity.*

Rule 702 further requires that the evidence or testimony "assist the trier of fact to understand the evidence or to determine a fact in issue." This condition goes primarily to relevance. "Expert testimony which does not relate to any issue in the case is not relevant and, ergo, non-helpful." 3 Weinstein and Berger, ¶702[02], p. 702-18. See also *United States* v. *Downing*, 753 F.2d 1224, 1242 (CA3 1985) ("An additional consideration under Rule 702—and another aspect of relevancy—is whether expert testimony proffered in the case is sufficiently tied to the facts of the case that it will aid the jury in resolving a factual dispute"). The consideration has been aptly described by Judge Becker as one of "fit." *Ibid.* "Fit" is not always obvious, and scientific validity for one purpose is not necessarily scientific validity for other, unrelated purposes. See Starrs, *Frye* v. *United States* Restructured and Revitalized: A Proposal to Amend Federal Evidence Rule 702, and 26 *Jurimetrics J.*, 249, 258 (1986). The study of the phases of the moon, for example, may provide valid scientific "knowledge" about whether a certain night was dark, and if darkness is a fact in issue, the knowledge will assist the trier of fact. However (absent creditable grounds supporting such a link), evidence that the moon was full on a certain night will not assist the trier of fact in determining whether an individual was unusually likely to have behaved irrationally on that night. Rule 702's "helpfulness" standard requires a valid scientific connection to the pertinent inquiry as a precondition to admissibility.

That these requirements are embodied in Rule 702 is not surprising. Unlike an ordinary witness, see Rule 701, an expert is permitted wide latitude to offer opinions, including those that are not based on first-hand knowledge or observation. See Rules 702 and 703. Presumably, this relaxation of the usual requirement of first-hand knowledge—a rule which represents "a 'most pervasive manifestation' of the common law insistence upon 'the most reliable sources of information,'" Advisory Committee's Notes on Fed. Rule Evid. 602 (citation omitted)—is premised on an assumption that the expert's opinion will have a reliable basis in the knowledge and experience of his discipline.

C

Faced with a proffer of expert scientific testimony, then, the trial judge must determine at the outset, pursuant to Rule 104(a),[10] whether the expert is proposing to testify to (1) scientific knowledge that (2) will assist the trier

---

[10] Rule 104(a) provides: "Preliminary questions concerning the qualification of a person to be a witness, the existence of a privilege, or the admissibility of evidence shall be determined by the court, subject to the provisions of subdivision (b) [pertaining to conditional admissions]. In making its determination it is not bound by the rules of evidence except those with respect to privileges." These matters should be established by a preponderance of proof. See *Bourjaily* v. *United States*, 483 U.S. 171, 175–176 (1987).

of fact to understand or determine a fact in issue.[11] This entails a preliminary assessment of whether the reasoning or methodology underlying the testimony is scientifically valid and of whether that reasoning or methodology properly can be applied to the facts in issue. We are confident that federal judges possess the capacity to undertake this review. Many factors will bear on the inquiry, and we do not presume to set out a definitive checklist or test. But some general observations are appropriate.

Ordinarily, a key question to be answered in determining whether a theory or technique is scientific knowledge that will assist the trier of fact will be whether it can be (and has been) tested. "Scientific methodology today is based on generating hypotheses and testing them to see if they can be falsified; indeed, this methodology is what distinguishes science from other fields of human inquiry." Green, at 645. See also C. Hempel, *Philosophy of Natural Science*, 49 (1966) ("[T]he statements constituting a scientific explanation must be capable of empirical test"); K. Popper, *Conjectures and Refutations: The Growth of Scientific Knowledge*, 37 (5th ed. 1989) ("[T]he criterion of the scientific status of a theory is its falsifiability, or refutability, or testability").

Another pertinent consideration is whether the theory or technique has been subjected to peer review and publication. Publication (which is but one element of peer review) is not a *sine qua non* of admissibility; it does not necessarily correlate with reliability, see S. Jasanoff, *The Fifth Branch: Science Advisors as Policymakers*, 61–76 (1990), and in some instances well-grounded but innovative theories will not have been published, see Horrobin, *The Philosophical Basis of Peer Review and the Suppression of Innovation*, 263 J. Am. Med. Assoc., 1438 (1990). Some propositions, moreover, are too particular, too new, or of too limited interest to be published. But submission to the scrutiny of the scientific community is a component of "good science," in part because it increases the likelihood that substantive flaws in methodology will be detected. See J. Ziman, *Reliable Knowledge: An Exploration of the Grounds for Belief in Science*, 130–133 (1978); Relman and Angell, How Good Is Peer Review?, 321 *New Engl. J. Med.*, 827 (1989). The fact of publication (or lack thereof) in a peer-reviewed journal thus will be a relevant, though not dispositive, consideration in assessing the scientific validity of a particular technique or methodology on which an opinion is premised.

Additionally, in the case of a particular scientific technique, the court ordinarily should consider the known or potential rate of error, see, *e.g.*,

---

[11] Although the *Frye* decision itself focused exclusively on "novel" scientific techniques, we do not read the requirements of Rule 702 to apply specially or exclusively to unconventional evidence. Of course, well-established propositions are less likely to be challenged than those that are novel, and they are more handily defended. Indeed, theories that are so firmly established as to have attained the status of scientific law, such as the laws of thermodynamics, properly are subject to judicial notice under Fed. Rule Evid. 201.

United States v. *Smith*, 869 F.2d 348, 353–354 (CA7 1989) (surveying studies of the error rate of spectrographic voice identification technique), and the existence and maintenance of standards controlling the technique's operation. See *United States* v. *Williams*, 583 F.2d 1194, 1198 (CA2 1978) (noting professional organization's standard governing spectrographic analysis), cert. denied, 439 U.S. 1117 (1979).

Finally, "general acceptance" can yet have a bearing on the inquiry. A "reliability assessment does not require, although it does permit, explicit identification of a relevant scientific community and an express determination of a particular degree of acceptance within that community." *United States* v. *Downing*, 753 F.2d, at 1238. See also 3 Weinstein and Berger, ¶702[03], pp. 702-41 to 702-42. Widespread acceptance can be an important factor in ruling particular evidence admissible, and "a known technique that has been able to attract only minimal support within the community," *Downing, supra,* at 1238, may properly be viewed with skepticism.

The inquiry envisioned by Rule 702 is, we emphasize, a flexible one.[12] Its overarching subject is the scientific validity—and thus the evidentiary relevance and reliability—of the principles that underlie a proposed submission. The focus, of course, must be solely on principles and methodology, not on the conclusions that they generate.

Throughout, a judge assessing a proffer of expert scientific testimony under Rule 702 should also be mindful of other applicable rules. Rule 703 provides that expert opinions based on otherwise inadmissible hearsay are to be admitted only if the facts or data are "of a type reasonably relied upon by experts in the particular field in forming opinions or inferences upon the subject." Rule 706 allows the court at its discretion to procure the assistance of an expert of its own choosing. Finally, Rule 403 permits the exclusion of relevant evidence "if its probative value is substantially outweighed by the danger of unfair prejudice, confusion of the issues, or misleading the jury... ." Judge Weinstein has explained: "Expert evidence can be both powerful and quite misleading because of the difficulty in evaluating it. Because of this risk, the judge in weighing possible prejudice against probative force under Rule 403 of the present rules exercises more control over experts than over lay witnesses." Weinstein, 138 *F.R.D.*, at 632.

---

[12] A number of authorities have presented variations on the reliability approach, each with its own slightly different set of factors. See, e.g., *Downing,* 753 F.2d 1238–1239 (on which our discussion draws in part); 3 Weinstein and Berger, ¶702[03], pp. 702-41 to 702-42 (on which the *Downing* court in turn partially relied); McCormick, Scientific Evidence: Defining a New Approach to Admissibility, 67 *Iowa L. Rev.*, 879, 911–912 (1982); and Symposium on Science and the Rules of Evidence, 99 *F.R.D.* 187, 231 (1983) (statement by Margaret Berger). To the extent that they focus on the reliability of evidence as ensured by the scientific validity of its underlying principles, all these versions may well have merit, although we express no opinion regarding any of their particular details.

III

We conclude by briefly addressing what appear to be two underlying concerns of the parties and *amici* in this case. Respondent expresses apprehension that abandonment of "general acceptance" as the exclusive requirement for admission will result in a "free-for-all" in which befuddled juries are confounded by absurd and irrational pseudoscientific assertions. In this regard respondent seems to us to be overly pessimistic about the capabilities of the jury, and of the adversary system generally. Vigorous cross-examination, presentation of contrary evidence, and careful instruction on the burden of proof are the traditional and appropriate means of attacking shaky but admissible evidence. See *Rock* v. *Arkansas*, 483 U.S. 44, 61 (1987). Additionally, in the event the trial court concludes that the scintilla of evidence presented supporting a position is insufficient to allow a reasonable juror to conclude that the position more likely than not is true, the court remains free to direct a judgment, *Fed. Rule Civ. Proc.* 50(a), and likewise to grant summary judgment, *Fed. Rule Civ. Proc.* 56. Cf., *e.g.*, *Turpin* v. *Merrell Dow Pharmaceuticals, Inc.*, 959 F.2d 1349 (CA6) (holding that scientific evidence that provided foundation for expert testimony, viewed in the light most favorable to plaintiffs, was not sufficient to allow a jury to find it more probable than not that defendant caused plaintiff's injury), cert. denied, 506 U.S. __ (1992); *Brock* v. *Merrell Dow Pharmaceuticals, Inc.*, 874 F.2d 307 (CA5 1989) (reversing judgment entered on jury verdict for plaintiffs because evidence regarding causation was insufficient), modified, 884 F.2d 166 (CA5 1989), cert. denied, 494 U.S. 1046 (1990); Green 680–681. These conventional devices, rather than wholesale exclusion under an uncompromising "general acceptance" test, are the appropriate safeguards where the basis of scientific testimony meets the standards of Rule 702.

Petitioners and, to a greater extent, their *amici* exhibit a different concern. They suggest that recognition of a screening role for the judge that allows for the exclusion of "invalid" evidence will sanction a stifling and repressive scientific orthodoxy and will be inimical to the search for truth. See, *e.g.*, Brief for Ronald Bayer et al. as *Amici Curiae*. It is true that open debate is an essential part of both legal and scientific analyses. Yet there are important differences between the quest for truth in the courtroom and the quest for truth in the laboratory. Scientific conclusions are subject to perpetual revision. Law, on the other hand, must resolve disputes finally and quickly. The scientific project is advanced by broad and wide-ranging consideration of a multitude of hypotheses, for those that are incorrect will eventually be shown to be so, and that in itself is an advance. Conjectures that are probably wrong are of little use, however, in the project of reaching a quick, final, and binding legal judgment—often of great conse-

quence—about a particular set of events in the past. We recognize that in
practice, a gatekeeping role for the judge, no matter how flexible, inevitably
on occasion will prevent the jury from learning of authentic insights and
innovations. That, nevertheless, is the balance that is struck by Rules of
Evidence designed not for the exhaustive search for cosmic understanding
but for the particularized resolution of legal disputes.[13]

IV

To summarize: "general acceptance" is not a necessary precondition to
the admissibility of scientific evidence under the Federal Rules of Evidence,
but the Rules of Evidence—especially Rule 702—do assign to the trial judge
the task of ensuring that an expert's testimony both rests on a reliable foundation and is relevant to the task at hand. Pertinent evidence based on
scientifically valid principles will satisfy those demands.

The inquiries of the District Court and the Court of Appeals focused
almost exclusively on "general acceptance," as gauged by publication and the
decisions of other courts. Accordingly, the judgment of the Court of Appeals
is vacated and the case is remanded for further proceedings consistent with
this opinion.

It is so ordered.

---

[13] This is not to say that judicial interpretation, as opposed to adjudicative factfinding, does
not share basic characteristics of the scientific endeavor: "The work of a judge is in one
sense enduring and in another ephemeral .... In the endless process of testing and retesting,
there is a constant rejection of the dross and a constant retention of whatever is pure and
sound and fine." B. Cardozo, *The Nature of the Judicial Process*, 178, 179 (1921).

SUPREME COURT OF THE UNITED STATES

KUMHO TIRE COMPANY, LTD., et al., PETITIONERS
v.
PATRICK CARMICHAEL, etc., et al.

No. 97-1709

ON WRIT OF CERTIORARI TO THE
UNITED STATES COURT OF APPEALS FOR THE ELEVENTH CIRCUIT

[March 23, 1999]

Justice Breyer delivered the opinion of the Court.

In *Daubert* v. *Merrell Dow Pharmaceuticals, Inc.*, 509 U.S. 579 (1993), this Court focused upon the admissibility of scientific expert testimony. It pointed out that such testimony is admissible only if it is both relevant and reliable. And it held that the Federal Rules of Evidence "assign to the trial judge the task of ensuring that an expert's testimony both rests on a reliable foundation and is relevant to the task at hand." *Ibid.*, at 597. The Court also discussed certain more specific factors, such as testing, peer review, error rates, and "acceptability" in the relevant scientific community, some or all of which might prove helpful in determining the reliability of a particular scientific "theory or technique." *Ibid.*, at 593–594.

This case requires us to decide how *Daubert* applies to the testimony of engineers and other experts who are not scientists. We conclude that *Daubert*'s general holding—setting forth the trial judge's general "gatekeeping" obligation—applies not only to testimony based on "scientific" knowledge, but also to testimony based on "technical" and "other specialized" knowledge. See Fed. Rule Evid., 702. We also conclude that a trial court may consider one or more of the more specific factors that *Daubert* mentioned when doing so will help determine that testimony's reliability. But, as the Court stated in *Daubert*, the test of reliability is "flexible," and *Daubert*'s list of specific factors neither necessarily nor exclusively applies to all experts or in every case. Rather, the law grants a district court the same broad latitude when it decides how to determine reliability as it enjoys in respect to its ultimate reliability determination. See *General Electric Co.* v. *Joiner*, 522 U.S. 136, 143 (1997) (courts of appeals are to apply "abuse of discretion" standard when reviewing district court's reliability determination). Applying these standards, we determine that the District Court's decision in this case—not to admit certain expert testimony—was within its discretion and therefore lawful.

I

On July 6, 1993, the right rear tire of a minivan driven by Patrick Carmichael blew out. In the accident that followed, one of the passengers died, and others were severely injured. In October 1993, the Carmichaels brought this diversity suit against the tire's maker and its distributor, whom we refer to collectively as Kumho Tire, claiming that the tire was defective. The plaintiffs rested their case in significant part upon deposition testimony provided by an expert in tire failure analysis, Dennis Carlson, Jr., who intended to testify in support of their conclusion.

Carlson's depositions relied upon certain features of tire technology that are not in dispute. A steel-belted radial tire like the Carmichaels' is made up of a "carcass" containing many layers of flexible cords, called "plies," along which (between the cords and the outer tread) are laid steel strips called "belts." Steel wire loops, called "beads," hold the cords together at the plies' bottom edges. An outer layer, called the "tread," encases the carcass, and the entire tire is bound together in rubber, through the application of heat and various chemicals. See generally, e.g., J. Dixon, *Tires, Suspension and Handling*, 68–72 (2nd ed. 1996). The bead of the tire sits upon a "bead seat," which is part of the wheel assembly. That assembly contains a "rim flange," which extends over the bead and rests against the side of the tire. See M. Mavrigian, *Performance Wheels and Tires*, 81, 83 (1998) (illustrations), and A. Markovich, *How To Buy and Care For Tires*, 4 (1994).

Carlson's testimony also accepted certain background facts about the tire in question. He assumed that before the blowout the tire had traveled far. (The tire was made in 1988 and had been installed some time before the Carmichaels bought the used minivan in March 1993; the Carmichaels had driven the van approximately 7,000 additional miles in the two months they had owned it.) Carlson noted that the tire's tread depth, which was 11/32 of an inch when new, App. 242, had been worn down to depths that ranged from 3/32 of an inch along some parts of the tire, to nothing at all along others. *Ibid.*, at 287. He conceded that the tire tread had at least two punctures which had been inadequately repaired. *Ibid.*, at 258–261, 322.

Despite the tire's age and history, Carlson concluded that a defect in its manufacture or design caused the blow-out. He rested this conclusion in part upon three premises which, for present purposes, we must assume are not in dispute: First, a tire's carcass should stay bound to the inner side of the tread for a significant period of time after its tread depth has worn away. *Ibid.*, at 208–209. Second, the tread of the tire at issue had separated from its inner steel-belted carcass prior to the accident. *Ibid.*, at 336. Third, this "separation" caused the blowout. *Ibid.*

Carlson's conclusion that a defect caused the separation, however, rested upon certain other propositions, several of which the defendants strongly dispute. First, Carlson said that if a separation is not caused by a certain kind of tire misuse called "overdeflection" (which consists of underinflating the tire or causing it to carry too much weight, thereby generating heat that can undo the chemical tread/carcass bond), then, ordinarily, its cause is a tire defect. *Ibid.*, at 193–195, 277–278. Second, he said that if a tire has been subject to sufficient overdeflection to cause a separation, it should reveal certain physical symptoms. These symptoms include (a) tread wear on the tire's shoulder that is greater than the tread wear along the tire's center, *Ibid.*, at 211; (b) signs of a "bead groove," where the beads have been pushed too hard against the bead seat on the inside of the tire's rim, *Ibid.*, at 196–197; (c) sidewalls of the tire with physical signs of deterioration, such as discoloration, *Ibid.*, at 212; and/or (d) marks on the tire's rim flange, *Ibid.*, at 219–220. Third, Carlson said that where he does not find at least two of the

172 Ethics in Forensic Science

four physical signs just mentioned (and presumably where there is no reason to suspect a less common cause of separation), he concludes that a manufacturing or design defect caused the separation. *Ibid.*, at 223–224.

Carlson added that he had inspected the tire in question. He conceded that the tire to a limited degree showed greater wear on the shoulder than in the center, some signs of "bead groove," some discoloration, a few marks on the rim flange, and inadequately filled puncture holes (which can also cause heat that might lead to separation). *Ibid.*, at 256–257, 258–261, 277, 303–304, 308. But, in each instance, he testified that the symptoms were not significant, and he explained why he believed that they did not reveal overdeflection. For example, the extra shoulder wear, he said, appeared primarily on one shoulder, whereas an overdeflected tire would reveal equally abnormal wear on both shoulders. *Ibid.*, at 277. Carlson concluded that the tire did not bear at least two of the four overdeflection symptoms, nor was there any less obvious cause of separation; and since neither overdeflection nor the punctures caused the blowout, a defect must have done so.

Kumho Tire moved the District Court to exclude Carlson's testimony on the ground that his methodology failed Rule 702's reliability requirement. The court agreed with Kumho that it should act as a *Daubert*-type reliability "gatekeeper," even though one might consider Carlson's testimony as "technical," rather than "scientific." See *Carmichael* v. *Samyang Tires, Inc.*, 923 F. Supp. 1514, 1521–1522 (SD Ala. 1996). The court then examined Carlson's methodology in light of the reliability-related factors that *Daubert* mentioned, such as a theory's testability, whether it "has been a subject of peer review or publication," the "known or potential rate of error," and the "degree of acceptance … within the relevant scientific community." 923 F. Supp., at 1520 (citing *Daubert*, 509 U.S., at 592–594). The District Court found that all those factors argued against the reliability of Carlson's methods, and it granted the motion to exclude the testimony (as well as the defendants' accompanying motion for summary judgment).

The plaintiffs, arguing that the court's application of the *Daubert* factors was too "inflexible," asked for reconsideration. And the Court granted that motion. *Carmichael* v. *Samyang Tires, Inc.*, Civ. Action No. 93-0860-CB-S (SD Ala., June 5, 1996), App. to Pet. for Cert. 1c. After reconsidering the matter, the court agreed with the plaintiffs that *Daubert* should be applied flexibly, that its four factors were simply illustrative, and that other factors could argue in favor of admissibility. It conceded that there may be widespread acceptance of a "visual-inspection method" for some relevant purposes. But the court found insufficient indications of the reliability of "the component of Carlson's tire failure analysis which most concerned the Court, namely, the methodology employed by the expert in analyzing the data obtained in the visual inspection, and the scientific basis, if any, for such an analysis." *Ibid.*, at 6c. It consequently affirmed its earlier order declaring Carlson's testimony inadmissable and granting the defendants' motion for summary judgment.

The Eleventh Circuit reversed. See *Carmichael* v. *Samyang Tire, Inc.*, 131 F.3d 1433 (1997). It "review[ed] ... de novo" the "district court's legal decision to apply *Daubert.*" *Ibid.*, at 1435. It noted that "the Supreme Court in *Daubert* explicitly limited its holding to cover only the 'scientific context,'" "adding that "a *Daubert* analysis" applies only where an expert relies "on the application of scientific principles," rather than "on skill- or experience-based observation." *Ibid.*, at 1435–1436. It concluded that Carlson's testimony, which it viewed as relying on experience, "falls outside the scope of *Daubert,*" that "the district court erred as a matter of law by applying *Daubert* in this case," and that the case must be remanded for further (non-*Daubert*-type) consideration under Rule 702. *Ibid.*, at 1436.

Kumho Tire petitioned for certiorari, asking us to determine whether a trial court "may" consider *Daubert*'s specific "factors" when determining the "admissibility of an engineering expert's testimony." We granted certiorari in light of uncertainty among the lower courts about whether, or how, *Daubert* applies to expert testimony that might be characterized as based not upon "scientific" knowledge, but rather upon "technical" or "other specialized" knowledge. Fed. Rule Evid. 702; compare, e.g., *Watkins* v. *Telsmith, Inc.*, 121 F.3d 984, 990–991 (CA5 1997), with, e.g., *Compton* v. *Subaru of America, Inc.*, 82 F.3d 1513, 1518–1519 (CA10), cert. denied, 519 U.S. 1042 (1996).

II

A

In *Daubert*, this Court held that Federal Rule of Evidence 702 imposes a special obligation upon a trial judge to "ensure that any and all scientific testimony ... is not only relevant, but reliable." 509 U.S., at 589. The initial question before us is whether this basic gatekeeping obligation applies only to "scientific" testimony or to all expert testimony. We, like the parties, believe that it applies to all expert testimony. See Brief for Petitioners 19; Brief for Respondents 17.

For one thing, Rule 702 itself says: "If scientific, technical, or other specialized knowledge will assist the trier of fact to understand the evidence or to determine a fact in issue, a witness qualified as an expert by knowledge, skill, experience, training, or education, may testify thereto in the form of an opinion or otherwise."

This language makes no relevant distinction between "scientific" knowledge and "technical" or "other specialized" knowledge. It makes clear that any such knowledge might become the subject of expert testimony. In *Daubert*, the Court specified that it is the Rule's word "knowledge," not the words (like "scientific") that modify that word, that "establishes a standard of evidentiary reliability." 509 U.S., at 589–590. Hence, as a matter of language, the Rule applies its reliability standard to all "scientific," "technical," or "other specialized" matters within its scope. We concede that the Court in *Daubert* referred only to "scientific" knowledge. But as the Court there said, it referred to "scientific" testimony "because that [wa]s the nature of the expertise" at issue. *Ibid.*, at 590, n. 8.

Neither is the evidentiary rationale that underlay the Court's basic *Daubert* "gatekeeping" determination limited to "scientific" knowledge. *Daubert* pointed out that Federal Rules 702 and 703 grant expert witnesses testimonial latitude unavailable to other witnesses on the "assumption that the expert's opinion will have a reliable basis in the knowledge and experience of his discipline." *Ibid.*, at 592 (pointing out that experts may testify to opinions, including those that are not based on firsthand knowledge or observation). The Rules grant that latitude to all experts, not just to "scientific" ones.

Finally, it would prove difficult, if not impossible, for judges to administer evidentiary rules under which a gatekeeping obligation depended upon a distinction between "scientific" knowledge and "technical" or "other specialized" knowledge. There is no clear line that divides the one from the others. Disciplines such as engineering rest upon scientific knowledge. Pure scientific theory itself may depend for its development upon observation and properly engineered machinery. And conceptual efforts to distinguish the two are unlikely to produce clear legal lines capable of application in particular cases. Cf. Brief for National Academy of Engineering as *Amicus Curiae* 9 (scientist seeks to understand nature while the engineer seeks nature's modification); Brief for Rubber Manufacturers Association as *Amicus Curiae* 14–16 (engineering, as an "applied science," relies on "scientific reasoning and methodology"); Brief for John Allen et al. as *Amici Curiae* 6 (engineering relies upon "scientific knowledge and methods").

Neither is there a convincing need to make such distinctions. Experts of all kinds tie observations to conclusions through the use of what Judge Learned Hand called "general truths derived from ... specialized experience." Hand, Historical and Practical Considerations Regarding Expert Testimony, 15 *Harv. L. Rev.* 40, 54 (1901). And whether the specific expert testimony focuses upon specialized observations, the specialized translation of those observations into theory, a specialized theory itself, or the application of such a theory in a particular case, the expert's testimony often will rest "upon an experience confessedly foreign in kind to [the jury's] own." *Ibid.* The trial judge's effort to assure that the specialized testimony is reliable and relevant can help the jury evaluate that foreign experience, whether the testimony reflects scientific, technical, or other specialized knowledge.

We conclude that *Daubert*'s general principles apply to the expert matters described in Rule 702. The Rule, in respect to all such matters, "establishes a standard of evidentiary reliability." 509 U.S., at 590. It "requires a valid ... connection to the pertinent inquiry as a precondition to admissibility." *Ibid.*, at 592. And where such testimony's factual basis, data, principles, methods, or their application are called sufficiently into question, see Part III, *infra*, the trial judge must determine whether the testimony has "a reliable basis in the knowledge and experience of [the relevant] discipline." 509 U.S., at 592.

B

The petitioners ask more specifically whether a trial judge determining the "admissibility of an engineering expert's testimony" may consider several more specific factors that *Daubert* said might "bear on" a judge's gate-keeping determination. These factors include:

–Whether a "theory or technique ... can be (and has been) tested";
–Whether it "has been subjected to peer review and publication";
–Whether, in respect to a particular technique, there is a high "known or potential rate of error" and whether there are "standards controlling the technique's operation"; and
–Whether the theory or technique enjoys "general acceptance" within a "relevant scientific community." 509 U.S., at 592–594.

Emphasizing the word "may" in the question, we answer that question yes.

Engineering testimony rests upon scientific foundations, the reliability of which will be at issue in some cases. See, e.g., Brief for Stephen Bobo et al. as *Amici Curiae* 23 (stressing the scientific bases of engineering disciplines). In other cases, the relevant reliability concerns may focus upon personal knowledge or experience. As the Solicitor General points out, there are many different kinds of experts, and many different kinds of expertise. See Brief for United States as *Amicus Curiae* 18–19, and n. 5 (citing cases involving experts in drug terms, handwriting analysis, criminal *modus operandi*, land valuation, agricultural practices, railroad procedures, attorney's fee valuation, and others). Our emphasis on the word "may" thus reflects *Daubert*'s description of the Rule 702 inquiry as "a flexible one." 509 U.S., at 594. *Daubert* makes clear that the factors it mentions do not constitute a "definitive checklist or test." *Ibid.*, at 593. And *Daubert* adds that the gatekeeping inquiry must be "'tied to the facts'" of a particular "case." *Ibid.*, at 591 (quoting *United States* v. *Downing*, 753 F.2d 1224, 1242 (CA3 1985)).

We agree with the Solicitor General that "[t]he factors identified in *Daubert* may or may not be pertinent in assessing reliability, depending on the nature of the issue, the expert's particular expertise, and the subject of his testimony." Brief for United States as *Amicus Curiae* 19. The conclusion, in our view, is that we can neither rule out, nor rule in, for all cases and for all time the applicability of the factors mentioned in *Daubert*, nor can we now do so for subsets of cases categorized by category of expert or by kind of evidence. Too much depends upon the particular circumstances of the particular case at issue.

Daubert itself is not to the contrary. It made clear that its list of factors was meant to be helpful, not definitive. Indeed, those factors do not all necessarily apply even in every instance in which the reliability of scientific testimony is challenged. It might not be surprising in a particular case, for example, that a claim made by a scientific witness has never been the subject of peer review, for the particular application at issue may never previously have interested any scientist. Nor, on the other hand, does the presence of *Daubert*'s general acceptance factor help show that an expert's testimony is reliable where the discipline itself lacks reliability, as, for example, do theories grounded in any so-called generally accepted principles of astrology or necromancy.

At the same time, and contrary to the Court of Appeals' view, some of *Daubert*'s questions can help to evaluate the reliability even of experience-based testimony. In certain cases, it will be appropriate for the trial judge to ask, for example, how often an engineering expert's experience-based methodology has produced erroneous results, or whether such a method is generally accepted in the relevant engineering community. Likewise, it will at times be useful to ask even of a witness whose expertise is based purely on experience, say, a perfume tester able to distinguish among 140 odors at a sniff, whether his preparation is of a kind that others in the field would recognize as acceptable.

We must therefore disagree with the Eleventh Circuit's holding that a trial judge may ask questions of the sort *Daubert* mentioned only where an expert "relies on the application of scientific principles," but not wherean expert relies "on skill- or experience-based observation." 131 F.3d, at 1435. We do not believe that Rule 702 creates a schematism that segregates expertise by type while mapping certain kinds of questions to certain kinds of experts. Life and the legal cases that it generates are too complex to warrant so definitive a match.

To say this is not to deny the importance of *Daubert*'s gatekeeping requirement. The objective of that requirement is to ensure the reliability and relevancy of expert testimony. It is to make certain that an expert, whether basing testimony upon professional studies or personal experience,

employs in the courtroom the same level of intellectual rigor that character-
izes the practice of an expert in the relevant field. Nor do we deny that, as
stated in *Daubert*, the particular questions that it mentioned will often be
appropriate for use in determining the reliability of challenged expert testimony. Rather, we conclude that the trial judge must have considerable leeway
in deciding in a particular case how to go about determining whether particular expert testimony is reliable. That is to say, a trial court should consider
the specific factors identified in *Daubert* where they are reasonable measures
of the reliability of expert testimony.

C

The trial court must have the same kind of latitude in deciding how to
test an expert's reliability, and to decide whether or when special briefing or
other proceedings are needed to investigate reliability, as it enjoys when it
decides whether that expert's relevant testimony is reliable. Our opinion in
Joiner makes clear that a court of appeals is to apply an abuse-of-discretion
standard when it "review[s] a trial court's decision to admit or exclude expert
testimony." 522 U.S., at 138–139. That standard applies as much to the trial
court's decisions about how to determine reliability as to its ultimate conclusion. Otherwise, the trial judge would lack the discretionary authority
needed both to avoid unnecessary "reliability" proceedings in ordinary cases
where the reliability of an expert's methods is properly taken for granted,
and to require appropriate proceedings in the less usual or more complex
cases where cause for questioning the expert's reliability arises. Indeed, the
Rules seek to avoid "unjustifiable expense and delay" as part of their search
for "truth" and the "jus[t] determin[ation]" of proceedings. Fed. Rule Evid.,
102. Thus, whether *Daubert*'s specific factors are, or are not, reasonable
measures of reliability in a particular case is a matter that the law grants the
trial judge broad latitude to determine. See *Joiner, supra*, at 143. And the
Eleventh Circuit erred insofar as it held to the contrary.

III

We further explain the way in which a trial judge "may" consider *Daubert*'s factors by applying these considerations to the case at hand, a matter
that has been briefed exhaustively by the parties and their 19 *amici*. The
District Court did not doubt Carlson's qualifications, which included a
masters degree in mechanical engineering, 10 years' work at Michelin America, Inc., and testimony as a tire failure consultant in other tort cases. Rather,
it excluded the testimony because, despite those qualifications, it initially
doubted, and then found unreliable, "the methodology employed by the
expert in analyzing the data obtained in the visual inspection, and the

scientific basis, if any, for such an analysis." Civ. Action No. 93-0860-CB-S (SD Ala., June 5, 1996), App. to Pet. For Cert. 6c. After examining the transcript in "some detail," 923 F. Supp., at 1518–519, n. 4, and after considering respondents' defense of Carlson's methodology, the District Court determined that Carlson's testimony was not reliable. It fell outside the range where experts might reasonably differ, and where the jury must decide among the conflicting views of different experts, even though the evidence is "shaky." *Daubert*, 509 U.S., at 596. In our view, the doubts that triggered the District Court's initial inquiry here were reasonable, as was the court's ultimate conclusion.

For one thing, and contrary to respondents' suggestion, the specific issue before the court was not the reasonableness in general of a tire expert's use of a visual and tactile inspection to determine whether overdeflection had caused the tire's tread to separate from its steel-belted carcass. Rather, it was the reasonableness of using such an approach, along with Carlson's particular method of analyzing the data thereby obtained, to draw a conclusion regarding the particular matter to which the expert testimony was directly relevant. That matter concerned the likelihood that a defect in the tire at issue caused its tread to separate from its carcass. The tire in question, the expert conceded, had traveled far enough so that some of the tread had been worn bald; it should have been taken out of service; it had been repaired (inadequately) for punctures; and it bore some of the very marks that the expert said indicated, not a defect, but abuse through overdeflection. See *supra*, at 3–5; App. 293–294. The relevant issue was whether the expert could reliably determine the cause of this tire's separation.

Nor was the basis for Carlson's conclusion simply the general theory that, in the absence of evidence of abuse, a defect will normally have caused a tire's separation. Rather, the expert employed a more specific theory to establish the existence (or absence) of such abuse. Carlson testified precisely that in the absence of at least two of four signs of abuse (proportionately greater tread wear on the shoulder; signs of grooves caused by the beads; discolored sidewalls; marks on the rim flange) he concludes that a defect caused the separation. And his analysis depended upon acceptance of a further implicit proposition, namely, that his visual and tactile inspection could determine that the tire before him had not been abused despite some evidence of the presence of the very signs for which he looked (and two punctures).

For another thing, the transcripts of Carlson's depositions support both the trial court's initial uncertainty and its final conclusion. Those transcripts cast considerable doubt upon the reliability of both the explicit theory (about the need for two signs of abuse) and the implicit proposition (about the significance of visual inspection in this case). Among other things, the expert could not say whether the tire had traveled more than 10, or 20, or 30, or

40, or 50 thousand miles, adding that 6,000 miles was "about how far" he could "say with any certainty." *Ibid.*, at 265. The court could reasonably have wondered about the reliability of a method of visual and tactile inspection sufficiently precise to ascertain with some certainty the abuse-related significance of minute shoulder/center relative tread wear differences, but insufficiently precise to tell "with any certainty" from the tread wear whether a tire had traveled less than 10,000 or more than 50,000 miles. And these concerns might have been augmented by Carlson's repeated reliance on the "subjective[ness]" of his mode of analysis in response to questions seeking specific information regarding how he could differentiate between a tire that actually had been overdeflected and a tire that merely looked as though it had been. *Ibid.*, at 222, 224–225, 285–286. They would have been further augmented by the fact that Carlson said he had inspected the tire itself for the first time the morning of his first deposition, and then only for a few hours. (His initial conclusions were based on photographs.) *Ibid.*, at 180.

Moreover, prior to his first deposition, Carlson had issued a signed report in which he concluded that the tire had "not been ... overloaded or underinflated," not because of the absence of "two of four" signs of abuse, but simply because "the rim flange impressions ... were normal." *Ibid.*, at 335–336. That report also said that the "tread depth remaining was 3/32 inch," *Ibid.*, at 336, though the opposing expert's (apparently undisputed) measurements indicate that the tread depth taken at various positions around the tire actually ranged from .5/32 of an inch to 4/32 of an inch, with the tire apparently showing greater wear along both shoulders than along the center, *Ibid.*, at 432–433.

Further, in respect to one sign of abuse, bead grooving, the expert seemed to deny the sufficiency of his own simple visual-inspection methodology. He testified that most tires have some bead groove pattern, that where there is reason to suspect an abnormal bead groove he would ideally "look at a lot of [similar] tires" to know the grooving's significance, and that he had not looked at many tires similar to the one at issue. *Ibid.*, at 212–213, 214, 217.

Finally, the court, after looking for a defense of Carlson's methodology as applied in these circumstances, found no convincing defense. Rather, it found (1) that "none" of the *Daubert* factors, including that of "general acceptance" in the relevant expert community, indicated that Carlson's testimony was reliable, 923 F. Supp., at 1521; (2) that its own analysis "revealed no countervailing factors operating in favor of admissibility which could outweigh those identified in *Daubert*," App. to Pet. for Cert. 4c; and (3) that the "parties identified no such factors in their briefs," *Ibid.* For these three reasons taken together, it concluded that Carlson's testimony was unreliable.

Respondents now argue to us, as they did to the District Court, that a method of tire failure analysis that employs a visual/tactile inspection is a reliable method, and they point both to its use by other experts and to Carlson's long experience working for Michelin as sufficient indication that that is so. But no one denies that an expert might draw a conclusion from a set of observations based on extensive and specialized experience. Nor does anyone deny that, as a general matter, tire abuse may often be identified by qualified experts through visual or tactile inspection of the tire. See Affidavit of H. R. Baumgardner 1–2, cited in Brief for National Academy of Forensic Engineers as *Amici Curiae* 16 (Tire engineers rely on visual examination and process of elimination to analyze experimental test tires). As we said before, *supra*, at 14, the question before the trial court was specific, not general. The trial court had to decide whether this particular expert had sufficient specialized knowledge to assist the jurors "in deciding the particular issues in the case." 4 J. McLaughlin, *Weinstein's Federal Evidence,* ¶702.05[1], p. 702-33 (2d ed. 1998); see also Advisory Committee's Note on Proposed Fed. Rule Evid. 702, Preliminary Draft of Proposed Amendments to the Federal Rules of Civil Procedure and Evidence: Request for Comment 126 (1998) (stressing that district courts must "scrutinize" whether the "principles and methods" employed by an expert "have been properly applied to the facts of the case").

The particular issue in this case concerned the use of Carlson's two-factor test and his related use of visual/tactile inspection to draw conclusions on the basis of what seemed small observational differences. We have found no indication in the record that other experts in the industry use Carlson's two-factor test or that tire experts such as Carlson normally make the very fine distinctions about, say, the symmetry of comparatively greater shoulder tread wear that were necessary, on Carlson's own theory, to support his conclusions. Nor, despite the prevalence of tire testing, does anyone refer to any articles or papers that validate Carlson's approach. Compare Bobo, Tire Flaws and Separations, in *Mechanics of Pneumatic Tires* 636–637 (S. Clark ed. 1981); C. Schnuth et al., Compression Grooving and Rim Flange Abrasion as Indicators of Over-Deflected Operating Conditions in Tires, presented to Rubber Division of the American Chemical Society, Oct. 21–24, 1997; J. Walter and R. Kiminecz, Bead Contact Pressure Measurements at the Tire-Rim Interface, presented to Society of Automotive Engineers, Feb. 24–28, 1975. Indeed, no one has argued that Carlson himself, were he still working for Michelin, would have concluded in a report to his employer that a similar tire was similarly defective on grounds identical to those upon which he rested his conclusion here. Of course, Carlson himself claimed that his method was accurate, but, as we pointed out in *Joiner,* "nothing in either *Daubert* or the Federal Rules of Evidence requires a district court to admit opinion evidence that is connected to existing data only by the *ipse dixit* of the expert." 522 U.S., at 146.

Respondents additionally argue that the District Court too rigidly applied *Daubert*'s criteria. They read its opinion to hold that a failure to satisfy any one of those criteria automatically renders expert testimony inadmissible. The District Court's initial opinion might have been vulnerable to a form of this argument. There, the court, after rejecting respondents' claim that Carlson's testimony was "exempted from *Daubert*-style scrutiny" because it was "technical analysis" rather than "scientific evidence," simply added that "none of the four admissibility criteria outlined by the *Daubert* court are satisfied." 923 F. Supp., at 1522. Subsequently, however, the court granted respondents' motion for reconsideration. It then explicitly recognized that the relevant reliability inquiry "should be 'flexible,'" that its "'overarching subject [should be] … validity' and reliability," and that "*Daubert* was intended neither to be exhaustive nor to apply in every case." App. to Pet. for Cert. 4c (quoting *Daubert*, 509 U.S., at 594–595). And the court ultimately based its decision upon Carlson's failure to satisfy either *Daubert*'s factors or any other set of reasonable reliability criteria. In light of the record as developed by the parties, that conclusion was within the District Court's lawful discretion.

In sum, Rule 702 grants the district judge the discretionary authority, reviewable for its abuse, to determine reliability in light of the particular facts and circumstances of the particular case. The District Court did not abuse its discretionary authority in this case. Hence, the judgment of the Court of Appeals is Reversed.

SUPREME COURT OF CALIFORNIA

THE PEOPLE, Plaintiff and Respondent,
v.
DONALD RICHARD NATION JR.,
Defendant and Appellant

26 Cal 3d 169 (1980)

[January 8,1980]

Opinion by Mosk, J.,
expressing the unanimous view of the court.

A.

Defendant appeals from a judgment of conviction entered on a jury verdict finding him guilty of lewd and lascivious conduct upon a child under 14 years of age (Pen. Code, § 288) while armed with a firearm (Pen. Code, § 12022).

The sole issue at trial was the identification of the defendant as the perpetrator of the crime. The facts of the crime and the somewhat convoluted identification process are as follows. In the twilight hours of February 14, 1976, Barbara, age 12, and 2 girlfriends, Lou and Therese, made a purchase at a doughnut shop. An employee of the shop later testified she noticed two men, also customers, watching the girls. She observed that one of the men had long dirty red hair and a beard, and had a gun in his pocket.

The three girls then walked over to the neighborhood school grounds to sit and talk. As they entered the grounds, they were approached by a white man whom they had earlier observed at the doughnut shop. He asked the girls if they would do him a favor, then produced a gun and ordered the girls to sit down. Lou began to cry and the other two girls tried to calm her. The man instructed Therese to remain with Lou and directed Barbara to follow him into some nearby bushes where he attempted to rape her; the victim did not confirm a penetration. The victim later testified that it was getting dark at this time and what she remembered most about the assailant was his long reddish brown hair and beard.

The victim reported the attack to the police and was examined by a police doctor later that same evening. The examination confirmed the presence of semen in the region of the victim's vagina. The semen sample was not tested to identify the donor class of the rapist; it was retained by the police on a smear slide but no further measures such as refrigeration were taken to assure its preservation for future identification analysis. Pursuant to discovery defense counsel later acquired the slide. Not until after trial, however, did a belated laboratory analysis reveal some type B blood group activity on the slide. A more extensive analysis could not be performed because the slide had not been properly preserved. As no blood sample was taken from the victim, it was never determined whether the observed blood type was that of the victim or the attacker.

Two weeks after the event, the three girls went to the police station to attempt to identify the attacker from police photographs. One of the girls, Lou, selected a mug shot of the defendant; she informed the other two girls she had found the assailant, and, after some discussion, the other girls agreed. The police officer gave the girls the defendant's mug shot to take home to show two other possible witnesses, one being the mother of one of the girls, Mrs. S. She had not been a witness to the crime, but had reported that on the evening of the attack a man had made a lewd remark to her in the vicinity of where the rape occurred later that night. When the girls showed Mrs. S. the mug shot they had picked out, she identified the photograph as depicting the man who had made the comment to her in the street.

The doughnut shop employee who had observed the armed man watching the girls on the night of the crime reported to the police that the same man had returned a few days later with his hair cut. She later testified that the defendant was definitely not this man.

Two months later Lou, Mrs. S., and the victim returned to the police station for further photographic identification. The police officer showed them eight photographs, one of which was the same photograph of the defendant that the girls had in their possession for a week and that Mrs. S. had previously identified. The victim selected two photographs from this group, the defendant and another, but discarded the latter after Lou selected the defendant's picture.

In early June a police lineup was conducted at defendant's request. Each person in the lineup was asked to say: "Hold it. I've got a gun." The witnesses were properly instructed not to talk to one another during the lineup. The victim and her two girlfriends all selected the person whose position in the lineup was number one, but he was not the defendant. Mrs. S. selected the defendant, whose position was number three, thus hers was the only corporeal identification of the defendant in the case. After the lineup the girls were informed by the police that they had selected the "wrong" man and Mrs. S. the "right" man.

At trial, the witnesses testified to the above pretrial identifications. The girls also identified in court the same photograph of the defendant they had originally selected as depicting the perpetrator of the crime. The girls testified that they could not identify the defendant in person, but attributed this to the fact that he had altered his appearance by changing his hair and shaving. (Page 26 Cal. 3d 175.)

Defendant raises two principal contentions on appeal. The first involves the duty of the prosecution to preserve material evidence. The defendant contends the prosecution had a duty to preserve the assailant's semen sample recovered from the victim so that the defense could attempt to prove by chemical analysis that the discharge could not have come from the defendant. The second contention is that the failure of defense counsel to object to the introduction of identification testimony resulting from obviously questionable pretrial procedures deprived the defendant of his constitutional right to effective assistance of counsel.

We conclude that if the state recovers a semen sample of one who has made a sexual assault, it has a duty to take reasonable steps to preserve that evidence and to make it available to the defense. However, in the circumstances of this case we hold the defendant has not demonstrated that the people failed in their responsibility to adequately preserve this evidence. On the second issue we hold that the defendant was denied effective assistance of counsel.

I

We first consider whether the prosecution's failure to adequately preserve the sample of the attempted rapist's semen deprived the defendant of a fair trial.

[1] It is clear that the Constitution does not require the prosecution to make a complete and detailed accounting to the defendant of all police investigatory work on a case. (*Moore* v. *Illinois* (1972) 408 U.S. 786, 795 [33 L.Ed.2d 706, 713, 92 S.Ct. 2562].) Yet it is well established that the suppression by the state of evidence favorable to an accused, after a request therefor, violates due process, irrespective of the good faith of the prosecution. (*Brady* v. *Maryland* (1963) 373 U.S. 83, 87 [10 L.Ed.2d 215, 218, 83 S.Ct. 1194].) This court has recognized the prosecutor's duty to disclose such material evidence favorable to the accused even in the absence of a request from the defense. (In re *Ferguson* (1971), 532 [96 Cal. Rptr. 594, 487 P.2d 1234].) In *People* v. *Hitch* (1974), 650 [117 Cal. Rptr. 9, 527 P.2d 361], we held that the obligation to disclose the existence of material evidence places on the state a correlative duty to preserve such evidence even without a request therefor,[1] and directed that in the future law enforcement agencies take reasonable measures to ensure its adequate preservation.

The People seek to distinguish *Hitch* on factual grounds. There, the defendant was convicted of driving under the influence of intoxicating liquor. The results of the breathalyzer test introduced by the prosecution were presumptive evidence of guilt. (Veh. Code, § 23126.) The accuracy of that test was dependent on the precise amount of testing solution used in the test ampoule. (Thus if the ampoule had been preserved, it might have provided a source of evidence to impeach the incriminating test results. In the present case, the People argue that the semen sample was not "material" evidence because (1) the defendant was charged with lewd conduct rather than rape, and hence the presence of semen was not a necessary element of the crime; and (2) the finding of semen merely confirmed the victim's testimony that an attack occurred, and was not used to identify the defendant.

As in *Hitch*, we are not in a position to examine the suppressed evidence to decide whether or not it is material. However, evidence lost to the defense because of its destruction by the authorities will be deemed material for the purpose of triggering the due process concerns of *Hitch* if there is a reasonable possibility that it would be favorable to the defendant on the issue of guilt or innocence. Contrary to the prosecution's contention, the rationale of *Hitch* is thus not limited to circumstances in which the destroyed evidence proves a necessary element of the crime.

At the trial, the police doctor who identified the existence of semen in the victim's vaginal smear testified that it might have been possible to determine from whom the semen had come. While there are many possible anal-

---

[1] The present case is typical of the problem covered by *Hitch*, in that defendant here was not charged at the time the police physician obtained the semen sample. If a request were a condition to the duty to preserve, the duty might not arise until it became impossible of performance.

yses that may be performed on semen to identify the donor, and by corollary, to eliminate others from the class of possible donors, the two analyses deemed most commonly feasible are ABO blood typing and identification of the genetic marker phosphoglucomutase (PGM). (Blake and Sensabaugh, Genetic Markers in Human Semen. II. Quantitation of Polymorphic Proteins (1978) 23 J. Forensic Sci., 717, 727.) A recent discrimination probability study of white males in California indicates that an analysis of ABO type and PGM would eliminate approximately 80 percent of such males as the donor of a particular semen sample.[2] (Page 26 Cal. 3d 177.)

Thus, an analysis of the semen sample in the present case might have not only impeached the credibility of the prosecution's witnesses (cf. *People v. Ruthford* (1975), 407–408 [121 Cal. Rptr. 261, 534 P.2d 1341]), but also might have completely exonerated the defendant. Whether or not the police deem the crime sufficiently important to warrant such an identification analysis, they cannot make this decision for the defendant.

[2] Accordingly, when a woman has been the victim of an attempted or actual rape and the police recover a semen sample of the assailant, the authorities must take reasonable measures to adequately preserve this evidence.

Such a rule protects not only the due process rights of the defendant, but also society's interest in the integrity of the judicial system. The duty to preserve critical evidence enhances the reliability of the trial process: if an accused is convicted of rape when available evidence would have exonerated him, not only is he unjustly incarcerated but the actual rapist remains at large. "Law enforcement has failed in its primary function, and has left society unprotected from the depredations of an active criminal." (*Manson* v. *Brathwaite* (1977) 432 U.S. 98, 127 [53 L.Ed.2d 140, 162, 97 S.Ct. 2243] (dis. opn. of Marshall, J.).)

[3] The duty of the prosecution is not simply to obtain convictions, but to "'fully and fairly present to the court the evidence material to the charge.'" (*People* v. *Ruthford, supra*, 405.)

[4] In the present case, while the state did retain the semen sample, it failed to meet its burden of establishing that it had "undertake[n] reasonable efforts to preserve the material evidence. ..." (Italics added.) (*People* v. *Hitch, supra*) However, under the particular circumstances of the case, the conviction may not be reversed on this ground.

As noted above, the state delivered the semen sample to the defense in response to a pretrial discovery request. At that time defense counsel neither

---

[2] Grunbaum et al., Frequency Distribution and Discrimination Probability of Twelve Protein Genetic Variants in Human Blood as Functions of Race, Sex, and Age (1978) 23 *J. Forensic Sci.* 577, 585, Table 10.

Since the genetic systems are statistically independent (*Ibid.*, at p. 583), the probability of two white males having the same ABO blood type and the same PGM type is not the sum but the product of the two individual probabilities.

submitted the slide to a laboratory for analysis nor took any measures to assure its preservation. Instead, it appears from the record that counsel gave the slide to the defendant's father, and only after the defendant was tried and convicted was the semen sample retrieved and sent to a laboratory for analysis. Even at this late date the laboratory was still able to identify the blood type of the sample. While it is theoretically possible that a more complete analysis might have been successfully undertaken had the state refrigerated the evidence (Page 26 Cal. 3d 178), in these circumstances we cannot say that the deterioration of the sample was caused by the state's inaction. Certainly the prosecution had no duty to preserve the evidence once it was in the hands of the defense.

II

[5a] The defendant's second contention is that he was denied effective assistance of counsel because his trial attorney did not object to the prosecution's introduction into evidence of impermissibly suggestive pretrial identifications. These identifications were the primary evidence linking him to the crime. The defendant claims that had his counsel made the obvious objections, the pretrial identification evidence might have been suppressed.

The right to effective assistance of counsel was first articulated by the United States Supreme Court in reversing the rape convictions of the "Scottsboro Boys." (Powell v. Alabama (1932) 287 U.S. 45, 71 [77 L.Ed. 158, 171, 53 S.Ct. 55, 84 A.L.R. 527].) A significant line of recent cases has expanded the constitutional guarantee of an accused's right to counsel (Gideon v. Wainwright (1963) 372 U.S. 335, 344 [9 L.Ed.2d 799, 805, 83 S.Ct. 792, 93 A.L.R.2d 733]) to include the right to the effective assistance of reasonably competent counsel. (McMann v. Richardson (1970) 397 U.S. 759, 771 [25 L.Ed.2d 763, 773, 90 S.Ct. 1441]; United States v. DeCoster (D.C.Cir. 1973) 487 F.2d 1197, 1202; People v. Pope (1979) 423–424 [152 Cal. Rptr. 732, 590 P.2d 859].)

[6] The right to adequate assistance of counsel, grounded on the Sixth Amendment of the United States Constitution and section 15 of article I of the California Constitution, is in addition to the general due process protection of a fair trial; it focuses "on the quality of the representation provided the accused." (People v. Pope, supra)

[7] In Pope a majority of the court articulated the analysis involved in a determination of whether a defendant has been denied adequate assistance of counsel. The appellant has the burden of showing "that trial counsel failed to act in a manner to be expected of reasonably competent attorneys acting as diligent advocates. In addition, appellant must establish that counsel's acts or omissions resulted in the withdrawal of a potentially meritorious defense." (Ibid. at p. 425.) The Pope standard is applicable to retained counsel. (People

v. *Frierson* (1979), 161–162 [158 Cal. Rptr. 281, 599 P.2d 587].) (Page 26 Cal. 3d 179.)

[8a] Turning to the case at bar, we note intially that a penetrating concern as to the propriety of a pretrial identification should be a commonplace consideration to any attorney engaged in criminal trials. "In any case in which the defendant has been identified at a pretrial confrontation conducted without counsel, defense counsel ... should consider an attack upon the identification procedure ... on the ground that the confrontation was unfair." (*Criminal Defense Techniques*, (Hall and Eisenstein, eds., 1979) § 2.01[2], p. 2–8.)

[5b] The record of the instant case strikingly reveals, from the first day of the trial, that the sole issue was the validity of the pretrial identification of the defendant as the assailant. During *voir dire*, every prospective juror was asked by the prosecutor whether he or she could vote for a conviction when the only evidence linking the accused to the crime was mere photographic identification. In addition, there was no in-court corporeal identification of the defendant by any witness. In these circumstances, if an objection to the identification evidence would have been potentially meritorious, and thus should have been argued to the trial court, counsel's failure to so object denied defendant a trial on the key issue of the case.

Since an objection to the identification evidence would have been adjudicated outside the presence of the jury, there could be no satisfactory tactical reason for not making a potentially meritorious objection. (*People* v. *Pope*, *supra*, at p. 426.)

[8b] In order to demonstrate that the alleged incompetency of his trial counsel in not objecting to the identification evidence denied him a potentially meritorious defense, the defendant must present a convincing argument that the pretrial identification procedure "resulted in such unfairness that it infringed his right to due process of law." (*Stovall* v. *Denno* (1967), 388 U.S. 293, 299 [18 L.Ed.2d 1199, 1205, 87 S.Ct. 1967]; *People* v. *Caruso* (1968), 184 [65 Cal. Rptr. 336, 436 P.2d 336].) Our task is thus to assess the facts and circumstances of the identifications to determine whether they were "so impermissibly suggestive as to give rise to a very substantial likelihood of irreparable misidentification." (*Simmons* v. *United States* (1968), 390 U.S. 377, 384 [19 L.Ed.2d 1247, 1253, 88 S.Ct. 967]; *People* v. *Blair* (1979), 659 [159 Cal. Rptr. 818, 602 P.2d 818].)

[5c] We have carefully reviewed the critical facts relating to identification. As previously noted, about two weeks after the crime the victim and her two girlfriends went to the police station to attempt to (Page 26 Cal. 3d 180) identify a suspect. No effort was made to separate the witnesses so as to assure independent appraisals. The defendant's mug shot was initially selected by Lou, and she told the other two girls that she had found the assailant. At that

time, Barbara, the victim, was considering another suspect's photograph. Barbara testified to what happened next: "I looked at the hair and mustache and stuff, and the color of the hair was a reddish brown, and he sorta looked like the guy. And the other [photograph] didn't look nothing hardly even like him. So we all agreed it was him."

The foregoing testimony suggests the witnesses felt constrained to select one of the mug shots as the assailant, and the defendant's photograph initially selected by one of the girls was then collectively declared to be the one most resembling the assailant. We do not doubt that it may be helpful for the police to determine which of their suspects most resembles an assailant, but this procedure does not address the ultimate question, *i.e.*, whether the defendant is in fact the assailant. Furthermore, it appears the identification here was a product of "mutual reinforcement of opinion" among the witnesses (*Clemons* v. *United States* (D.C.Cir. 1968) 408 F.2d 1230, 1241, 1245 & fn. 16), and it is unclear from the record whether or not the girls could have independently identified the defendant. It is clear they did not do so. Furthermore, they were unable to do so at the ensuing lineup.

Once the defendant's mug shot had been selected in this fashion, the police officer gave the photograph to the girls to take home with them to show Lou's mother, Mrs. S. Although the record is ambiguous, it appears the girls retained the defendant's photograph at home for at least a week. When the girls showed Mrs. S. the single mug shot they had selected as the assailant, she agreed it was the same man who had made a lewd remark to her on the night of the crime.

It would be difficult to conceive a more impermissibly suggestive identification procedure. The mere showing of suspects singly to a witness for identification has been widely condemned. (*Stovall* v. *Denno, supra*, 388 U.S. 293, 302 [18 L.Ed.2d 1199, 1206]; *Foster* v. *California* (1969), 394 U.S. 440, 443 [22 L.Ed.2d 402, 406, 89 S.Ct. 1127].) Here, Mrs. S. was effectively told, "this is the man who molested your daughter's friend." The danger of error in identification is at its greatest when the police display only the picture of a single individual and it is heightened when the witness has indications that there is other evidence that the person in the photograph committed the crime. (*Simmons* v. *United States, supra* (Page 26 Cal. 3d 181), 390 U.S. 377, 383 [19 L.Ed.2d 1247, 1252].) The extraordinary suggestiveness of this identification procedure raises considerable doubt that the prosecution would have been able to introduce Mrs. S.'s identification over a timely objection by defense counsel.

We next consider whether Mrs. S.'s subsequent identification of the defendant at a lineup was also objectionable. The question is whether the identification she made at the properly conducted lineup resulted from her prior viewing of defendant's photograph "or instead [from] means sufficiently distinguishable to be purged of the primary taint." (*People* v. *Martin* (1970), 831 [87 Cal. Rptr. 709, 471 P.2d 29]; *Wong Sun* v. *United States* (1963), 371 U.S. 471, 488 [9 L.Ed.2d 441, 455, 83 S.Ct. 407].) The danger is that the witness, having seen a suggestively displayed picture, will "retain in [her] memory the image of the photograph rather than of the person actually seen... ." (*Simmons* v. *United States, supra*, 390 U.S. 377, 383–384 [19 L.Ed.2d 1247, 1253].) If trial counsel had made the appropriate objection, the prosecution would have had the burden of establishing by clear and convincing evidence that Mrs. S.'s lineup identification was purged of the taint of the prior illegal procedure. (*People* v. *Caruso, supra*, 189–190.)

It is at least questionable whether the prosecution could have met this burden.[3] The mere fact that Mrs. S. testified at trial that her identifications stemmed from her observation at the time and place of the street encounter begs the critical inquiry, *i.e.*, "How did her testimony as to her specific observations tend to show that her in-court identification was not infected with the taint of the illegal pretrial confrontation?" (*People* v. *Martin, supra*, 833.) By her own admission, Mrs. S. had only seconds to glance at a passerby who made a crude remark to her; compared to that miniscule time span, she had more recent access of at least a week to the defendant's photograph.

For the foregoing reasons we conclude that trial counsel's failure to obtain an adjudication of the admissibility of the critical identification evidence against his client deprived the defendant of constitutionally adequate assistance.[4] The "trial" that might have determined the defendant's fate could very well have taken place not in the courtroom but in (Page 26 Cal. 3d 182) the illegally suggestive pretrial identification procedures. (Cf. *United States* v. *Wade* (1967), 388 U.S. 218, 235–236 [18 L.Ed.2d. 1149, 1162, 87 S.Ct. 1926].)

The judgment is reversed.

Bird, C. J., Tobriner, J., Clark, J., Richardson, J., Manuel, J., and Newman, J., concurred.

[3] We do not decide the issue on this appeal, and thus do not foreclose the prosecution from attempting to meet its burden upon retrial.
[4] In view of the foregoing incidents of inadequacy of representation, we need not reach defendant's additional claims of his counsel's incompetence.

SUPREME COURT OF THE UNITED STATES

ARIZONA
v.
LARRY YOUNGBLOOD

488 U.S. 51 (1988)

ON WRIT OF CERTIORARI TO THE
COURT OF APPEALS OF ARIZONA

Argued October 11, 1988
Decided November 29, 1988

CHIEF JUSTICE REHNQUIST delivered the opinion of the court.

The victim, a 10-year-old boy, was molested and sodomized by a middle-aged man for 1½ hours. After the assault, the boy was taken to a hospital where a physician used a swab from a "sexual assault kit" to collect semen samples from the boy's rectum. The police also collected the boy's clothing, which they failed to refrigerate. A police criminologist later performed some tests on the rectal swab and the boy's clothing, but he was unable to obtain information about the identity of the boy's assailant. At trial, expert witnesses testified that respondent might have been completely exonerated by timely performance of tests on properly preserved semen samples. Respondent was convicted of child molestation, sexual assault, and kidnaping in an Arizona state court. The Arizona Court of Appeals reversed the conviction on the ground that the state had breached a constitutional duty to preserve the semen samples from the victim's body and clothing.

Held:

The Due Process Clause of the Fourteenth Amendment did not require the state to preserve the semen samples even though the samples might have been useful to respondent. Unless a criminal defendant can show bad faith on the part of the police, failure to preserve potentially useful evidence does not constitute a denial of due process of law. Here, the police's failure to refrigerate the victim's clothing and to perform tests on the semen samples can at worst be described as negligent. None of this information was concealed from respondent at trial, and the evidence—such as it was—was made available to respondent's expert, who declined to perform any tests on the samples. The Arizona Court of Appeals noted in its opinion—and this Court agrees—that there was no suggestion of bad faith on the part of the police. Moreover, the Due Process Clause was not violated because the state failed to perform a newer test on the semen samples. The police do not have a constitutional duty to perform any particular tests. Pp. 55–59, 153 Ariz. 50, 734 P.2d 592, reversed.

REHNQUIST, C. J., delivered the opinion of the Court, in which WHITE, O'CONNOR, SCALIA, and KENNEDY, JJ., joined. STEVENS, J., filed an opinion concurring in the judgment, post, p. 59. BLACKMUN, J., filed a dissenting opinion, in which BRENNAN and MARSHALL, JJ., joined, post, p. 61. [488 U.S. 51, 52]

John R. Gustafson argued the cause for petitioner. With him on the brief were Stephen D. Neely, James M. Howard, and Deborah Strange Ward.

Daniel F. Davis argued the cause and filed a brief for respondent.

CHIEF JUSTICE REHNQUIST delivered the opinion of the Court.

Respondent Larry Youngblood was convicted by a Pima County, Arizona, jury of child molestation, sexual assault, and kidnaping. The Arizona Court of Appeals reversed his conviction on the ground that the state had failed to preserve semen samples from the victim's body and clothing. 153 Ariz. 50, 734 P.2d 592 (1986). We granted certiorari to consider the extent to which the Due Process Clause of the Fourteenth Amendment requires the state to preserve evidentiary material that might be useful to a criminal defendant.

On October 29, 1983, David L., a 10-year-old boy, attended a church service with his mother. After he left the service at about 9:30 p.m., the boy went to a carnival behind the church, where he was abducted by a middle-aged man of medium height and weight. The assailant drove the boy to a secluded area near a ravine and molested him. He then took the boy to an unidentified, sparsely furnished house where he sodomized the boy four times. Afterwards, the assailant tied the boy up while he went outside to start his car. Once the assailant started the car, albeit with some difficulty, he returned to the house and again sodomized the boy. The assailant then sent the boy to the bathroom to wash up before he returned him to the carnival. He threatened to kill the boy if he told anyone about the attack. The entire ordeal lasted about 1½ hours.

After the boy made his way home, his mother took him to Kino Hospital. At the hospital, a physician treated the boy for rectal injuries. The physician also used a "sexual assault kit" to collect evidence of the attack. The Tucson Police Department [488 U.S. 51, 53] provided such kits to all hospitals in Pima County for use in sexual assault cases. Under standard procedure, the victim of a sexual assault was taken to a hospital, where a physician used the kit to collect evidence. The kit included paper to collect saliva samples, a tube for obtaining a blood sample, microscopic slides for making smears, a set of Q-Tip-like swabs, and a medical examination report. Here, the physician used the swab to collect samples from the boy's rectum and mouth. He then made a microscopic slide of the samples. The doctor also obtained samples of the boy's saliva, blood, and hair. The physician did not examine the samples at any time. The police placed the kit in a secure refrigerator at the police station. At the hospital, the police also collected the boy's underwear and T-shirt. This clothing was not refrigerated or frozen.

Nine days after the attack, on November 7, 1983, the police asked the boy to pick out his assailant from a photographic lineup. The boy identified respondent as the assailant. Respondent was not located by the police until four weeks later; he was arrested on December 9, 1983.

On November 8, 1983, Edward Heller, a police criminologist, examined the sexual assault kit. He testified that he followed standard department procedure, which was to examine the slides and determine whether sexual contact had occurred. After he determined that such contact had occurred, the criminologist did not perform any other tests, although he placed the assault kit back in the refrigerator. He testified that tests to identify blood group substances were not routinely conducted during the initial examination of an assault kit and in only about half of all cases in any event. He did not test the clothing at this time.

Respondent was indicted on charges of child molestation, sexual assault, and kidnaping. The state moved to compel respondent to provide blood and saliva samples for comparison with the material gathered through the use of the sexual assault kit, but the trial court denied the motion on the [488 U.S. 51, 54] ground that the state had not obtained a sufficiently large semen sample to make a valid comparison. The prosecutor then asked the state's criminologist to perform an ABO blood group test on the rectal swab sample in an attempt to ascertain the blood type of the boy's assailant. This test failed to detect any blood group substances in the sample.

In January 1985, the police criminologist examined the boy's clothing for the first time. He found one semen stain on the boy's underwear and another on the rear of his T-shirt. The criminologist tried to obtain blood group substances from both stains using the ABO technique, but was unsuccessful. He also performed a P-30 protein molecule test on the stains, which indicated that only a small quantity of semen was present on the clothing; it was inconclusive as to the assailant's identity. The Tucson Police Department had just begun using this test, which was then used in slightly more than half of the crime laboratories in the country.

Respondent's principal defense at trial was that the boy had erred in identifying him as the perpetrator of the crime. In this connection, both a criminologist for the State and an expert witness for respondent testified as to what might have been shown by tests performed on the samples shortly after they were gathered, or by later tests performed on the samples from the boy's clothing had the clothing been properly refrigerated. The court instructed the jury that if they found the state had destroyed or lost evidence, they might "infer that the true fact is against the state's interest." 10 Tr. 90.

The jury found respondent guilty as charged, but the Arizona Court of Appeals reversed the judgment of conviction. It stated that "'when identity is an issue at trial and the police permit the destruction of evidence that could eliminate the defendant as the perpetrator, such loss is material to the defense and is a denial of due process.'" 153 Ariz., at 54, 734 P.2d, at 596, quoting *State* v. *Escalante*, 153 Ariz. 55, 61, 734 P.2d 597, 603 (App. 1986). The Court of Appeals [488 U.S. 51, 55] concluded on the basis of the expert testimony at trial that timely performance of tests with properly preserved semen samples could have produced results that might have completely exonerated respondent. The Court of Appeals reached this conclusion even though it did "not imply any bad faith on the part of the state." 153 Ariz., at 54, 734

P.2d, at 596. The Supreme Court of Arizona denied the state's petition for review, and we granted certiorari. 485 U.S. 903 (1988). We now reverse.

Decision of this case requires us to again consider "what might loosely be called the area of constitutionally guaranteed access to evidence." *United States* v. *Valenzuela-Bernal*, 458 U.S. 858, 867 (1982). In *Brady* v. *Maryland*, 373 U.S. 83 (1963), we held that "the suppression by the prosecution of evidence favorable to the accused upon request violates due process where the evidence is material either to guilt or to punishment, irrespective of the good faith or bad faith of the prosecution." *Ibid.*, at 87. In *United States* v. *Agurs*, 427 U.S. 97 (1976), we held that the prosecution had a duty to disclose some evidence of this description even though no requests were made for it, but at the same time we rejected the notion that a "prosecutor has a constitutional duty routinely to deliver his entire file to defense counsel." *Ibid.*, at 111; see also *Moore* v. *Illinois*, 408 U.S. 786, 795 (1972) ("We know of no constitutional requirement that the prosecution make a complete and detailed accounting to the defense of all police investigatory work on a case").

There is no question but that the state complied with *Brady* and *Agurs* here. The state disclosed relevant police reports to respondent, which contained information about the existence of the swab and the clothing, and the boy's examination at the hospital. The state provided respondent's expert with the laboratory reports and notes prepared by the police criminologist, and respondent's expert had access to the swab and to the clothing. [488 U.S. 51, 56]

If respondent is to prevail on federal constitutional grounds, then, it must be because of some constitutional duty over and above that imposed by cases such as *Brady* and *Agurs*. Our most recent decision in this area of the law, *California* v. *Trombetta*, 467 U.S. 479 (1984), arose out of a drunken driving prosecution in which the state had introduced test results indicating the concentration of alcohol in the blood of two motorists. The defendants sought to suppress the test results on the ground that the state had failed to preserve the breath samples used in the test. We rejected this argument for several reasons: first, "the officers here were acting in 'good faith and in accord with their normal practice,'" *Ibid.*, at 488, quoting *Killian* v. *United States*, 368 U.S. 231, 242 (1961); second, in the light of the procedures actually used, the chances that preserved samples would have exculpated the defendants were slim, 467 U.S., at 489; and, third, even if the samples might have shown inaccuracy in the tests, the defendants had "alternative means of demonstrating their innocence." *Ibid.*, at 490. In the present case, the likelihood that the preserved materials would have enabled the defendant to exonerate himself appears to be greater than it was in *Trombetta*, but here, unlike in *Trombetta*, the state did not attempt to make any use of the materials in its own case in chief.[1] [488 U.S. 51, 57]

Our decisions in related areas have stressed the importance for constitutional purposes of good or bad faith on the part of the government when the claim is based on loss of evidence attributable to the government. In *United States* v. *Marion*, 404 U.S. 307 (1971), we said that "[n]o actual prejudice to the conduct of the defense is alleged or proved, and there is no showing that the government intentionally delayed to gain some tactical advantage over appellees or to harass them." *Ibid.*, at 325; see also *United States* v. *Lovasco*, 431 U.S. 783, 790 (1977). Similarly, in *United States* v. *Valenzuela-Bernal, supra*, we considered whether the government's deportation of two witnesses who were illegal aliens violated due process. We held that the prompt deportation of the witnesses was justified "upon the Executive's good-faith determination that they possess no evidence favorable to the defendant in a criminal prosecution." *Ibid.*, at 872.

The Due Process Clause of the Fourteenth Amendment, as interpreted in *Brady*, makes the good or bad faith of the state irrelevant when the state fails to disclose to the defendant material exculpatory evidence. But we think the Due Process Clause requires a different result when we deal with the failure of the state to preserve evidentiary material of which no more can be said than that it could have been subjected to tests, the results of which might have exonerated the defendant. Part of the reason for the difference in treatment is found in the observation made by the Court in *Trombetta, supra*, at 486, that "[w]henever potentially exculpatory [488 U.S. 51, 58] evidence is permanently lost, courts face the treacherous task of divining the import of materials whose contents are unknown and, very often, disputed." Part of it stems from our unwillingness to read the "fundamental fairness" requirement of the Due Process Clause, see *Lisenba* v. *California*, 314 U.S. 219, 236 (1941), as imposing on the police an undifferentiated and absolute duty to retain and to preserve all material that might be of conceivable evidentiary significance in a particular prosecution. We think that requiring a defendant to show bad faith on the part of the police both limits the extent of the police's obligation to preserve evidence to reasonable bounds and confines it to that class of cases where the interests of justice most clearly require it, *i.e.*, those cases in which the police themselves by their conduct indicate that the evidence could form a basis for exonerating the defendant. We therefore hold that unless a criminal defendant can show bad faith on the part of the police, failure to preserve potentially useful evidence does not constitute a denial of due process of law.

In this case, the police collected the rectal swab and clothing on the night of the crime; respondent was not taken into custody until six weeks later. The failure of the police to refrigerate the clothing and to perform tests on the semen samples can at worst be described as negligent. None of this information was concealed from respondent at trial, and the evidence—such as it was—was made available to respondent's expert who declined to perform any tests on the samples. The Arizona Court of Appeals noted in its opinion—and we agree—that there was no suggestion of bad faith on the part of the police. It follows, therefore, from what we have said, that there was no violation of the Due Process Clause.

The Arizona Court of Appeals also referred somewhat obliquely to the state's "inability to quantitatively test" certain semen samples with the newer P-30 test. 153 Ariz., at 54, 734 P.2d, at 596. If the court meant by this statement [488 U.S. 51, 59] that the Due Process Clause is violated when the police fail to use a particular investigatory tool, we strongly disagree. The situation here is no different than a prosecution for drunken driving that rests on police observation alone; the defendant is free to argue to the finder of fact that a breathalyzer test might have been exculpatory, but the police do not have a constitutional duty to perform any particular tests.

The judgment of the Arizona Court of Appeals is reversed, and the case is remanded for further proceedings not inconsistent with this opinion.

Reversed.

JUSTICE STEVENS, concurring in the judgment.

Three factors are of critical importance to my evaluation of this case. First, at the time the police failed to refrigerate the victim's clothing, and thus negligently lost potentially valuable evidence, they had at least as great an interest in preserving the evidence as did the person later accused of the crime. Indeed, at that time it was more likely that the evidence would have been useful to the police—who were still conducting an investigation—and to the prosecutor—who would later bear the burden of establishing guilt beyond a reasonable doubt—than to the defendant. In cases such as this, even without a prophylactic sanction such as dismissal of the indictment, the state has a strong incentive to preserve the evidence.

Second, although it is not possible to know whether the lost evidence would have revealed any relevant information, it is unlikely that the defendant was prejudiced by the state's omission. In examining witnesses and in her summation, defense counsel impressed upon the jury the fact that the state failed to preserve the evidence and that the state could have conducted tests that might well have exonerated the defendant. See App. to Pet. for Cert. C21–C38, C42–C45; 9 Tr. 183–202, 207–208; 10 Tr. 58–61, 69–70. More significantly, the trial judge instructed the jury: "If you find that the state has ... allowed to be destroyed or lost any evidence whose [488 U.S. 51, 60] content or quality are in issue, you may infer that the true fact is against the state's interest." 10 Tr. 90. As a result, the uncertainty as to what the evidence might have proved was turned to the defendant's advantage.

Third, the fact that no juror chose to draw the permissive inference that proper preservation of the evidence would have demonstrated that the defendant was not the assailant suggests that the lost evidence was "immaterial." Our cases make clear that "[t]he proper standard of materiality must reflect our overriding concern with the justice of the finding of guilt," and that a state's failure to turn over (or preserve) potentially exculpatory evidence therefore "must be evaluated in the context of the entire record." *United States* v. *Agurs*, 427 U.S. 97, 112 (1976) (footnotes omitted); see also *California* v. *Trombetta*, 467 U.S. 479, 488 (1984) (duty to preserve evidence "must be limited to evidence that might be expected to play a significant role in the suspect's defense"). In declining defense counsel's and the court's invitations to draw the permissive inference, the jurors in effect indicated that, in their view, the other evidence at trial was so overwhelming that it was highly improbable that the lost evidence was exculpatory. In *Trombetta*, this Court found no due process violation because "the chances [were] extremely low that preserved [breath] samples would have been exculpatory." *Ibid.*, at 489. In this case, the jury has already performed this calculus based on its understanding of the evidence introduced at trial. Presumably, in a case involving a closer question as to guilt or innocence, the jurors would have been more ready to infer that the lost evidence was exculpatory.

With these factors in mind, I concur in the Court's judgment. I do not, however, join the Court's opinion because it announces a proposition of law that is much broader than necessary to decide this case. It states that "unless a criminal defendant can show bad faith on the part of the police, failure to preserve potentially useful evidence does not constitute a [488 U.S. 51, 61] denial of due process of law." *Ante*, at 58. In my opinion, there may well be cases in which the defendant is unable to prove that the state acted in bad faith but in which the loss or destruction of evidence is nonetheless so critical to the defense as to make a criminal trial fundamentally unfair. This, however, is not such a case. Accordingly, I concur in the judgment.

JUSTICE BLACKMUN, with whom JUSTICE BRENNAN and JUSTICE MARSHALL join, dissenting.

The Constitution requires that criminal defendants be provided with a fair trial, not merely a "good faith" try at a fair trial. Respondent here, by what may have been nothing more than police ineptitude, was denied the opportunity to present a full defense. That ineptitude, however, deprived respondent of his guaranteed right to due process of law. In reversing the judgment of the Arizona Court of Appeals, this Court, in my view, misreads the import of its prior cases and unduly restricts the protections of the Due Process Clause. An understanding of due process demonstrates that the evidence which was allowed to deteriorate was "constitutionally material," and that its absence significantly prejudiced respondent. Accordingly, I dissent.

I

The Court, with minimal reference to our past cases and with what seems to me to be less than complete analysis, announces that "unless a criminal defendant can show bad faith on the part of police, failure to preserve potentially useful evidence does not constitute a denial of due process of law." *Ante*, at 58. This conclusion is claimed to be justified because it limits the extent of police responsibility "to that class of cases where the interests of justice most clearly require it, *i.e.*, those cases in which the police themselves by their conduct indicate that the evidence could form a basis for exonerating the defendant." *Ibid.* The majority has identified clearly one type of violation, for police action affirmatively [488 U.S. 51, 62] aimed at cheating the process undoubtedly violates the Constitution. But to suggest that this is the only way in which the Due Process Clause can be violated cannot be correct. Regardless of intent or lack thereof, police action that results in a defendant's receiving an unfair trial constitutes a deprivation of due process.

The Court's most recent pronouncement in "what might loosely be called the area of constitutionally guaranteed access to evidence," *United States* v. *Valenzuela-Bernal*, 458 U.S. 858, 867 (1982), is in *California* v. *Trombetta*, 467 U.S. 479 (1984). *Trombetta* addressed "the question whether the Amendment ... demands that the state preserve potentially exculpatory evidence on behalf of defendants." *Ibid.*, at 481. JUSTICE MARSHALL, writing for the Court, noted that while the particular question was one of first impression, the general standards to be applied had been developed in a number of cases, including *Brady* v. *Maryland*, 373 U.S. 83 (1963), and *United States* v. *Agurs*, 427 U.S. 97 (1976).[2] Those [488 U.S. 51, 63] cases in no way require that government actions that deny a defendant access to material evidence be taken in bad faith in order to violate due process.

As noted by the majority, *ante*, at 55, the Court in *Brady* ruled that "the suppression by the prosecution of evidence favorable to an accused upon request violates due process where the evidence is material either to guilt or to punishment, irrespective of the good faith or bad faith of the prosecution." 373 U.S., at 87. The *Brady* Court went on to explain that the principle underlying earlier cases, e.g., *Mooney* v. *Holohan*, 294 U.S. 103 (1935) (violation of due process when prosecutor presented perjured testimony), is "not punishment of society for misdeeds of a prosecutor but avoidance of an unfair trial to the accused." 373 U.S., at 87. The failure to turn over material evidence "casts the prosecutor in the role of an architect of a proceeding that does not comport with standards of justice, even though, as in the present case, his action is not 'the result of guile.'" *Ibid.*, at 88 (quoting lower court opinion).

In *Trombetta*, the Court also relied on *United States* v. *Agurs*, 427 U.S., at 107, which required a prosecutor to turn over to the defense evidence that was "clearly supportive of a claim of innocence" even without a defense request. The Court noted that the prosecutor's duty was not one of constitutional dimension unless the evidence was such that its "omission deprived the defendant of a fair trial," *Ibid.*, at 108, and explained:

"Nor do we believe the constitutional obligation is measured by the moral culpability, or the willfulness, of the prosecutor. If evidence highly probative of innocence is in his file, he should be presumed to recognize its significance even if he has actually overlooked it. ... If the suppression of evidence results in constitutional error, it is because of the character of the evidence, not [488 U.S. 51, 64] the character of the prosecutor." *Ibid.*, at 110.

Agurs thus made plain that the prosecutor's state of mind is not determinative. Rather, the proper standard must focus on the materiality of the evidence, and that standard "must reflect our overriding concern with the justice of the finding of guilt." *Ibid.*, at 112.

Brady and *Agurs* could not be more clear in their holdings that a prosecutor's bad faith in interfering with a defendant's access to material evidence is not an essential part of a due process violation.[4] Nor did *Trombetta* create such a requirement. *Trombetta's* initial discussion focused on the due process requirement "that criminal defendants be afforded a meaningful opportunity to present a complete defense," 467 U.S., at 485, and then noted that the delivery of exculpatory evidence to the defendant "protect[s] the innocent from erroneous [488 U.S. 51, 65] conviction and ensur[es] the integrity of our criminal justice system." *Ibid.* Although the language of *Trombetta* includes a quotation in which the words "in good faith" appear, those words, for two reasons, do not have the significance claimed for them by the majority. First, the words are the antecedent part of the fuller phrase "in good faith and in accord with their normal practice." *Ibid.*, at 488. That phrase has its source in *Killian* v. *United States*, 368 U.S. 231, 242 (1961), where the Court held that the practice of discarding investigators' notes, used to compile reports that were then received in evidence, did not violate due process.[5] In both *Killian* and *Trombetta*, the importance of police compliance with usual procedures was manifest. Here, however, the same standard of conduct cannot be claimed. There has been no suggestion that it was the usual procedure to ignore the possible deterioration of important evidence, or generally to treat material evidence in a negligent or reckless manner. Nor can the failure to refrigerate the clothing be squared with the careful steps taken to preserve the sexual-assault kit. The negligent or reckless failure to preserve important evidence just cannot be "in accord with ... normal practice."

Second, and more importantly, *Trombetta* demonstrates that the absence of bad faith does not end the analysis. The determination in *Trombetta* that the prosecution acted in good faith and according to normal practice merely prefaced the primary inquiry, which centers on the "constitutional materiality" of the evidence itself. 467 U.S., at 489. There is [488 U.S. 51, 66] nothing in *Trombetta* that intimates that good faith alone should be the measure.[6]

The cases in this area clearly establish that police actions taken in bad faith are not the only species of police conduct that can result in a violation of due process. As *Agurs* points out, it makes no sense to overturn a conviction because a malicious prosecutor withholds information that he mistakenly believes to be material, but which actually would have been of no help to the defense. 427 U.S., at 110. In the same way, it makes no sense to ignore the fact that a defendant has been denied a fair trial because the state allowed evidence that was material to the defense to deteriorate beyond the point of usefulness, simply because the police were inept rather than malicious.

I also doubt that the "bad faith" standard creates the bright-line rule sought by the majority. Apart from the inherent difficulty a defendant would have in obtaining evidence to show a lack of good faith, the line between "good faith" and "bad faith" is anything but bright, and the majority's formulation may well create more questions than it answers. What constitutes bad faith for these purposes? Does a defendant have to show actual malice, or would recklessness, or the deliberate failure to establish standards for maintaining and preserving evidence, be sufficient? Does "good faith police work" require a certain minimum of diligence, or will a lazy officer, who does not walk the few extra steps to the evidence refrigerator, be considered to be acting in good faith? While the majority leaves these questions for [488 U.S. 51, 67] another day, its quick embrace of a "bad faith" standard has not brightened the line; it only has moved the line so as to provide fewer protections for criminal defendants.

II

The inquiry the majority eliminates in setting up its "bad faith" rule is whether the evidence in question here was "constitutionally material," so that its destruction violates due process. The majority does not say whether "evidentiary material of which no more can be said than that it could have been subjected to tests, the results of which might have exonerated the defendant," *ante*, at 57, is, for purposes of due process, material. But because I do not find the question of lack of bad faith dispositive, I now consider whether this evidence was such that its destruction rendered respondent's trial fundamentally unfair.

Trombetta requires that a court determine whether the evidence possesses "an exculpatory value that was apparent before the evidence was destroyed," and whether it was "of such a nature that the defendant would be unable to obtain comparable evidence by other reasonably available means." 467 U.S., at 489. In *Trombetta* neither requirement was met. But it is important to note that the facts of *Trombetta* differed significantly from those of this case. As such, while the basic standards set by *Trombetta* are controlling, the inquiry here must be more finely tuned.

In *Trombetta*, samples of breath taken from suspected drunk drivers had been discarded after police had tested them using an Intoxilyzer, a highly accurate and reliable device for measuring blood-alcohol concentration levels. *Ibid.*, at 481–482. The Court reasoned that the likelihood of the post-test samples proving to be exculpatory was extremely low, and further observed that the defendants were able to attack the reliability of the test results by presenting evidence of the ways in which the Intoxilyzer might have malfunctioned. This case differs from *Trombetta* in that here no [488 U.S. 51, 68] conclusive tests were performed on the relevant evidence. There is a distinct possibility in this case, one not present in *Trombetta*, that a proper test would have exonerated respondent, unrebutted by any other conclusive test results. As a consequence, although the discarded evidence in *Trombetta* had impeachment value (*i.e.*, it might have shown that the test results were incorrect), here what was lost to the respondent was the possibility of complete exoneration. *Trombetta*'s specific analysis, therefore, is not directly controlling.

The exculpatory value of the clothing in this case cannot be determined with any certainty, precisely because the police allowed the samples to deteriorate. But we do know several important things about the evidence. First, the semen samples on the clothing undoubtedly came from the assailant. Second, the samples could have been tested, using technology available and in use at the local police department, to show either the blood type of the assailant, or that the assailant was a nonsecreter, *i.e.*, someone who does not secrete a blood-type "marker" into other body fluids, such as semen. Third, the evidence was clearly important. A semen sample in a rape case where identity is questioned is always significant. See *Hilliard* v. *Spalding*, 719 F.2d 1443, 1446–1447 (CA9 1983); *People* v. *Nation*, 26 Cal. 3d 169, 176–177, 604 P.2d 1051, 1054–1055 (1980). Fourth, a reasonable police officer should have recognized that the clothing required refrigeration. Fifth, we know that an inconclusive test was done on the swab. The test suggested that the assailant was a nonsecreter, although it was equally likely that the sample on the swab was too small for accurate results to be obtained. And, sixth, we know that respondent is a secreter.

If the samples on the clothing had been tested, and the results had shown either the blood type of the assailant or that the assailant was a nonsecreter, its constitutional materiality would be clear. But the state's conduct has deprived the defendant, and the courts, of the opportunity to determine with certainty the import of this evidence: it has "interfere[d] with [488 U.S. 51, 69] the accused's ability to present a defense by imposing on him a requirement which the government's own actions have rendered impossible to fulfill." *Hilliard* v. *Spalding*, 719 F.2d, at 1446. Good faith or not, this is intolerable, unless the particular circumstances of the case indicate either that the evidence was not likely to prove exculpatory, or that the defendant was able to use effective alternative means to prove the point the destroyed evidence otherwise could have made.

I recognize the difficulties presented by such a situation.[7] The societal interest in seeing criminals punished rightly requires that indictments be dismissed only when the unavailability of the evidence prevents the defendant from receiving a fair trial. In a situation where the substance of the lost evidence is known, the materiality analysis laid out in *Trombetta* is adequate. But in a situation like the present one, due process requires something more. Rather than allow a state's ineptitude to saddle a defendant with an impossible burden, a court should focus on the type of evidence, the possibility it might prove exculpatory, and the existence of other evidence going to the same point of contention in determining whether the failure to preserve the evidence in question violated due process. To put it succinctly, where no comparable evidence is likely to be available to the defendant, police must preserve physical evidence of a type that they reasonably should know has the potential, if tested, to reveal immutable characteristics of the criminal, and hence to exculpate a defendant charged with the crime. [488 U.S. 51, 70]

The first inquiry under this standard concerns the particular evidence itself. It must be of a type which is clearly relevant, a requirement satisfied, in a case where identity is at issue, by physical evidence which has come from the assailant. Samples of blood and other body fluids, fingerprints, and hair and tissue samples have been used to implicate guilty defendants, and to exonerate innocent suspects. This is not to say that all physical evidence of this type must be preserved. For example, in a case where a blood sample is found, but the circumstances make it unclear whether the sample came from the assailant, the dictates of due process might not compel preservation (although principles of sound investigation might certainly do so). But in a case where there is no doubt that the sample came from the assailant, the presumption must be that it be preserved.

A corollary, particularly applicable to this case, is that the evidence embody some immutable characteristic of the assailant which can be determined by available testing methods. So, for example, a clear fingerprint can be compared to the defendant's fingerprints to yield a conclusive result; a blood sample, or a sample of body fluid which contains blood markers, can either completely exonerate or strongly implicate a defendant. As technology develops, the potential for this type of evidence to provide conclusive results on any number of questions will increase. Current genetic testing measures, frequently used in civil paternity suits, are extraordinarily precise. See *Clark v. Jeter*, 486 U.S. 456, 465 (1988). The importance of these types of evidence is indisputable, and requiring police to recognize their importance is not unreasonable.

The next inquiry is whether the evidence, which was obviously relevant and indicates an immutable characteristic of the actual assailant, is of a type likely to be independently exculpatory. Requiring the defendant to prove that the particular piece of evidence probably would be independently exculpatory [488 U.S. 51, 71] would require the defendant to prove the content of something he does not have because of the state's misconduct. Focusing on the type of evidence solves this problem. A court will be able to consider the type of evidence and the available technology, as well as the circumstances of the case, to determine the likelihood that the evidence might have proved to be exculpatory. The evidence must also be without equivalent in the particular case. It must not be cumulative or collateral, cf. *United States* v. *Agurs*, 427 U.S., at 113–114, and must bear directly on the question of innocence or guilt.

Due process must also take into account the burdens that the preservation of evidence places on the police. Law enforcement officers must be provided the option, as is implicit in *Trombetta*, of performing the proper tests on physical evidence and then discarding it.[8] Once a suspect has been arrested the police, after a reasonable time, may inform defense counsel of plans to discard the evidence. When the defense has been informed of the existence of the evidence, after a reasonable time the burden of preservation may shift to the defense. There should also be flexibility to deal with evidence that is unusually dangerous or difficult to store.

III

Applying this standard to the facts of this case, I conclude that the Arizona Court of Appeals was correct in overturning respondent's conviction. The clothing worn by the victim contained samples of his assailant's semen. The appeals court found that these samples would probably be larger, less contaminated, and more likely to yield conclusive test results than would the samples collected by use of the assault kit. 153 Ariz. 50, 54, 734 P.2d 592, 596

(1986). The clothing [488 U.S. 51, 72] and the semen stains on the clothing therefore obviously were material.

Because semen is a body fluid which could have been tested by available methods to show an immutable characteristic of the assailant, there was a genuine possibility that the results of such testing might have exonerated respondent. The only evidence implicating respondent was the testimony of the victim.[9] There was no other eyewitness, and the only other significant physical evidence, respondent's car, was seized by police, examined, turned over to a wrecking company, and then dismantled without the victim's having viewed it. The police also failed to check the car to confirm or refute elements of the victim's testimony.[10] [488 U.S. 51, 73]

Although a closer question, there was no equivalent evidence available to respondent. The swab contained a semen sample, but it was not sufficient to allow proper testing. Respondent had access to other evidence tending to show that he was not the assailant, but there was no other evidence that would have shown that it was physically impossible for respondent to have been the assailant. Nor would the preservation of the evidence here have been a burden upon the police. There obviously was refrigeration available, as the preservation of the swab indicates, and the items of clothing likely would not tax available storage space.

Considered in the context of the entire trial, the failure of the prosecution to preserve this evidence deprived respondent of a fair trial. It still remains "a fundamental value determination of our society that it is far worse to convict an innocent man than to let a guilty man go free." In re *Winship*, 397 U.S. 358, 372 (1970) (concurring opinion). The evidence in this case was far from conclusive, and the possibility that the evidence denied to respondent would have exonerated him was not remote. The result is that he was denied a fair trial by the actions of the state, and consequently was denied due process of law. Because the Court's opinion improperly limits the scope of due process, and ignores its proper focus in a futile pursuit of a bright-line rule,[11] I dissent.

Footnotes

[Footnote 1] In this case, the Arizona Court of Appeals relied on its earlier decision in *State v. Escalante*, 153 Ariz. 55, 734 P.2d 597 (1986), holding that "'when identity is an issue at trial and the police permit destruction of evidence that could eliminate a defendant as the perpetrator, such loss is material to the defense and is a denial of due process.'" 153 Ariz. 50, 54, 734 P.2d 592, 596 (1986), quoting *Escalante, supra*, at 61, 734 P.2d, at 603 (emphasis added). The reasoning in *Escalante* and the instant case mark a sharp departure from *Trombetta* in two respects. First, *Trombetta* speaks of evidence whose exculpatory value is "apparent." 467 U.S., at 489. The possibility that the semen samples could have exculpated respondent if preserved or tested is not enough to satisfy the standard of constitutional materiality in *Trombetta*. Second, we made clear in *Trombetta* that the exculpatory value of the evidence must be apparent [488 U.S. 51, 57] "before the evidence was destroyed." *Ibid.* (emphasis added). Here, respondent has not shown that the police knew the semen samples would have exculpated him when they failed to perform certain tests or to refrigerate the boy's clothing; this evidence was simply an avenue of investigation that might have led in any number of directions. The presence or absence of bad faith by the police for purposes of the Due Process Clause must necessarily turn on the police's knowledge of the exculpatory value of the evidence at the time it was lost or destroyed. Cf. *Napue* v. *Illinois*, 360 U.S. 264, 269 (1959).

[Footnote 2] The Court's discussion in *Trombetta* also noted other cases: In *Napue* v. *Illinois*, 360 U.S. 264 (1959), the prosecution failed to inform the defense and the trial court that one of its witnesses had testified falsely that he had not been promised favorable treatment in return for testifying. The Court noted that a conviction obtained by the knowing use of such testimony must fall, and suggested that the conviction is invalid even when the perjured testimony is "'not the result of guile or a desire to prejudice ... for its impact was the same, preventing, as it did, a trial that could in any real sense be termed fair.'" *Ibid.*, at 270, quoting *People* v. *Savvides*, 1 N.Y. 2d 554, 557, 136 N.E. 2d 853, 854–855 (1956). In *Giglio* v. *United States*, 405 U.S. 150 (1972), the Court required a federal prosecutor to reveal a promise of nonprosecution if a witness testified, holding that "whether the nondisclosure was a result of negligence or design, it is the responsibility of the prosecutor." *Ibid.*, at 154. The good faith of the prosecutor thus was irrelevant for purposes of due process. And in *Roviaro* v. *United States*, 353 U.S. 53 (1957), the Court held that in some cases the government must disclose to the defense the identity of a confidential informant. There was no discussion of any requirement of bad faith.

[Footnote 3] The *Agurs* Court went on to note that the standard to be applied in considering the harm suffered by the defendant was different from the standard applied when new evidence is discovered by a neutral source after trial. The prosecutor is "the 'servant of the law, the twofold aim of which is that guilt shall not escape or innocence suffer.'" 427 U.S., at 111 , quoting *Berger* v. *United States*, 295 U.S. 78, 88 (1935). Holding the prosecution to a higher standard is necessary, lest the "special significance to the prosecutor's obligation to serve the cause of justice" be lost. 427 U.S., at 111.

[Footnote 4] Nor does *United States* v. *Valenzuela-Bernal*, 458 U.S. 858 (1982), provide support for the majority's "bad faith" requirement. In that case a defendant was deprived of certain testimony at his trial when the government deported potential witnesses after determining that they possessed no material evidence relevant to the criminal trial. These deportations were not the result of malice or negligence, but were carried out pursuant to immigration policy. *Ibid.*, at 863–866. Consideration of the government's motive was only the first step in the due process inquiry. Because the government acted in good faith, the defendant was required to make "a plausible showing" that "the evidence lost would be both material and favorable to the defense." *Ibid.*, at 873. In *Valenzuela-Bernal*, the defendant was not able to meet that burden. Under the majority's "bad faith" test, the defendant would have no opportunity to try.

[Footnote 5] In *Killian*, the notes in question related to witnesses' statements, were used to prepare receipts which the witnesses then signed, and were destroyed in accord with usual practice. 368 U.S., at 242. Had it not been the usual practice of the agents to destroy their notes, or if no reports had been prepared from those notes before they were destroyed, a different question, closer to the one the Court decides today, would have been presented.

[Footnote 6] The cases relied upon by the majority for the proposition that bad faith is necessary to show a due process violation, *United States* v. *Marion*, 404 U.S. 307 (1971), and *United States* v. *Lovasco*, 431 U.S. 783 (1977), concerned claims that preindictment delay violated due process. The harm caused by such delay is certainly more speculative than that caused by the deprivation of material exculpatory evidence, and in such cases statutes of limitations, not the Due Process Clause, provide the primary protection for defendants' interests. Those cases are a shaky foundation for the radical step taken by the Court today.

[Footnote 7] We noted in *California* v. *Trombetta*, 467 U.S. 479, 486 (1984): "The absence of doctrinal development in this area reflects, in part, the difficulty of developing rules to deal with evidence destroyed through prosecutorial neglect or oversight. Whenever potentially exculpatory evidence is permanently lost, courts face the treacherous task of divining the import of materials whose contents are unknown and, very often, disputed." While the inquiry is a difficult one, I do not read *Trombetta* to say, nor do I believe, that it is impossible. Respect for constitutional rights demands that the inquiry be made.

[Footnote 8] There is no need in this case to discuss whether the police have a duty to test evidence, or whether due process requires that police testing be on the "cutting edge" of technology. But uncertainty as to these questions only highlights the importance of preserving evidence, so that the defense has the opportunity at least to use whatever scientifically recognized tests are available. That is all that is at issue in this case.

[Footnote 9] This Court "has recognized the inherently suspect qualities of eyewitness identification evidence." *Watkins* v. *Sowders*, 449 U.S. 341, 350 (1981) (BRENNAN, J., dissenting). Such evidence is "notoriously unreliable," *Ibid.*; see *United States* v. *Wade*, 388 U.S. 218, 228 (1967); *Manson* v. *Brathwaite*, 432 U.S. 98, 111–112 (1977), and has distinct impacts on juries. "All the evidence points rather strikingly to the conclusion that there is almost nothing more convincing than a live human being who takes the stand, points a finger at the defendant, and says, 'That's the one!'" E. Loftus, *Eyewitness Testimony* 19 (1979).

Studies show that children are more likely to make mistaken identifications than are adults, especially when they have been encouraged by adults. See generally Cohen and Harnick, The Susceptibility of Child Witnesses to Suggestion, 4 *Law Human Behav.*, 201 (1980). Other studies show another element of possible relevance in this case: "Crossracial identifications are much less likely to be accurate than same race identifications." Rahaim and Brodsky, Empirical Evidence versus Common Sense: Juror and Lawyer Knowledge of Eyewitness Accuracy, 7 *Law Psychol. Rev.*, 1, 2 (1982). These authorities suggest that eyewitness testimony alone, in the absence of corroboration, is to be viewed with some suspicion.

[Footnote 10] The victim testified that the car had a loud muffler, that country music was playing on its radio, and that the car was started using a key. Respondent and others testified that his car was inoperative on the night of the incident, that when it was working it ran quietly, that the radio did not work, and that the car could be started only by using a screwdriver. The police did not check any of this before disposing of the car. See 153 Ariz. 50, 51–52, 734 P.2d 592, 593–594 (App. 1986).

[Footnote 11] Even under the standard articulated by the majority the proper resolution of this case should be a remand to consider whether the police did act in good faith. The Arizona Court of Appeals did not state in its opinion that there was no bad faith on the part of the police. Rather, it held that the proper standard to be applied was a consideration of whether the failure to preserve the evidence deprived respondent of a fair trial, and that, as a result, its holding did "not imply any bad faith on the part of the state." *Ibid.*, at 54, 734 P.2d, at 596. But there certainly is a sufficient basis on this record for a finding that the police acted in bad faith. The destruction of respondent's car by the police (which in itself may serve on remand as an alternative ground for finding a constitutional violation, see *Ibid.*, [488 U.S. 51, 74] at 55, 734 P.2d, at 597 (question left open)) certainly suggests that the police may have conducted their investigation with an improper animus. Although the majority provides no guidance as to how a lack of good faith is to be determined, or just how egregious police action must be, the police actions in this case raise a colorable claim of bad faith. If the Arizona courts on remand should determine that the failure to refrigerate the clothing was part of an overall investigation marred by bad faith, then, even under the majority's test, the conviction should be overturned. [488 U.S. 51, 74]

Index

A

AAFS Code of Ethics and Conduct, 27–28,
123
    professional practice applications, 58–59,
64, 68, 72, 76, 81, 86, 92
    technical competence applications, 92,
97, 109, 118–119
    text, 123
AAFS Good Forensic Practices Committee,
28–29
AAFS Good Forensic Practices Guidelines,
143–144
ABC *Code of Ethics*, 153
ABC Rules of Professional Conduct
    professional practice applications, 59,
64–65, 69, 72–73, 77, 81, 86, 92–93
    technical competence applications,
92–93, 97, 108–109, 118
    text, 153–154
Accountability, 150
Accreditation, 151
American Academy of Forensic Sciences, *see*
AAFS entries
American Board of Criminalists (ABC) *Code
of Ethics*, 153, *see also* ABC *Rules of
Professional Conduct*
American Institute for the Advancement of
Science, 163
American Society for Testing and Materials
(ASTM), 108
Appeal, of complaint procedures, 39,
140–142
Applications of ethics
    to case work, 43–45
    to client interactions, 45–48
    to collegial interactions, 48–50
    to competence issues, 89–119, *see also*
Competence scenarios
    to professional practice, 53–87, *see also*
Professional practice scenarios
Arizona v. Youngblood, 193–211
ASCLD *Guidelines for Forensic Laboratory
Management Practices*, 103, 109 110,
145–152
Attorney–client relationship, 59–60, 75
Attorneys
    approach as compared with scientists',
12–13
    interactions with, 48
    obligations regarding discovery, 55–56
    professional province of, 48–49
Avoidance of cross-examination, 78–81

B

Beech Aircraft Corp. v. Rainey, 161, 162
Blood evidence, 12, 49
Blood stain analysis scenario, 99–111
Bourjaily v. United States, 164
Brady v. Maryland, 186, 197, 198, 201–202
Brock v. Merrell Dow Pharmaceuticals, Inc.,
167

C

CAC *Code of Ethics*, 27, 29–31, 125–130
    enforcement, 131–141
    professional practice applications, 59–60,
63–64, 68–69, 73, 76–77, 81, 87, 93–94

technical competence applications,
    93–94, 98, 105–109, 117–118
California Association of Criminalists
    (CAC), 7, 10, *see also* CAC *Code of
    Ethics*
California v. Trombetta, 197, 201, 202–203,
    204–206, 208, 209
Carmichael v. Samyang Tires, 172–173
Certification, 151
Charges (complaints), 32–39, *see also*
    Complaints
Children, as witnesses, 210
Clark v. Jeter, 206
Clemons v. United States, 190
Client interactions, 45–48, *see also* Lawyers
Codes of ethics, *see also* specific codes
    applications, 43–50, *see also* Applications;
        Professional practice scenarios
    complaint process under, 32–39
    enforcement of, 8–9, 31–32
    existing, 6
    importance in forensics, 4–6, 11–12
    models of, 27–31
    rationales for professional, 11–26
    revision of, 30–31
    sanctions under, 9–10, 40–41, 139–140
Communication, 148
    privileged, 49
Comparisons, inconclusive, 47–48
Competence, 22–25, 43–44, 148
Competence scenarios, 89–119
    blood stain analysis, 99–111
    consulting criminalist and inaccurate or
        incompetent work, 94–99
    gun identification, 89–94
    preservation of test results, 111–119
Complaints (charges), 32–39
    appeal procedures, 39
    cooperation with, 37–38
    expansion of investigation, 38
    funding of, 35–36
    hearing/review procedures, 38–39
    investigating body composition and
        scope, 36–37
    investigative procedures, 34–35
    making of, 32–34
    process of bringing charge, 34
    representation of accused, 37
    sanctions under, 9–10, 40–41, 139–140
Compton v. Subaru of America, Inc., 173

Conflict of interest, 149
Council for the Registration of Forensic
    Practitioners (CRFP) code of conduct,
    155–156
Credibility, 16–19
Crime scene, evidence preservation at, 113
Criminalist(s)
    applicability of ethics codes to, 4
    competence of, 74–78, *see also*
        Competence
    evidence discovered by defense, 81–87
    licensing of, 20
    moral principles and, 15–16
    professional background of, 3
    professional status of, 4, 6–7
    unethical, 74–78
Criminalist–client relationship, 59–60
Criminalistics, 112
Cross-examination, avoidance of, 78–81
Crossover electrophoresis (CEP), 111–112

D

*Daubert v. Merrell Dow Pharmaceuticals,
    Inc.*, 13, 157–168, 170, 172–174,
    175–177, 179, 180, 181
Defense criminalist
    evidence discovered by, 81–87
    recovery of physical evidence by, 53–60
DeLuca v. Merrell Dow Pharmaceuticals, Inc.,
    160
Disclosure, 48–50, 150, *see also* Recorded
    versus unrecorded observations
Discovery, 49, 54–60, 150
DNA profiling, 7, 11

E

Employment practices, 147
Enforcement, 8, 31–32, 31–34, 135–140, *see
    also* Complaints; Sanctions
    CAC *Code of Ethics* provisions, 131–141
Erie R. Co. v. Tompkins, 162
Ethics
    as compared with morals, 14–16
    as compared with professional rules,
        21–22
    competence as related to, 22–25

credibility as reason for, 16–19
legal vs. scientific practices, 12–14
obligations of expert witness, 19–21
rationales for professional, 11–26
Evidence, *see also* specific types
discovery by defense criminalist, 81–87
identification of other examiner's markings, 70–74
legal requirements for scientific, 13
preservation of, 110–119
as prosecution or defense property, 57
required properties of, 48–49
selective examination of, 65–70
Expert witnesses, obligations of, 19–21

F

Fiber evidence, 49
Firearms identification scenario, 89–94
Fiscal practices, 149
Frye v. United States, 159, 160, 161, 162–163
Funding, of complaint investigations, 35–36

G

General Electric Co. v. Joiner, 170, 177
Gideon v. Wainwright, 188
Good Forensic Practices Guidelines, 28-29
Gun identification scenario, 89–94

H

Hearings, 137–140
of appeal, 141–142
of complaints (charges), 38–39
Hilliard v. Spalding, 204, 205

I

Inaccuracy, 94–99, *see also* Competence scenarios
Incompetence, 94–99, *see also* Competence scenarios
Inconclusive comparisons, 47
Inconclusive results, 105–106
Institutional privilege, 49–50

Investigating committees, 36–37
Investigation, of complaints, 34–38, *see also* Complaints

K

Killian v. United States, 197, 202–203, 209
Kumho Tire Company, Ltd, et al. v. Patrick Carmichael, etc., et al., 113, 169–181

L

Lawyers, *see* Attorneys
Legal practices, as compared with scientific, 12–14
Licensing, 20
Lisenba v. California, 198

M

Management information systems, 147
Manson v. Brathwaite, 187
McMann v. Richardson, 188
Models, for codes of ethics, 27–31, *see also* specific models
Mooney v. Holohan, 198, 201–202
Moore v. Illinois, 186, 197
Morals, as compared with ethics, 14–16

N

National Academy of Engineering, 174

P

Peer organizations, 151
People v. Blair, 189
People v. Caruso, 189, 191
People v. Donald Richard Nation Jr., 112, 183–191, 204
People v. Frierson, 188–189
People v. Hitch, 186, 187
People v. Martin, 191
People v. Pope, 188–189
People v. Ruthford, 187

People v. Savvides, 208
PGM blood typing, 99–111
Photographic evidence, 113–114
Physical evidence
    discovery by defense investigator, 82–87
    ownership of, 57
    preservation of, 56–57, 58
    recovery by defense investigator, 53–60
Powell v. Alabama, 188
Preservation of evidence, 110–119
Privileged communication, 49
Professional practice scenarios, 53–87
    avoidance of cross-examination, 78–81
    criticism of work not done, 60–65
    defense investigator recovery of physical
        evidence, 53–60
    defense re-examination of evidence, 70–74
    evidence discovered by defense
        investigator, 82–87
    incompetent or unethical consultant,
        74–78
    selective evidence examination, 65–70
Professional recommendations, 150
Professional responsibility, 150–151
Professional staffing, 149
Proprietary privilege, 49–50
Public responsibility, 149
Public versus private sanctions, 40–41

Q

Qualifications, of laboratory managers,
    147–148
Quality assurance, 110, 150

R

Recommendations, professional, 150
Recorded versus unrecorded observations,
    46–47, *see also* Disclosure
Relevance, 44
Research, 151
Review, of complaint procedures, 38–39
Reviewability, 45
Revision, 30–31
Rock v. Arkansas, 167
Roviaro v. United States, 208
Rubber Manufacturers of America, 174

Rules, as compared with codes of ethics, 21–22

S

Safety, 147
Sanctions, 9–10, 40–41, 139–140
Scientific method, 18, 91
Scientific Working Groups, 108
Security measures, 147
Selective examination of evidence, 65–70
Simmons v. United States, 189, 190, 191
Staff development, 148
Staffing, 149
State v. Escalante, 196–197, 206–207
Stovall v. Denno, 189, 190
Supervision, 110, 149

T

Technical competence, *see* Competence
Thoroughness, 44
Training, of laboratory managers, 148
Truth telling, definitions of, 5
Turpin v. Merrell Dow Pharmaceuticals, Inc.,
    167

U

Undone work, 60–65
Unethical criminalists, 74–78
United States v. Abel, 161–162
United States v. Agurs, 197, 201, 202, 203,
    206, 208
United States v. DeCoster, 188
United States v. Downing, 164, 166
United States v. Kilgus, 159
United States v. Lovasco, 198, 209
United States v. Marion, 198, 209
United States v. Shorter, 160
United States v. Smith, 166
United States v. Solomon, 159
United States v. Valenzuela-Bernal, 197, 198,
    209
United States v. Wade, 191, 210
United States v. Williams, 166
Unrecorded versus recorded observations,
    46–47, *see also* Disclosure

W

Watkins v. Sowders, 210
Watkins v. Telsmith, Inc., 173

Wong Sun v. United States, 191
Work environment, 148
Work not done, 60–65